THE ART OF THE BUILDER

ELEVATING PRE-CONSTRUCTION PLANNING

BOOK 2- THE FIRST PLANNER® SYSTEM

AN  IPCS™ SYSTEM
FPS™ | TPS® | LPS®

JASON SCHROEDER

Thank You!

I want to send a special "Thank You" to Daryle Delafosse and Joel Hamilton for their contributions to this work. They provided considerable commentary and suggestions to guide the direction of the book.

Daryle Delafosse GSC is a trade person, PM, and 'fixer' of projects challenged by poor communication. He introduces Lean practices, trains, coaches and blogs on how to translate Trade-talk, Management-speak and Business value to the industry. His focus is to show where profit fade really happens in his program Recognizing & Managing Impacts.

Joel Hamilton is an Albertan Ironworker PM (or Steel Specialist as his LinkedIn profile states). Joel has been a part of many projects large and small, traversing Canada, coast to coast (and even just south of the North Pole). While currently overseeing the Steel Reinforcing Scope for Edmonton's (Alberta) new Light Rail Transit Project with A&H Steel, Joel also consults and raises industry awareness by being a trade ambassador to the next generation. When Joel isn't managing steel construction, he and his wife, Sarah, are building the Hamilton Homestead surrounded by their four kids and their gaggle of animals on the outskirts of Leduc, AB. He enjoys volunteering within their community and church as well and is an avid audiobook 'reader' and daily podcast listener.

DARYLE
DELAFOSSE

JOEL
HAMILTON

Our goal at Elevate Construction is to be the help you need. We are Alfred when you're Bruce. Morpheus to your Neo. the Morgan Freeman of construction. You get it. We see you out there getting your ass kicked or kicking ass every damn day. We're here to help. Like any wise old mentor and mentee relationship, we're going to tell you the truth and guide you to construction enlightenment. You're going to have to listen to us and you're going to have to grow. It's fine for you to disagree, but it makes more sense to hear us out first. Let your guard down and listen. We spend a shit ton of time and money trying to change the construction industry because we see waste and abuse. So let's approach this like you are here to find a better way and we will share everything we can to help you reach your potential and change the industry for the better. If you're still here, that means you consent to the feedback and education you are about to receive. Buckle up.

Integrated Production Control System™

The Integrated Production Control System™ has three components: the First Planner System™, the Takt Production System®, and the Last Planner® System. They cover the planning of a project, the project systems for running a lean project, and scheduling/controlling a project. Each system must be understood independently, and as it relates to the other two. Only when you are operating with the Integrated Production Control System™, unifying all phases and teams, are you able to reduce variation to the point of no impact, control the flow, and predict project success.

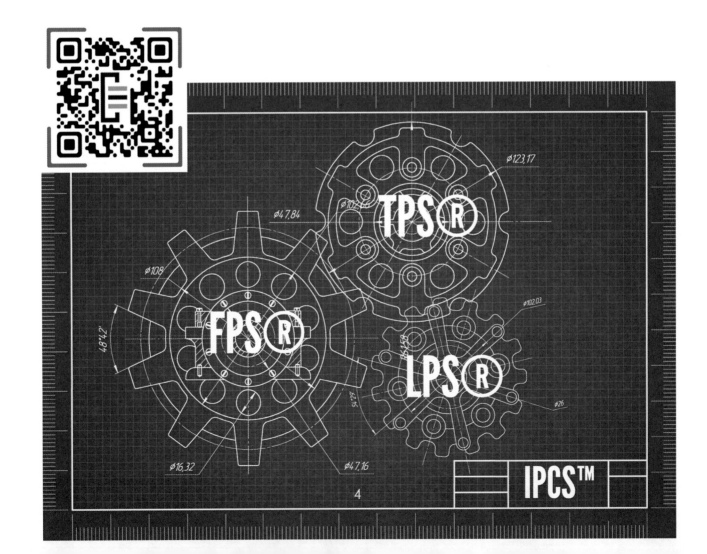

Integrated Production Control System™

INCEPTION

NTP

COMPLETION

MEETING & HUDDLE SYSTEM	DELIVER-ABLES	EXPECT-ATIONS

LAST PLANNER® SYSTEM

TAKT PLAN	ZONE & LOGISTICS MAPS	4-6 WEEK LOOK AHEAD	TRAILER SIGNAGE & ORG CHART	PRO-CUREMENT LOG

TAKT PLANNING

CONSTRAINT MANAGEMENT	ROADBLOCK REMOVAL	ZONE CONTROL	DELAY MANAGEMENT	ACCOUNT-ABILITY

TAKT STEERING & CONTROL

TAKT PRODUCTION SYSTEM®

PROPOSAL PHASE	BUILD TEAM/ SET PARAMETERS	ADAPT & ENABLE	PLAN WITH BUILDERS	PREPARE TO START STRONG

DESIGN & PRE-CONSTRUCTION

TEAM	PLAN	SUPPLY CHAIN	CULTURE	TRAINING

THE PRODUCTION SYSTEM

FIRST PLANNER SYSTEM™

PARADIGM OF THE OWNERS	MINDSETS	GOAL OF THE SYSTEM	STRUCTURE OF THE PROJECT	RULES OF THE SYSTEM

SYSTEM LEVERAGE POINTS

PEOPLE FIRST

The Integrated Production Control System™ brings people together through three systems--TPS®, FPS™, and LPS®. This integrated First and Last Planner® team controls production from start to finish. There must be a First Planner System™ to support last Planners® and a rhythm to keep them in a production flow.

FIRST PLANNERS™

LAST PLANNERS®

The Last Planner® System

I'm assuming you're very familiar with the Last Planner® system, so I'll keep the recap brief. The system is designed to involve the front-line leaders of the project team that are last in the planning cycle. Connecting early decision makers with front line leaders enables better planning and commitment throughout the process. It's comprised of the meeting system, key planning deliverables, and behavioral expectations.

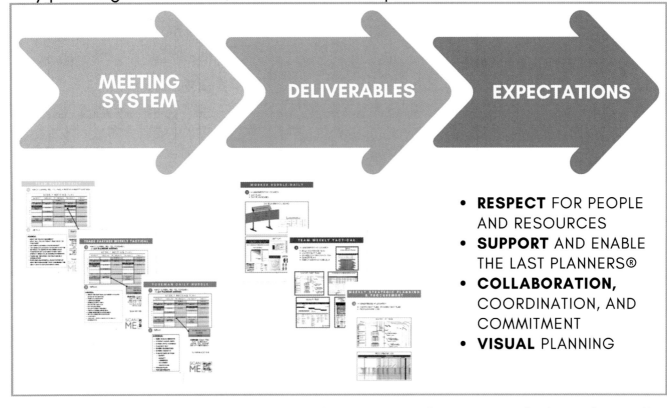

MEETING SYSTEM ➤ **DELIVERABLES** ➤ **EXPECTATIONS**

- **RESPECT** FOR PEOPLE AND RESOURCES
- **SUPPORT** AND ENABLE THE LAST PLANNERS®
- **COLLABORATION**, COORDINATION, AND COMMITMENT
- **VISUAL** PLANNING

These Last Planners® coordinate and commit to short-interval plans that will align the labor, materials, information, and permissions together in an execution plan. The fact that we have a Last Planner® System automatically implies and necessitates the creation of the First Planner System™.
I'm your huckleberry.

RESOURCES:

The Takt Production System®

Every lean transformation should begin with production planning or Takt Planning. This system sets tasks to a specific pace, improving efficiency, reducing waste, and ensuring a smooth workflow through standardized zones and visual management tools on our projects. We will keep a high level approach in this book, so for more information you can reference our last book, "Takt Planning," to fully understand the system.

TAKTPLANNING
-what we want to happen-

TAKT PLAN

ZONE & LOGISTICS MAPS

LPS® INTEGRATION

TRAILER SIGNAGE & ORG CHART

PROCUREMENT LOG

TAKT PRODUCTION SYSTEM®

LEVELING WORK

MANAGE PRODUCTION

FOREMAN & SUPER CONTROL

CREATING STABILITY

QUALITY PRODUCT

ROADBLOCK REMOVAL

TAKT STEERING & CONTROL
-how we manage reality-

RESOURCES:

TAKT CONSTRUCTION
● LEAN TAKT

THE ART OF THE BUILDER
TAKT PLANNING
LEAN CONSTRUCTION SCHEDULING WITH THE TAKT PRODUCTION SYSTEM® AND LAST PLANNER®

JASON SCHROEDER
with
LEAN TAKT
AN ELEVATED COMPANY

The *First Planner System*™

This book will walk you through how to properly plan and setup a project by covering the design and pre-construction phase and the system that must be setup for lean project delivery.

DESIGN & PRE-CONSTRUCTION

PROPOSAL PHASE ▸ BUILD TEAM ▸ ADAPT & ENABLE DESIGN ▸ PLAN WITH BUILDERS ▸ PREPARE & START STRONG

WE USE OUR TIME IN DESIGN & PRE-CONSTRUCTION TO SETUP THE RIGHT LEAN PROJECT MANAGEMENT SYSTEM.

PLAN · SUPPLY CHAIN · CULTURE · TRAINING · TEAM

THE PRODUCTION SYSTEM

WE SET OUR TRADES UP FOR SUCCESS BY ONBOARDING THEM TO OUR SYSTEMS.

BUYOUT · PRE-CON MTGS · PRE-MOB · FOLLOW-UP · FINAL INSPECTION · INITIAL INSPECTION

TRADE PARTNER PREPARATION PROCESS

This is an outline showing these components together in a framework.

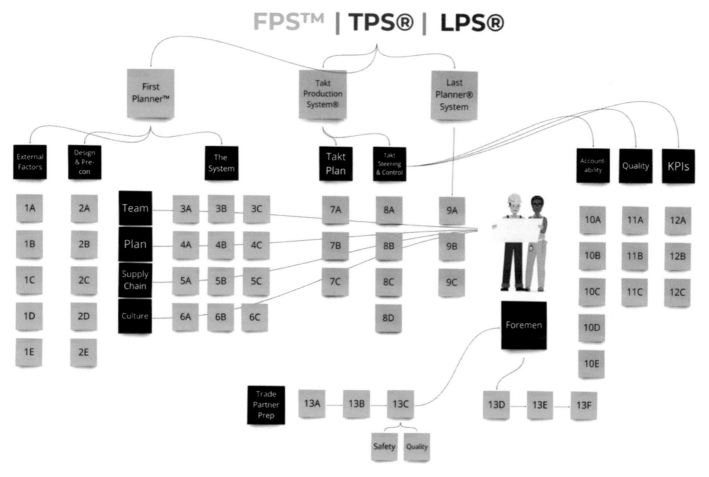

*This is the system in a horizontal timeline, according to implementation.

Outline:
1A - Power to See the Paradigm
1B - Mindsets & Paradigms
1C - Goals of the System
1D - Structure of the System
1E - Rules of the System
2A - Project Proposal
2B - Build the Design Team
2C - Enable Design
2D - Builder Planning
2E - Start Strong
3A - Build the Project Team
3B - Team Balance
3C - Individual Balance
4A - The Production Plan
4B - Lean in Contracts
4C - Manage Risks

5A - Procure Resources
5B - Prefabrication
5C - Logistics
6A - Win over the Workforce
6B - Clean, Safe, & Organized Project
6C - Onboarding & Orientation
7A - Takt Plan Creation
7B - Plan Use & Management
7C - First & Last Planner® Coordination
8A - Constraint Management
8B - Roadblock Removal
8C - Zone Control
8D - Delay Management
9A - Meeting & Huddle System
9B - Collaboration
9C - Planning Deliverables
10A - Zero Tolerance
10B - Daily Correction System
10C - Quality at the Source
10D - Contractor Grading
10E - Team Health Score

11A - Continuous Improvement
11B - Customer Needs & Wants
11C - Conditions of Satisfaction
12A - Leading Indicators
12B - Lagging Indicators
12C - Foremen
13A - Buyout
13B - Pre-mobilization Meeting
13C - Preconstruction Meeting
13D - First-in-place Inspection
13E - Follow-up Inspection
13F - Final Inspection

This framework combines many lean and operational frameworks together into one. To create this I overlayed the This Is Lean, LeanCore, AGC Lean, 14 Toyota Way Principles, 2 Second Lean, Military Doctrine, Human Systems, How Big Things Get Done, and Built To Fail frameworks to make sure it was complete and covered the bare minimum of what it means to have a complete system.

IPCS™

FPS™ | TPS® | LPS®

| First Planner™ | | Takt Production System® | Last Planner® System |

External Factors	Design & Pre-con	The System				Takt Plan	Takt Steering & Control		Account-ability	Quality	KPIs
1A	2A	Team	3A	3B	3C	7A	8A	9A	10A	11A	12A
1B	2B	Plan	4A	4B	4C	7B	8B	9B	10B	11B	12B
1C	2C	Supply Chain	5A	5B	5C	7C	8C	9C	10C	11C	12C
1D	2D	Culture	6A	6B	6C		8D		10D		
1E	2E								10E		

Foremen

| Trade Partner Prep | 13A | 13B | 13C | | 13D | 13E | 13F |

Safety   Quality

The First Planner System™, shown in these segments above, is comprised of three phases: Design & Pre-construction, the Production System, and the Trade Partner Preparation Process. We use our time in design & pre-construction to setup the right lean project management system that can stabilize all operations onsite. In this book we will show you what system we are are making, how to get trade partners involved, and how to make the system in pre-construction.

Respect for people-- FIRST!

The First Planner System™ is successfully implemented when the team and the individual are healthy and balanced. We believe that a work/life balance means that we can be fulfilled and successful at work, and therefore take our satisfaction and contentment home and continue to build upon those feelings. Grouchy at work generally means grouchy at home, and we're champions of breaking that cycle. Construction is energizing and exciting. We believe in winning at work and winning at home. We've covered these topics in Elevating Construction Senior Superintendents-Book One [Elevating Construction Project Teams]. With the team and individual healthy and balanced, we're ready to implement the systems needed to win on the project.

IF PEOPLE DON'T HAVE CAPACITY, THEY WON'T HAVE TIME FOR LEAN!

RESOURCES:

GRAB A COPY FOR REFERENCE OR LISTEN TO IT ON THE PODCAST!

11

IPCS™ & FPS™ *is* Foremen focused

The Integrated Production Control System™ and its component system the First Planner System™ is designed to get the Foremen everything they need, every single day. They are leading the crews that actually build the damn thing. I can't emphasize enough that they are the unsung heroes and deserve all the help and support that we can possibly give them. You must facilitate their success. If you hear someone blaming the foremen for a project in trouble, tell them they're an ass. I'm just kidding; that's not having respect for people. Direct them to the IPCS™ & FPS™ because they are confused about who is responsible for the faulty system. The workers and Foremen get the work done--they just need support.

GENERAL CONTRACTOR RESPONSIBILITIES TO FOREMEN

- QUALITY/SAFETY EXPECTATIONS
- MATERIALS
- LAYOUT
- INFORMATION
- PLAN
- STABILITY
- RESPECT

EMPLOYER RESPONSIBILITIES TO FOREMEN

- TRAINING
- LABOR
- TOOLS
- EQUIPMENT

LAST PLANNERS®

RESOURCES:

THE ART OF THE BUILDER
ELEVATING CONSTRUCTION FOREMEN

12

Playing the *hand* you've been *dealt*

We appreciate your expertise. We commend you for learning and growing professionally; we respect the years you've put into your craft and career. We told you that so we can tell you this--the deck may be stacked against you as you attempt to enable foremen, and no matter what hand you play, the house always wins. We're not against owners, but they can make it difficult, if not impossible, to implement lean systems successfully. We believe in protecting workers and foremen with lean practices. These are a few areas where you may need to formulate a strategic plan to offset the owner's greed, ignorance, or ego. I list these here so you can see them early and do what you can to remove them or work around them.

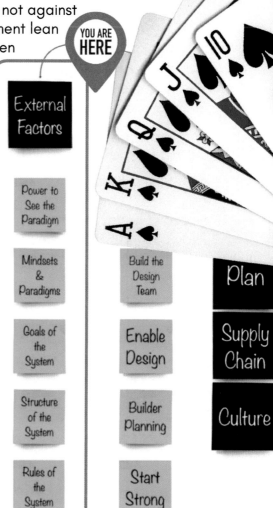

YOU ARE HERE

External Factors

Power to See the Paradigm

Mindsets & Paradigms

Goals of the System

Structure of the System

Rules of the System

Build the Design Team

Enable Design

Builder Planning

Start Strong

Plan

Supply Chain

Culture

We will continue to fill out this outline throughout the book so you can grasp the entire system

PARADIGMS

Do the Owners, Designers, & Builders see the lean paradigm? Do they respect people, support stability, and encourage flow? If you have an owner that wants to push people and cut costs, the system will not work.

MINDSET

Do the Stakeholders & Leaders have a mindset that respects people? Is it their top priority? If you have owners that tend to say, "add people, work overtime, work weekends, or work faster in more areas," you have decision makers that don't respect people. The project will suffer because of it.

GOALS OF THE SYSTEM

Is the goal of the project to finish on time? If you have an owner, owner's rep, or government influencer that wants to look good and grandstand, then the goal of the project will switch from finishing on time with happy people, to cutting budgets and holding to old methods. If you have a fire-fighting Super, the focus will be fighting fires rather than preventing them. Always find the actual goal of the project.

STRUCTURE OF THE SYSTEM

Is the project delivery structure proper for the goal? If you have an owner or business leaders that will not allow the use of lean methods, lean production plans, and proper project planning, the project will likely fail.

RULES OF THE SYSTEM

Do rules allow the team to succeed? If the owner or government specifies rules that hinder the project like being forced to use tradition CPM, dictating the overburden of trades, and denying reasonable delay claims, the team will suffer and fail.

13

You are the solution

Everywhere I go I hear comments like:
"We just don't have anyone who wants to work anymore."
"This new generation is lazy."
"You just can't get good people anymore."
"Our subs are just horrible."
"No one cares about their work anymore."

Admitting mistakes, taking ownership, and developing a plan to overcome challenges are integral to any successful team. Extreme Ownership. Leaders must own everything in their world. There is no one else to blame.

Jocko Willink

Even if this were true, is it helping us? If it's someone else's fault or problem then we are helpless victims, trapped in a miserable cycle. You can't be happy in a career if you think you're a victim and there's no hope. Good news. You're about to be empowered with knowledge and competence.

Here is the straight truth--workers and foremen are finishing our projects! In spite of poor planning on our part, bad systems, and a lack of fundamental respect and training, they are pushing through and driving results. They are the heroes and we are the problem. If you don't believe me, go read, "The Essential Deming," or, "Out of Crisis." **We can't blame the people that don't have the power to fix the problem.** It's up to us. This is that moment where you're mad at me but I'm stating facts. Accept that you're part of the problem so you can own the solution. So let' begin and solve this together for good!

TABLE OF CONTENTS

We are going to use a cake analogy for this book. What to make, who its for, and how to make it...

PART One- What is the Cake?
The Production System to Operate

PART Two- Who Eats the Cake?
How to get Trade Partners to participate

PART Three- How To Make the Cake?
Designing Your Production System

WHY?

If you know me at all, you know I love watching the Great British Baking Show, the home baker and the professional versions. I love watching the effort, the fails, and the successes. I recognize the dedication and passion that goes into each of the bakes and who doesn't wish that they could somehow taste through the screen? So baking a cake is the analogy we are using to help convey the First Planner System™. Let's begin with why we would even need cake in the first place-- and stay with me here, no one actually needs cake, but everyone in construction

AN OUNCE OF PREVENTION

The role of a First Planner®

Murphy's Law warns that anything that can go wrong will go wrong and at the worst possible time. I'm not here to argue whether or not that's hyperbole--I'm here to get in front of it. Benjamin Franklin saw enough fiery devastation and sad experiences to warn that an ounce of prevention is worth a pound of cure, and Flyvbjerg and Gardner drive the point home in the highly recommended book, "How Big Things Get Done." The authors compiled research from over 16,000 projects to illustrate the causes of poor project execution, and I have reduced them to 3 major factors.

PLANS — Projects are improperly planned. We do the bare minimum in planning and try to figure things out as we go.

WHY DO PROJECTS FAIL?

SYSTEM — We use improper systems & processes throughout the design process, the contracting system, and for project scheduling.

PEOPLE — We no longer train our professionals properly. People are running mega projects with inadequate training.

How Big Things Get Done: The Surprising Factors That Determine the Fate of Every Project, from Home Renovations to Space Exploration and Everything In Between

Authors: Bent Flyvbjerg and Dan Gardner

PLANNING

In general, we don't plan our projects properly. We are typically awarded the project and told to build it as soon as possible.

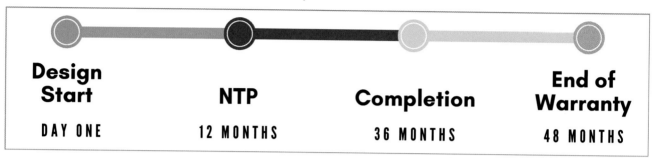

Current planning practices usually start pre-con just before we break ground. That would be like giving a keynote speech in front of thounsands of people with 5 minutes to prepare. Or showing up the morning of a wedding, ready to bake the bake. It is just not done.

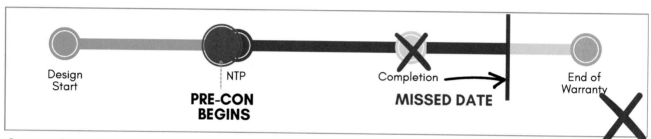

If you plan that way, you will fail. We must have a 1/3 to 2/3 ratio when it comes to project planning and execution. You need at least one third of the total project time to be spent in planning, and two thirds for execution. For example, if your project construction duration is 20 months, plan on 10 months for proper planning.

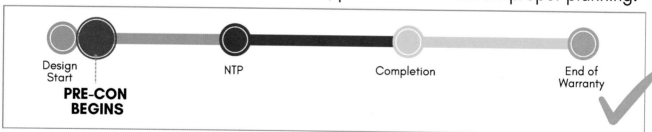

You may be thinking that I'm being dramatic and that this is unrealistic, but friend, the data doesn't support the dogma. Let me share an example from *How Big Things Get Done*. I read about a bullet train that was originally designed to go from San Diego to Sacramento and San Francisco. Due to a lack of planning, experience, and due diligence, the bullet train line will now end in Bakersfield, which is about half of the planned distance. It will be over 10 years late and will cost $67 billion more than the original estimate. In case you don't grasp the magnitude of this failure, a million seconds is about 2 weeks. A billion seconds is around 32 years--67 billion dollars is a lot of money.   18

Let's compare that fiasco to the Empire State building, a project that finished ahead of schedule, way under budget, and is known throughout the world as a massive success in most aspects of construction. It's an example of proper planning, experienced teams, and using the correct systems. As you can see to the right, the team is using a time by location schedule. Planners understood what they needed to build, how to build it, and how to keep the work flowing. This is how it needs to be done. We have everything we need to make this the standard. There is no excuse that times have changed and we build differently now. What has changed is that we no longer place emphasis in the right place.

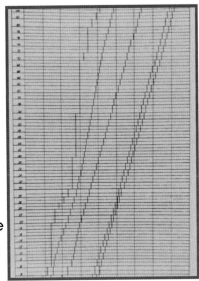

The shift we need to make is to think slow and act fast. We need to plan projects, build them right as we go, and finish strong as we go. Currently our industry does a poor job of planning, puts a lot of focus on building in the moment, and we finish okay.

PLAN IT FIRST	BUILD IT RIGHT	FINISH AS YOU GO
• Plan the project • Anchor to past experience • Assess and prevent risks • Pixar Planning • Build the project on paper first • Include the builders	• Execute the plan • Monitor costs • Monitor schedule • Collaborate with trades • Solve problems • Adjust to unforeseen conditions	• Meet quality expectations • Finish the work • Commission systems • Deliver the project as promised • Demobilize

If you don't properly plan your project, it will fail. You will realize problems that could have been prevented and spend 10 times the cost you would have spent by finding them in pre-construction and planning around them.

Every project has problems, whether we want them or not, and planning will allow us to prevent them to a great extent. A concept that I love from *How Big Things Get Done* is to neutralize or eliminate the **Window of Doom**.

YOUR PROJECT HAS X AMOUNT OF PROBLEMS:

☐ ☐ ☐ ☐ ☐ ☐ ☐ ☐

If you don't plan, you will find these problems in the field and it will cost you time, money, and morale. This leaves the **window** of the project duration **open** longer than needed, leaving more opportunities for uncertainties, one offs, and black swans (severe risks) to occur.

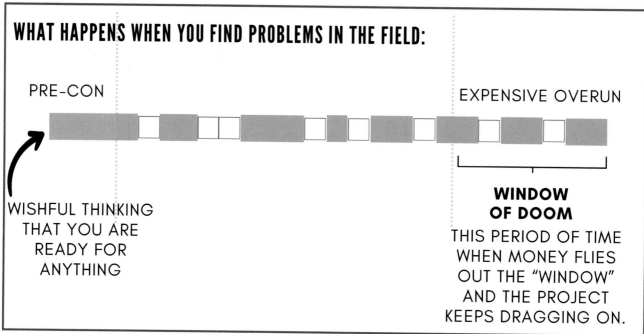

WHAT HAPPENS WHEN YOU FIND PROBLEMS IN THE FIELD:

PRE-CON

EXPENSIVE OVERRUN

WISHFUL THINKING THAT YOU ARE READY FOR ANYTHING

WINDOW OF DOOM

THIS PERIOD OF TIME WHEN MONEY FLIES OUT THE "WINDOW" AND THE PROJECT KEEPS DRAGGING ON.

I'm suggesting that you leverage the wisdom of the team and learn from the sad experiences of others--find the problems in pre-construction where the worst thing that can happen is that you have to re-plan and erase the white board or re-print the pdfs. You can largely predict project failure in one form or another and mitigate the damage.

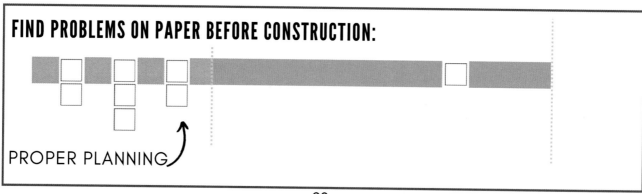

FIND PROBLEMS ON PAPER BEFORE CONSTRUCTION:

PROPER PLANNING

People tend to think that they are the exception but since you're here, I'm going to assume that you are humble enough to accept the data presented below, taken from *How Big Things Get Done*. These numbers represent the data compiled from over 16,000 projects throughout the world.

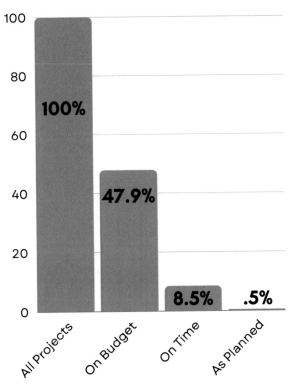

Over 50% of projects do not meet their budgets--they average **65% over budget**. That is an astronomical amount of error made by the team.

Over 90% of projects don't finish on time--they average **58 days behind schedule**. That represents a knowledge gap within the team.

Projects don't go wrong--they start wrong. They start without proper planning, systems, training, and experience.

How Big Things Get Done calls out several commonly held beliefs that need to be eliminated from all construction, and I'd like touch on them here. Please read the book if you're interested in digging deeper.

These fallacies are pervasive beliefs held by many leaders and owners. We have to call this out so that thought leaders and decision makers can see the harm these fallacies are doing to the industry and people.

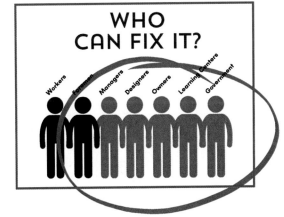

The Need for Speed

This concept is fine if you're a TOPGUN, but rushing, pushing, and being in a hurry won't help projects win. It will cut planning and preparation, which leads to a spiraling mess of rework, low quality work, prioritizing profits over people, and decreased safety on-site. Generating speed in any way other than through creating flow is unsafe. I don't like it because it's dangerous. Sorry to disappoint the Mavericks in the group.

Pushing Makes Haste

This fallacy pretends pushing people, pushing milestones too soon, and rushing work will make haste and help projects to progress and finish. The truth is that pushing creates pressure, which leads to:

- quick and erratic decision-making.
- unclear, chaotic, or ineffective communication.
- team members losing focus on priorities.
- a decrease in creativity and problem-solving.
- an increase in finger pointing and blame.
- declines in productivity as energy is wasted on managing panic.
- diminished trust within the team.
- a loss in morale and motivation.
- possible decrease in the quality of work.
- the team becoming more susceptible to making mistakes or overlooking critical details.

The Commitment Fallacy

The commitment fallacy is when owners, designers, or contractors think that getting a project started and a contractor on the hook will provide the motivation to make haste and compete it with urgency and efficiency. This is false. This actually only scales a mess. If the contractor began without proper planning, it's likely they do not know what they are doing, and they will be too busy catching up and covering their interests to properly manage the project.

Strategic Misrepresentation

My favorite to hate is strategic misrepresentation. This is when owners, designers, or contractors misrepresent existing conditions, complexity, or the full scope of a project/effort in order to push risk on another party or get the other party to begin work and push through what would otherwise be a change in cost or time. It's a fallacy to believe that the end justifies the means. This is disgusting and inexcusable behavior.

All of these fallacies will hurt you. If you experience any of them, you can anticipate that they will prevent the kind of planning and stability needed to run a remarkable project. Additionally you can add these to the list of idiotic ideas:

1. Why are workers not in every zone? I want to see busyness throughout this building.
2. You don't need more staff for change orders. You should be able to cover the changes with your current staff.
3. I know the design is not finished, but we should be fine. We just need to get started somewhere.
4. Just get it done as quickly as possible, no matter what.
5. Cut corners wherever you can to save time and money.
6. We're not concerned about quality, just meet the deadline.
7. Ignore safety regulations if it helps speed up the process.
8. We won't pay for delays, so make sure everything stays on schedule.
9. Don't worry about proper permits or approvals, we'll bypass the bureaucracy.
10. We expect you to work overtime without compensation to meet our timeline.
11. If you can't deliver on time, we'll find someone else who can.
12. We don't need to review the plans thoroughly, just start building.
13. We'll hold back payment until the project is completed, regardless of delays or issues.
14. You're responsible for any cost overruns, so keep expenses low at all costs.
15. Don't bother with thorough inspections, we trust that everything will be fine.
16. If you can't handle the pressure, we'll find someone who can.
17. You just need to have your trades work overtime.

If you hear any of these you must hold the line, do what is right, and push back, or you will and your team will suffer through a crash landed project that will hurt you, your people, and your families.

NO!!!

Ways a GC or trade can hold the line:
- Communicate the need for flow in the work
- Establish a clear schedule with needed predecessors
- Continually ask for work to made ready ahead of you
- When asked to push, refocus the conversation on preparing work
- Do not do any work unless it is financially approved, the crew has the capacity, and it is clean, safe, and organized.

Pushing from leaders creates pressure which leads to panic. I observed and tracked the outcomes of projects over a period of years in Arizona and found clear and frustrating results when comparing the execution of projects that push in comparison to a control group. **Most general contractors would undercut their proposal schedule by approximately 20% when submitting on a project.** They would end up overrunning what the project should have taken according to accurate historical anchors.

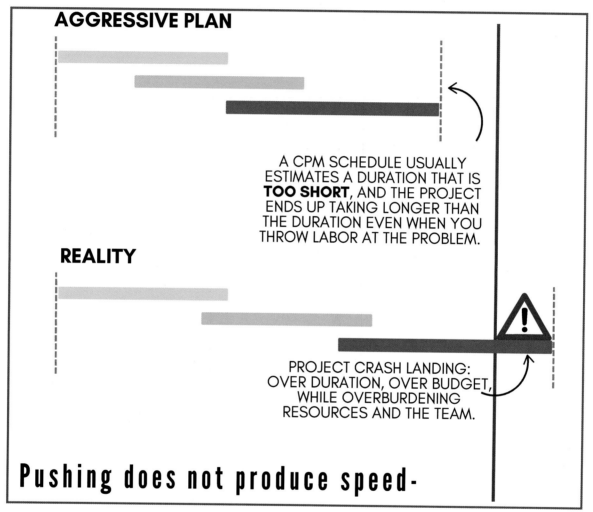

AGGRESSIVE PLAN

A CPM SCHEDULE USUALLY ESTIMATES A DURATION THAT IS **TOO SHORT**, AND THE PROJECT ENDS UP TAKING LONGER THAN THE DURATION EVEN WHEN YOU THROW LABOR AT THE PROBLEM.

REALITY

PROJECT CRASH LANDING: OVER DURATION, OVER BUDGET, WHILE OVERBURDENING RESOURCES AND THE TEAM.

Pushing does not produce speed.

This triggered an effort to understand the trends. I discovered that those projects never attempted to recover the time they needed in pre-construction, the teams began the project **knowing they did not have enough time**, and then they began to push, rush, and panic. This then led to the irresponsible addition of labor, batching, context switching, large team sizes, more complex communication, change in foremen, change in crew composition, unnecessary onboarding, overtime, fatigue, lack of quality, rework, distraction, loss of focus in planning, and then stops and restarts. Pushing does not make haste. Pushing creates pressure which leads to panicked behavior and decisions. Panic makes for late projects.

THE RIGHT SYSTEM - TAKT PLANNING

In that same 7 year period of observation I noticed the results of thoroughly planning a project with Takt. When projects were planned to create flow with a healthy overall total project duration, the team would experience delays, but on average, they finished on time or up to 5% early.

If you follow a good plan that is stable and reasonable you can meet or beat the plan.

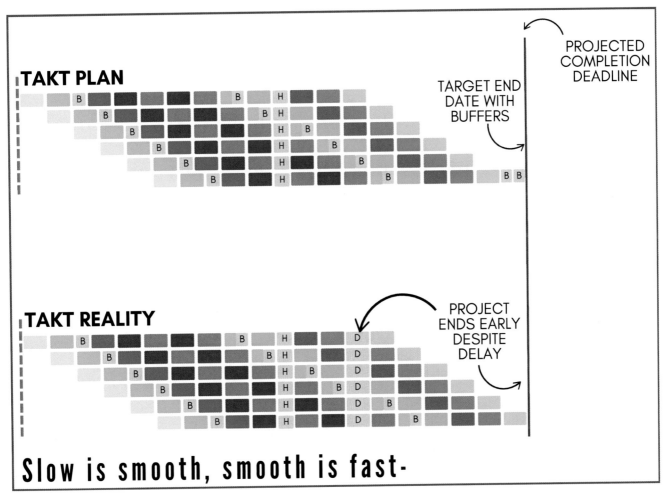

TAKT PLAN

PROJECTED COMPLETION DEADLINE

TARGET END DATE WITH BUFFERS

TAKT REALITY

PROJECT ENDS EARLY DESPITE DELAY

Slow is smooth, smooth is fast-

What we must implement is properly estimating the duration for projects and allowing our trades to flow. Workers and foremen are brilliant at improving their work and going faster when they have repetition, flow, and predictability. Takt planning means using crucial buffers to absorb delays and forces planners to establish reasonable and obtainable milestones. If you use Takt, your deadlines will be justified and manageable.

No seriously-we are totally underselling this! You must use Takt.

25

ITERATIONS

Lean thinking will encourage you to plan and iterate fast, but I want to emphasize that we work through these iterations in the planning process, before construction begins. Iterating will uncover problems, so everything that can be done in planning should be done as thoroughly as possible. The project plan will only have a correct overall total project duration if you iterate on paper, before you get to the field.

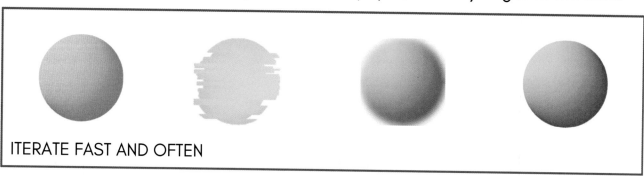

ITERATE FAST AND OFTEN

The authors of *How Big Things Get Done* stress the importance of learning from the best of the best to get planning right. No Hollywood movie studio is as successful as Pixar and it is their exhaustive planning that ensures each movie they create is a hit.

A writer will take one interesting thought and use multiple rounds of peer reviews to build that thought into a story outline of about 12 pages long. When the story outline is approved, a rough draft is written and then presented to a peer audience of Pixar employees. The draft is critiqued in a feedback session, and the process begins again; the only requirement is that the draft must improve. Several rounds of draft, feedback and improvement take place.

Once the writer has a fairly decent script, the movie is made in storyboard form. This is about 2,700 drawings complied into a movie with basic sound effects and voiced by Pixar employees. The movie is shown to a new audience within Pixar and the movie is picked apart. To this point, the process has taken about 4 months and is a considerable investment, but the investment is minor compared to the cost of actual production.

The storyboard movie is remade and critiqued, usually around 8 times in all. This extensive process allows people to be **creative and imaginative without consequences**. Every part of the plan is subjected to intense scrutiny and experimentation. The pressure to get things perfect the first time is removed by understanding that others will challenge the plan and help connect and correct the story.

The real production finally begins, with true animation, professional voice actors, a score and sounds effects pulled together for the final time. This is the film that is released by the studio, generally the ninth iteration of the movie.

Most construction projects start with a plan that isn't even completely finished, let alone one that's been reviewed and revised 9 times. If we are going to improve our industry and elevate our productivity, we must adapt a new mindset: the first plan is the worst plan. Let's noramlize admitting that we are learning as we go and that we want to improve the plan before we implement it. Let's normalize asking for advice and help. Lean means that we continuously improve our plan. Let's stop bringing an incomplete mess to the trades and forcing them to make sense of it. This is why you are here--you're a First Planner™ and you have the power to elevate the industry.

| FIRST DRAFT | SECOND DRAFT | THIRD DRAFT | FOURTH DRAFT | FINAL DRAFT |

- Problem solve creatively
- Experiment with new technology

- Scrutinize every part
- Challenge your biases

- Ask for feedback
- Explain details to find the unrealistic beliefs

Rework in planning is inexpensive compared to the cost of rework during production. Do your due diligence by planning extensively for the benefit of everyone who will have the privilege of being a part of your project.

Pixar starts their planning with an interesting idea. We start our planning with a conceptual design. Pixar begins production with a script and visual guides in place. We begin construction with a plan and visual guides as well. There is no guesswork in a final Pixar production, and there is none in a fully planned project either. Architect Frank Gehry designed and built a 76 story skyscraper in Manhattan with no change orders because he doesn't let clients build before the design is complete. It's possible to complete planning before construction begins; here are the requirements:

We need the following before we break ground:

Takt Plan & Zone Maps	Org Accountability Chart
Procurement Log	Risk & Opportunity Register
Logistics Plan	Well Established Budget
Trailer & Signage Design	Master Builder and Experienced Team

It is critical to have these components in place before construction begins, and it must be done with the help and buy-in of the First and Last Planners®. I believe it is unethical to hold a project team accountable for a project they did not plan. We need a maximum virtual product developed by the team that will build the project. Over 60% of project success is determined before NTP, so when that notice comes, you'll be ready to win with these in place.

This is the *why*

Preventing problems through planning is the reason this book exists and why we are spending our time trying to raise awareness. You can prevent most of the difficulty you have in construction by creating and maintaining a project production system for your project. You ready? Set? On we go! 28

The First Planner System™

NEVER PLAN A PROJECT AS YOU START IT. PLAN IT BEFORE YOU BUILD using the right system! This book and the Takt Planning book will be your training.

This is how to plan

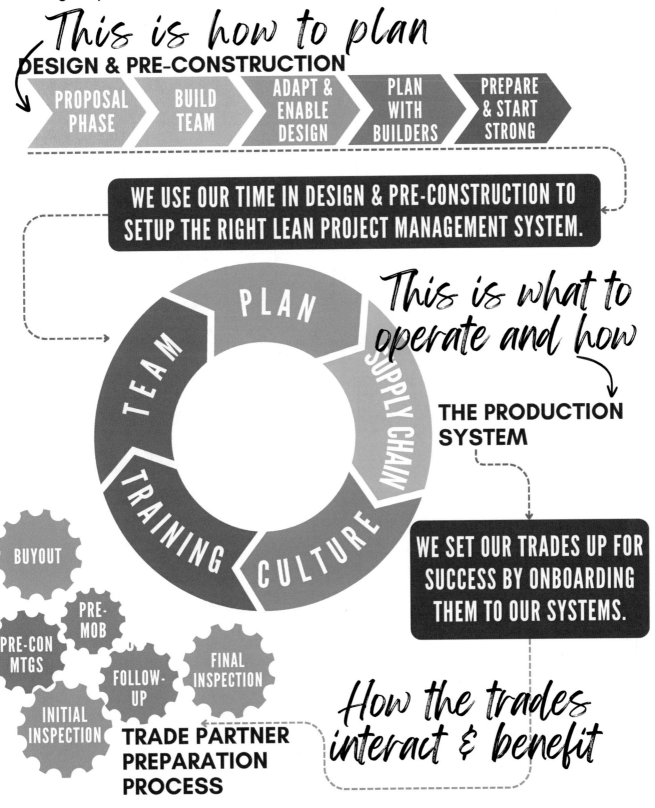

DESIGN & PRE-CONSTRUCTION

PROPOSAL PHASE → BUILD TEAM → ADAPT & ENABLE DESIGN → PLAN WITH BUILDERS → PREPARE & START STRONG

WE USE OUR TIME IN DESIGN & PRE-CONSTRUCTION TO SETUP THE RIGHT LEAN PROJECT MANAGEMENT SYSTEM.

This is what to operate and how

PLAN — SUPPLY CHAIN — CULTURE — TRAINING — TEAM

THE PRODUCTION SYSTEM

WE SET OUR TRADES UP FOR SUCCESS BY ONBOARDING THEM TO OUR SYSTEMS.

BUYOUT
PRE-MOB
PRE-CON MTGS
FOLLOW-UP
FINAL INSPECTION
INITIAL INSPECTION

TRADE PARTNER PREPARATION PROCESS

How the trades interact & benefit

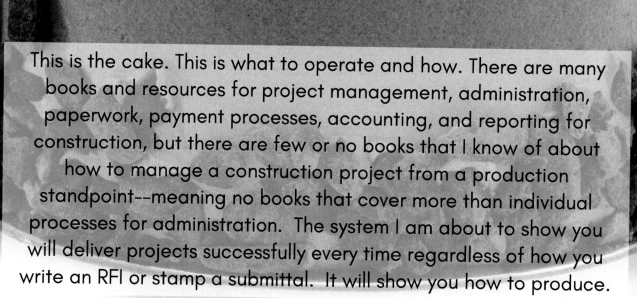

THE *What*
Part 1 – The Production System

This is the cake. This is what to operate and how. There are many books and resources for project management, administration, paperwork, payment processes, accounting, and reporting for construction, but there are few or no books that I know of about how to manage a construction project from a production standpoint--meaning no books that cover more than individual processes for administration. The system I am about to show you will deliver projects successfully every time regardless of how you write an RFI or stamp a submittal. It will show you how to produce.

The First Planner™ Production System

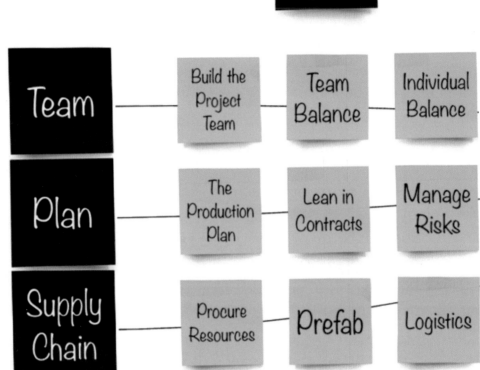

The Production System

Team	Build the Project Team	Team Balance	Individual Balance
Plan	The Production Plan	Lean in Contracts	Manage Risks
Supply Chain	Procure Resources	Prefab	Logistics
Culture	Win over The Workforce	Clean, Safe, & Organized Project	Onboarding & Orientation

Building a Project Team

It is critical to understand that you can plan a project according to all the best practices I'm referencing, engineer a flawless production plan for your project, and still fail miserably if your team is not healthy & high functioning. That is the push back I give to the industry experts. It's not enough to have the perfect plan and design.

I've spent a significant portion of my adult life problem solving construction issues, and the majority of the solutions I create include resolving team conflicts. Work being produced or installed on-site can be adversely affected by something as small as personality differences causing tension and a lack of communication by people upstream to that specific work. There are many books on the subject of team building and leadership, and I encourage you to read them and implement the practices and strategies that will benefit your unique team. I want to focus on what I see as the three crucial needs of your project team; these are the team issues most detrimental/beneficial to the entire project.

the CRITICAL NEEDS *of a* TEAM

1 A cohesive team that owns the project

2 Strenuous performance goals

3 Multiplier Leaders

COHESIVE TEAM THAT OWNS THE PROJECT

In *The Five Dysfunctions of a Team*, Patrick Lencioni shares the common behavioral tendencies that diminish team health and safety. As a team leader, you must focus on preventing the negative patterns/habits by promoting the attributes that foster a cohesive work environment.

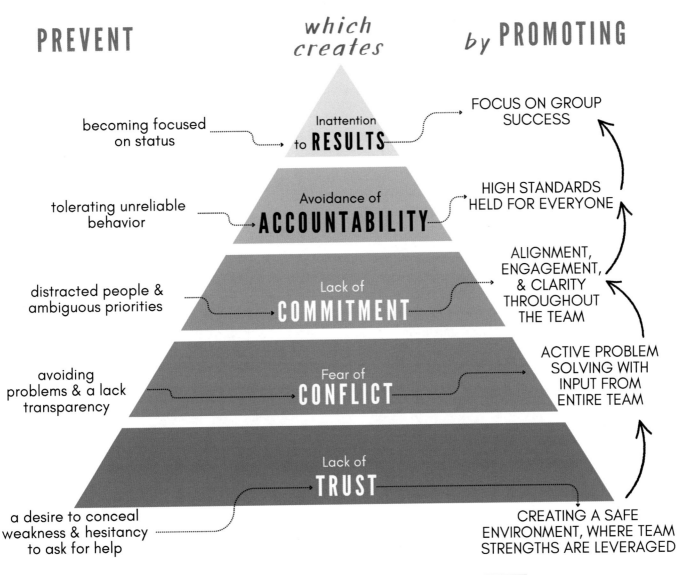

PREVENT · *which creates* · *by* PROMOTING

becoming focused on status → Inattention to **RESULTS** → FOCUS ON GROUP SUCCESS

tolerating unreliable behavior → Avoidance of **ACCOUNTABILITY** → HIGH STANDARDS HELD FOR EVERYONE

distracted people & ambiguous priorities → Lack of **COMMITMENT** → ALIGNMENT, ENGAGEMENT, & CLARITY THROUGHOUT THE TEAM

avoiding problems & a lack transparency → Fear of **CONFLICT** → ACTIVE PROBLEM SOLVING WITH INPUT FROM ENTIRE TEAM

a desire to conceal weakness & hesitancy to ask for help → Lack of **TRUST** → CREATING A SAFE ENVIRONMENT, WHERE TEAM STRENGTHS ARE LEVERAGED

The Five Dysfunctions of a Team: A Leadership Fable

Author: Patrick Lencioni

Henny Portman, a consultant and expert on traditional project management, took Lencioni's five tendencies and added ideas for teams and leaders to follow for best possible team outcomes. We've added our ideas where we saw the need.

	IDEAS FOR THE TEAM	IDEAS FOR THE LEADER
RESULTS	• Recognize contributions & achievements publicly	• Be objective and helpful • Focus on group results; do not encourage asshole superstars
ACCOUNTABILITY	• Display goals & standards • Review progress with daily/weekly status reports • Reward the team	• Encourage team to hold each other accountable first • Arbitrate and discipline fairly when needed
COMMITMENT	• Set realistic deadlines and encourage buy-in • Empower ownership with team solving the "how" • Allow for decision making at the "lowest" possible level	• Establish the "what" and let the team decide the how • Empower decision making at every possible step • Clarify possible risks or worst-case scenarios so the team can feel safe in their commitment
CONFLICT	• Mine for conflicts & misunderstanding often; facilitate resolution • Allow every voice to be heard and understood before closing issues • Encourage vulnerability through "I feel" statements (a feeling has to follow, not an accusation)	• Model healthy conflict resolution • Demonstrate restraint • Focus on impact rather than accusation; be patient and understanding
TRUST	• Develop a 360 degree feedback protocol • Use assessments to create team empathy • Accept individual weaknesses for what they are and seek to overcome them with the strength of the team when possible	• Be genuine • Create a safe environment; teach, coach, and mentor vs berate, belittle, and threaten • Demonstrate vulnerability first

As the team begins to eliminate conflicts and develop a sense of belonging, you will see the true ownership emerging. The team understands the "why" of their work as goals and standards are maintained. **Delegation** and problem solving gives the team an increased sense of value and purpose, which empowers everyone to excel in their scope. As a leader, you will blame problems and systems, rather than people, which means your team will be inclined to collaborate to solve issues, rather than feel punished or disenchanted by personal failure. **Celebrate** when you see the team empowered in their decision making and being truly responsible for creating their own success. Something I have done to promote ownership is to ask a person what they would do in a particular situation, listen to their answer and ask for clarification if needed, and then ask them to follow-up in a week/month to see how the solution is working. I like the following approach as well: "I intend to ..." where they propose the solution and provide the clarity needed for me to understand the issue and their ability to solve it. This gives me the opportunity to weigh in or stop them if they are headed in a wrong direction, but it puts the onus on them to identify and strategize without me needing to micromanage the how. The leader determines the "why" and "what" and gives support--the team can determine the "how." Anything else will lead to the five dysfunctions.

2 STRENUOUS PERFORMANCE GOALS

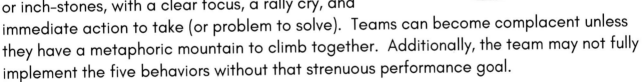

If you have a team nailing the five behaviors, they then need a strenuous performance goal. In construction that means intermediate milestones or inch-stones, with a clear focus, a rally cry, and immediate action to take (or problem to solve). Teams can become complacent unless they have a metaphoric mountain to climb together. Additionally, the team may not fully implement the five behaviors without that strenuous performance goal.

I remember a project that had enough money, time, what seemed to be the best available people, and the best resources in the company. Right out of the gate the team lost 3 months on the schedule from complacency. After discussing the critical needs pattern with the team, an assistant Super spoke up and said, "We need to move our mat placement date up. We are not targeting even close to what we could accomplish." They moved the date up by 6 weeks which was not impossibly aggressive, but also not conservative. The team immediately rallied and their dynamic became obvious. After fixing two or three other major issues within the team, they hit their new target within 6 days and soon after pulled the schedule back in and recovered the entire 3 months in a healthy way.

3 MULTIPLIER LEADERSHIP

In *Multipliers: How the Best Leaders Make Everyone Smarter*, author Liz Wiseman teaches us, "It isn't how much you know that matters. What matters is how much access you have to what other people know." One of the eight wastes of construction is not leveraging the wisdom of the team, underutilizing capabilities, and delegating tasks with inadequate training--all of these can be traced back to diminishing or accidental diminishing leadership. Compare ideal leadership behaviors and their negative counterparts below. These people tend to be the a-hole bosses you dread working for, meaning they generally understand their behavior is negatively affecting the team, but persist regardless of impact. I'm not here to try to understand their motivation; they are not reading this book. I need you to be self-aware enough to understand if this is you, and how can you adopt better leadership behaviors.

MULTIPLIERS V/S DIMINISHERS

Talent Magnets
Hire talented people, help them succeed, & a cycle of attraction is created

Empire Builders
Hire talented people, underutilize them, talent is stunted, a cycle of decline is created.

Liberators
Intense, stable environment that demands the best performance. Team free to think/act boldly.

Tyrants
Create a tense environment, anxiety limits ability to perform, people are cautious and don't speak up.

Challengers
Directives motivate people to stretch, discover, and innovate. Failure is normalized as critical to innovation.

Know-it-Alls
Define directives to help spotlight the leader's expertise; team learning is stifled.

Debate Maker
Encourages rigorous debate to land at collaborative solutions and sound decisions.

Decision Makers
Make decisions without the team (or with a tight inner circle); team feels uninvolved and confused.

Investors
Team is able to perform their work & be accountable for themselves. Leader gives insight, but team maintains ownership.

Micromanagers
Do everything personally; don't trust the team with the how, which creates an over-dependence on leader.

ACCIDENTAL DIMINISHING LEADERSHIP

Wiseman also shares six types of accidental diminishing behaviors that leaders practice; often these well-intentioned leaders are unaware of the impact they have on their team. These can be really frustrating because this is when you're trying your best, but the impact is not at all in line with your intention and expectation. This is where most of us will find our flaws. I personally struggle to understand the impact of my Rapid Responder behavior at times; my team is getting good at asking me how to restructure their priorities to accommodate the new tasks they have received. The struggle is real!

	INTENTION	IMPACT	SOLUTIONS
The Optimist	Create a belief that the team can do it!	No room for failure, belief that leader lacks empathy or effort not valued.	Acknowledge the struggles; encourage conversation about mistakes to normalize the opportunity for growth.
The Rapid Responder	Keep everything moving fast!	Overload of team due to speed of leader; traffic jams.	Prioritize work; understand WWP & how many tasks are being added daily.
The Pacesetter	Set a high standard for quality or pace!	Team becomes spectators to the leader.	Slow down; give time for people to learn and grow.
The Rescuer	Ensure success and protect reputations!	People lose confidence and depend on leader.	Ask questions to improve problem solving; encourage honey badgers.
The Idea Guy/Gal	Stimulate ideas in team with brilliant ideas!	Distraction, overwhelm, and time wasted chasing big things.	Put your ideas in a holding tank until they need to be discussed.
Always On	Create infectious energy with your point of view!	Take up too much space; people tune out.	Say less and create opportunities for others to take the floor.

Going back to the story I began in the strenuous performance goal section, I will report that the remaining team issues in that example were the results of diminishing leaders. The senior project manager and project director were ineffective and not multiplying the team. Even though it is not typically done, we made the hard decision to fire the PM and reassign the PD. Then the team started to thrive.

The PM was the Know-it-All Diminisher that wanted to maintain the status quo. The PD was a weak leader that would not correct his PM, nor did he attempt to build the team. Without a strenuous performance goal and multiplying leadership, the team was plagued with the five dysfunctional behaviors. And interestingly, once a better goal was put in place, the other two critical needs being unmet became obvious.

As a builder, I've see this pattern emerge over and over again. Your team can fail even if there is a good plan when you are not prioritizing critical needs. Your responsibility in all of this is to pattern your leadership style after healthy, multiplying behaviors and then utilize the people, plan, and resources in a way that expands the initial capacity, ability, and reach of the individuals. I love how Simon Sinek has redefined the concept of being an alpha leader. Alpha leaders are not simply the authority figure on the job, someone assigned to be in charge. Real alpha leaders are those with the resources and confidence to face any approaching danger. As an alpha, you do more work and put yourself at risk to take care of the team. The team is willing to follow where you lead, knowing that they have your help and protection along the way.

"We know this, that intelligence—it languishes. It shrinks essentially when it's not used. And when intelligence is challenged and used and applied, it grows. We literally get smarter and more capable around certain kinds of leaders and people and colleagues and roommates and family members. And that is really the multiplier effect. It's getting all of people's capability plus a growth dividend. And then the dynamic that happens across an organization where people come to work knowing that not only are they going to be fully utilized, they're going to be challenged. That you need to show up, game ready. That's the multiplier effect." Liz Wiseman

Multipliers, Revised and Updated: How the Best Leaders Make Everyone Smarter

Author: Liz Wiseman

REFLECTION-BUILDING A PROJECT TEAM

The purpose of this component in the First Planner System™ is as the apparatus with which all other systems and components are delivered. The team will implement every other component of the system to the degree that the team is functioning. If your team enjoys coming to work, engages in healthy conflict and works together to create flow, you are meeting the critical needs of the team . An unhealthy team has diminished capability, capacity and inherent motivation. If the team is fragmented and not aligned in the right ways, tensions and siloing will take over and more time and effort will be required to produce value-add work.

Component Scoring: (1%-100%)
1. Is your team:
    a. taking time to know each other?____
    b. building trust?____
    c. engaging in healthy conflict?____
    d. making decisions and setting goals/standards together?____
    e. holding each other accountable?____
    f. a high performing group?____
2. Does your team have a strenuous performance goal that is pulling the team towards alignment, mutual trust, and accountability to the group?____
3. Have you been intentional about creating your team culture?____
4. Is your team focused on finding the real cause of problems in the system rather than blaming individuals?____
5. Do you have a multiplier leader that:
    a. builds the team?____
    b. has difficult conversations when and how they need to take place?____
    c. manages, coaches, mentors, and trains direct reports without micromanagement?____
    d. ensures remarkable meetings are taking place?____
    e. scales communication and clarity effectively about the vision and direction of the project?____

What is your final score, taking the average of all answers? ____

If your score is below 80%, what specific actions do you need to take to elevate your team and leadership?

NOTE

Balance the Team

Once you have a functioning team with the right behaviors, goal, and leader, you will need to purposefully maintain balance. In *Built to Fail*, Todd Zabelle explains that when you exceed the capacity of a system, you extend the cycle time and throughput time. If you overburden the project team, the time it takes to complete work increases and you have an increased risk of errors. Overburden can come from:

- Too much administration.
- Wasteful paperwork and permissions.
- Useless meetings and requirements.
- Too many changes to the project without additional help.
- Too much owner-driven variation.

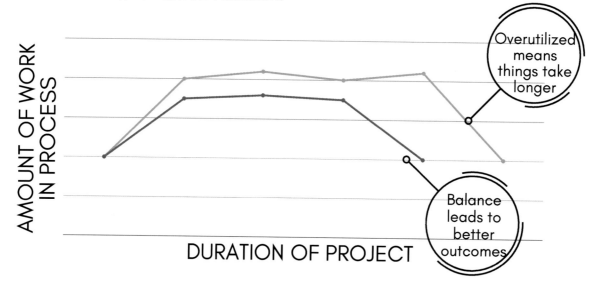

If you want to prevent wasting unnecessary time, keeping your team balanced and healthy is your top priority. The easiest metrics to evaluate are people and positions, work schedules, and team conditions.

Built to Fail: Why Construction Projects Take So Long, Cost Too Much, and How to Fix It

Author: Todd R Zabelle

1 PEOPLE & POSITIONS

Here are the questions you will ask to understand balance–
- Do you have the right people on and off the team?
- Are team members in the right roles?

This is the moment to gauge if you have too few people doing too many roles or if you are utilizing people for roles that are better suited to someone else. The more you know your team, the better able you are to assess that everyone is functioning well in their proper role. Consider removing high performing assholes from the team--yes, they accomplish a lot, but they are generally not worth the damage they do to team morale.

2 PERSONAL ORGANIZATION & SCHEDULES

Here are the questions you will ask to understand balance–
- Does each team member follow leader standard work and have a personal organization system?
- Are standard coverage schedules followed for the team to have a good blend between work and home?
- Are there any team members overburdened?

When you are a leader, no longer an authority, you will truly care about the people on your team. You have the power to improve their working conditions and should never abuse that power. When you can see someone is working too hard, it's unacceptable to intentionally exploit them for the benefit of the team. Would you want your child to be treated the way you are treating your team? Use your skills to leverage the wisdom of the team and help everyone to pull equally. Furthermore, insist that the team is transparent about their personal organization system, schedules, and leader standard work and that it is all seen at a glance. Make them visual and share them in a common place so you can be a protector of their time.

Shift your mindset from feeling like you need to squeeze more work out of everyone to how can I get people home on time.

Click for more on LSW

3 PROJECT CONDITIONS

To understand balance, ask if there are any project conditions that overburden the team. The following issues need to be assessed:

- **Design changes & change orders.** Isolate the changed areas and keep your team's focus on contract work. If they have capacity they can work on the changes. If they don't, you need more trained help, and the owner needs to pay for it.

- **Constant variation.** If your team experiences variation, you need to create consistency anywhere possible--especially in meeting systems, agendas, standard work, planning, and processes. Every time you add a one off or new task, consider the cost in time to absorb the variation.

- **Not enough onsite or remote support.** If you don't have the resources for the project, get them. Hire additional people, ask for company help, or outsource some of your needs. Sometimes projects fail simply because we don't have enough coverage.

- **Too many assignments.** If your project team has too many projects, side projects, corporate projects, or assignments creating context switching and wasted time, you need to focus them.

- **Too many people on the team above needed levels.** Sometimes having too many people will cause you problems because communication gets harder with larger teams. So if you've panicked and added too many people to help you, consider right sizing your team.

- **Too much waste in their environment.** Waste can drag down a team like nothing else. You must have your Paul Akers goggles on as the leader and remove any waste or wasted efforts from your team.

- **Unhealthy conflict.** This is the ninth waste in construction. If your team is experiencing unhealthy conflict with the owner, designers, contracts, requirements or other relationships on the project, it must be addressed and remedied immediately. This is the responsibility of the leader.

Use the scorecard to assess your team. Each person on the team will fill this out monthly; then you will aggregate the overall score and dig deep into topics that have lower scores. It's a remarkable way to keep the team balanced and stable.

TEAM HEALTH SCORECARD- BALANCE & STABILITY

KEY INDICATOR	SCORE BASED ON:	SCORE
Team in roles	Each member of the team in their proper role to ensure success.	
Team balanced	The team is balanced and not working too much, overloaded, disproportionate responsibilities, unorganized, etc.	
Leader Standard Work followed	All leaders have and stick to critical standard work each week.	
Team Standard Work followed	The team is following their standard work, with good hours, balanced meetings, and standardized schedules.	
Individual & Team Work/Life blend	Team has an appropriate blend of work life and family life, with neither aspect negatively affecting the other.	
Individual health of team members	Team is physically and emotionally healthy, and taking care of mental and physical needs.	
Team stabilized	The team is stable, focused, driving forward, determined and aligned.	
Healthy conflict	The team is practicing healthy conflict, and eliminating unhealthy conflict.	
Health of team chemistry	The team can relax and have fun together.	
Company or team politics	The team avoids politics and placing their status above the needs of others.	
Wider team health	The Trade Partners, Designers, and Owners Reps are organized into a well functioning team.	
Labor quality/quantity	There is enough labor, and quality labor is being performed on the project.	
"Bus" organized--let go/move people	We fire, move, and promote people as needed and deserved.	
Design & engineering balance	The engineers and architects are fostering balance onsite and within the team.	
RFI's acceptable	The RFI's remain at an acceptable number, not impacting the project with burden or imbalance.	
Design changes within reason	The design changes are not negatively affecting the construction site and team.	
Design responsibility balanced	Contractor and designers are balanced in the ongoing design efforts.	

REFLECTION-BALANCING THE PROJECT TEAM

The purpose of this component in the First Planner System™ is to ensure your team stays healthy throughout the duration of the project. Team building efforts will be overrun if you are not able to balance the changes your team will face as outside elements join your team. The project owner, owner's rep, designers, trades and even your own corporate policies have the potential to create an imbalance as you struggle to incorporate them and their demands into your own team dynamics. Once you and your team are over capacity, your project will begin to spiral. Simply put, the energy to control the project cannot be more than the combined team energy they have to offer. Your focus is to keep them balanced with high morale, at all costs.

Component Scoring: (1%-100%)
- Are you shielding your project team from impacts that will cause imbalance? ___
- Are you reducing variation and creating flow within your project leadership team?___
- Does your team have all the right people on and off the bus?___
- Does your team have all the right people in all the right seats on the bus?___

What is your final score, taking the average of all answers? ___

If your score is below 80%, what specific actions do you need to take to elevate your team and leadership?

NOTE

44

PLAN
SUPPLY CHAIN
CULTURE
TRAINING

Individual Balance

We've touched on this as a component to the wider team health and balance, but this is where leadership is going to have to be personal and intentional. People feel like we have a good work/home life balance when we feel like work doesn't suck away the best parts of who we are. The more we are emotionally drained at work, the less we have to give at home. It's not simply about working too many hours, although too much time at work can contribute to an imbalance. The imbalance is created from the hormones people experience when they are at work. Who knew that was coming? Now I'm not a medical professional and this is not medical advice, but if you want to keep your team balanced, you have to do your part to decrease the stress the team feels when they're working. You can't control anyone's emotions, nor should you try, but you are in control of the environment and you have the tools to reduce stress in their workplace/role. You're able to directly influence the anxiety people feel when working for you; continued elevated levels of cortisol (stress hormone) lead to anxiety, depression, and a depleted immune system. Simply put--mental health leads to better physical health and total health of the entire production system is of great benefit to you. It's the right thing to do, but it's also a better financial decision if we are just being honest.

Your responsibility as a leader is to assess and address each individual's mindset, aspirations, capability, and capacity.

MINDSET

It's my experience that there are no complete fixed or growth mindsets--just people that have fixed thoughts about certain subjects until they are able to learn more. At times we are adventurous or curious about a subject, which means we have a growth mindset. When we're quite close-minded about something, meaning we're resistant to new ideas and conversations, we have a fixed mindset.

Your challenge as a leader is to continually gauge the team for resistance to change, and use collaborative problem solving to shift perceptions and open minds. Pressure, threats (perceived or actual), stress, overwhelm and demoralizing behavior will cause a fixed mind. It isn't within your control to change someone else's mindset, however there is a leadership opportunity to provide the personalized help your team/teammate needs to soften their heart and open their minds. Help may look like providing more resources, making time to have an in-depth conversation to understand the fear or threat they feel like they are facing, and meeting people where they are. Sometimes an approach is to recognize that they may not believe in the new concept yet, but you do and you will be with them along the way. We see this resistance almost daily as we try to influence the world to accept Takt. It's new, it's scary, and immediately Takt seems like a threat to the older ways of doing construction. Being able to acknowledge why someone is closed off, and validate their experience is a skill all leaders need. From that place of empathy, you can sincerely ask for the team to trust your judgement and that you will be there as the team faces new challenges.

ASPIRATIONS

It's human nature to seek to broaden our horizons, develop new skills, and enhance our knowledge of the world. Setting goals and striving to achieve them leads to personal growth-both intellectually and emotionally. Most people have to feel like they can aspire to more in their career to maintain engagement and enjoyment at work. There are many career opportunities and individuals are leaving when their development opportunities are perceived as below average.

Your challenge as a leader is help your team by supporting their career and personal aspirations. You must provide clarity to your team and help them set realistic goals. If you view yourself as a protector of your team, you will be aware of how you can lead them towards their goals, or even facilitate their efforts through your connections or expertise.

To help your team with clarity, we suggest the Clarity-Action-Influence exercise with the entire team. You will work backwards from your life purpose, to your 5-10 year goals, and from there establish milestones and individual goals. In the example, you see that our fictional Super, Steve Rogers, has outlined his clarity all the way to his next milestone and defining goals.

CLARITY – ACTION – INFLUENCE PLAN FOR :   *Steve Rogers*

STRENGTHS

positive communication

leader of people

team connection

contextual teaching

ability to coach others

VALUES
1. *transparency*
2. *respect*
3. *building the team*
4. *integrity*
5. *generosity*

MISSION
VALUES
ACTION

MISSION | PURPOSE - 100 YEAR
To become a General Superintendent in my company and develop training programs for all other supers in the company. To develop enough personal wealth to start my children in life so they can continue the family legacy of giving and contributing to the world.

BHAG (BIG HAIRY AUDACIOUS GOAL) - 5- 10 YEAR
To learn the position of senior superintendent and to learn everything I can about project scheduling and project controls in the next 5 years.

NEXT MILESTONE - 4-18 MONTHS
Become proficient with project scheduling in the next ten months.

DEFINING GOALS

Take a Takt planning course; become a certified Takt Master –Master Scheduler	*Actively create and update current project schedule and provide weekly/monthly schedule updates*	*Find a mentor– Senior Super– and shadow them in their scheduling process*	*Reflect on the success of the schedule and improve on any mistakes that were made*	*Learn the Last Planner® system and become proficient with Pull Planning*

Strengths are important to understand so you can align your life with your talents.
Values help you direct your actions and behaviors.
Your purpose and mission will highlight what you plan to accomplish by the end of your life.
Your BHAG will harness your strengths and values, galvanize you to action, and ensure a relentless pursuit of a long term, mission driven goal.
Your next milestone is clarity on what is important right now.
And your defining goals, or "inch-stones" are the steps that will get you to your next milestone.

CAPABILITY & CAPACITY

In each facet of life, we must juggle our immediate needs and wants. At work, we balance the time it takes to complete our tasks with the learning of new skills. As we learn and increase our abilities, our capacity to manage work is increased. We can't learn and grow beyond our capacity if we don't have a system to support the growth. We can also underutilize our ability to learn if we are overburdened with too many tasks.

Your challenge as a leader is to support highly efficient routines for your project and to encourage or require an effective personal organization system for the entire team. You will find better outcomes when the systems are visible, used by everyone, and intuitive to the personality of the team. Here is how we recommend establishing capacity based on ability through personal organization.

Have everyone take the Clarity-Action-Influence Plan and time block your leader standard work (LSW) week in this order:
- You – Your needs for your health, wellness, sleep, training & five **goals**.
- Your family – The needs and wants of your family.
- Your LSW – The leader standard work you have for your role/project. These are the things that only you can do and should do in addition to the things that will help your career progress.

Once these are plugged into a calendar you can then schedule meetings and deal with the needs of the project.

Please note that personal, family, and work needs are all scheduled in the example. This is a win, win, win. It **must** be in this order. If you reverse it, you will never get past the needs of the project and will end up with a lose, lose, lose situation. We can't consider the project a success if it came at the expense of the team and/or their families-ever. It is anti-Lean because it does not respect people. That is the reason we are fighting this fight--to stop the disrespect of people in the construction industry. And no, I never get tired of harping on this; it's the hill I will die on.

LEADER STANDARD WORK WEEK | FIND THE WIN-WIN-WIN

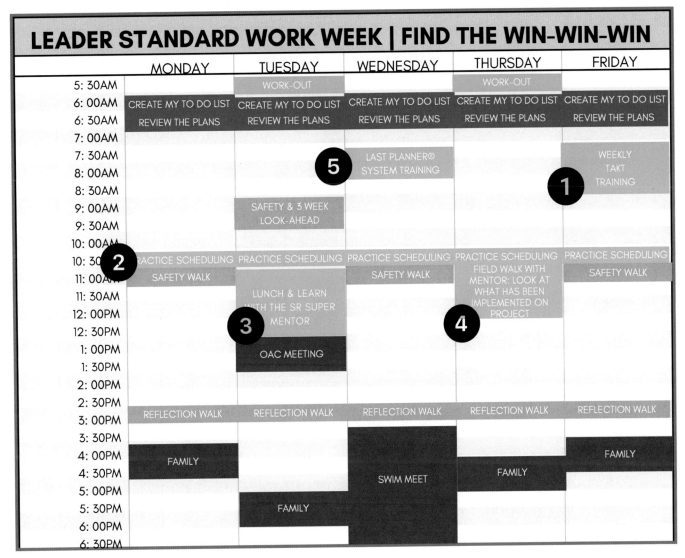

	MONDAY	TUESDAY	WEDNESDAY	THURSDAY	FRIDAY
5:30AM		WORK-OUT		WORK-OUT	
6:00AM	CREATE MY TO DO LIST	CREATE MY TO DO LIST	CREATE MY TO DO LIST	CREATE MY TO DO LIST	CREATE MY TO DO LIST
6:30AM	REVIEW THE PLANS	REVIEW THE PLANS	REVIEW THE PLANS	REVIEW THE PLANS	REVIEW THE PLANS
7:00AM					
7:30AM			LAST PLANNER® SYSTEM TRAINING (5)		WEEKLY TAKT TRAINING (1)
8:00AM					
8:30AM					
9:00AM		SAFETY & 3 WEEK LOOK-AHEAD			
9:30AM					
10:00AM					
10:30AM	(2) PRACTICE SCHEDULING	PRACTICE SCHEDULING	PRACTICE SCHEDULING	PRACTICE SCHEDULING	PRACTICE SCHEDULING
11:00AM	SAFETY WALK		SAFETY WALK	FIELD WALK WITH MENTOR: LOOK AT WHAT HAS BEEN IMPLEMENTED ON PROJECT (4)	SAFETY WALK
11:30AM		LUNCH & LEARN WITH THE SR SUPER MENTOR (3)			
12:00PM					
12:30PM					
1:00PM		OAC MEETING			
1:30PM					
2:00PM					
2:30PM					
3:00PM	REFLECTION WALK	REFLECTION WALK	REFLECTION WALK	REFLECTION WALK	REFLECTION WALK
3:30PM			SWIM MEET		
4:00PM	FAMILY			FAMILY	FAMILY
4:30PM					
5:00PM					
5:30PM		FAMILY			
6:00PM					
6:30PM					

■ DEFINING GOALS

Take a Takt planning course; become a certified Takt Master –Master Scheduler	*Actively create and update current project schedule and provide weekly/monthly schedule updates*	*Find a mentor– Senior Super– and shadow them in their scheduling process*	*Reflect on the success of the schedule and improve on any mistakes that were made*	*Learn the Last Planner System and become proficient with Pull Planning*

*Steve has purposefully prioritized his five defining goals, which will help him achieve his next milestone.

■ For the project needs, each of the team needs to keep a to do list that:

- Gets all ideas out of your head.
- Puts it all in one location.
- Is prioritized, and,
- Is clear and well described.

49

Once you have your concise to do list and your work week plan, you will build your day plans by adding tasks from the to do list. This can be done for the entire week to help you make use of each day.

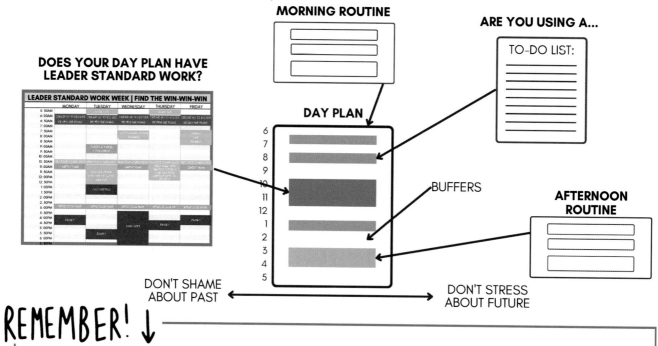

REMEMBER! ↓

- Don't become a victim to emails throughout the day.
- Add buffers between tasks so you can actually finish each task. This will save you 1-4 hours per day.
- Focus on tasks when in a flow-set yourself up for success.
- Only allow yourself to be distracted when the item is actually urgent.

This is a production system (within the larger production systems) that you will be able to see at work in each team member's personal and professional lives, and you'll be able to see it at a glance. Every time one of our team mentions how stressed they are or that they need more help, we can easily see the problems in their system by looking at their personal organization system. It's not about trying to control anyone's time; it's about our ability to see the issues at a glance. People are not the problem--the system is the problem and we have the ability to engineer near perfection for our personal organization systems.

Success Formula

CLARITY   **MINDSET**   **PERSONAL ORG SYSTEM**   **MORNING ROUTINE**

At Elevate Construction, we've created multiple personal organization planners to help you and your team prioritize everything that you're facing. They include:
- Role specific information
- Life planners
- Clarity documents
- PTO planners
- Day planners
- and other amazing tools

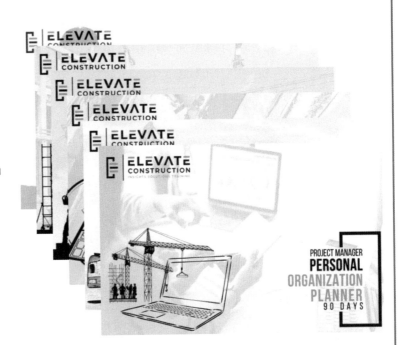

Just search "[Role] Personal Organization Planner" on Amazon for the following roles:
- Project Manager
- Project Engineer
- Superintendent
- Field Engineer
- Foreman
- Surveyor

An additional reference for the team component is Elevating Construction Project Teams also titled Elevating Construction Senior Superintendents. This book covers the Leader and the Team in depth and is a precursor to this book.

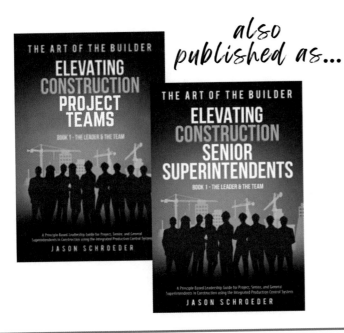

also published as...

REFLECTION-INDIVIDUAL BALANCE

The purpose of this component in the First Planner System™ is to ensure each person on the team is able to live a balanced and happy life and blend his or her work and family in a way that they can experience a win-in. If this component is not in place the team will not have the time to implement anything else in the system.

Component Scoring: (1%-100%)
- Does each person know about the fixed vs. growth mindset?____
- Does each person on your team have a clarity document?____
- Does each person have a personal organization system?____
- Does each person have a morning routine that sets them up for the day?____
- Are team members using to do lists?____
- Does every member have Leader Standard Work?____
- Are team members time blocking their days with buffers and focus?____

What is your final score, taking the average of all answers? ____
If your score is below 80%, what specific actions do you need to take to elevate your team and leadership?

NOTE

FPS™ | TPS® | LPS®

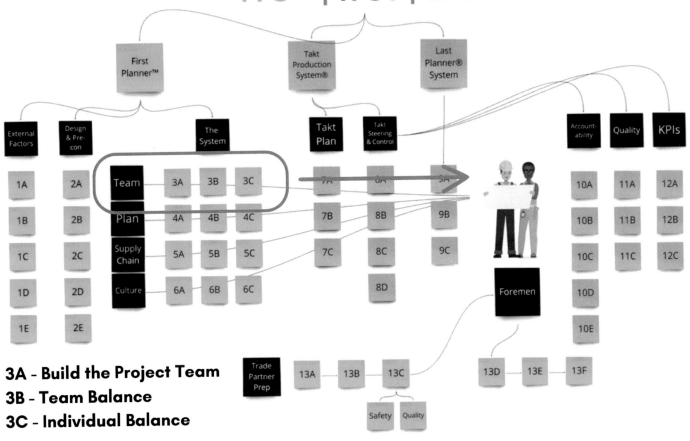

3A - Build the Project Team
3B - Team Balance
3C - Individual Balance

As we discuss components and phases of the First Planner System™ we will anchor you to the outline. At this point you have a project leadership team (First Planners™) that can reinforce the efforts of the foremen. Everything in this system is engineered to support the foremen installing work with workers in a work package within a zone.

now your foremen have a team to support them.

The Production Plan

Once you have a team that is formed and balanced, with each member having the capacity to implement lean, it's time to make a production plan, align trades to that plan, and clear the path for flow. I'd love to get everyone on the same page right now. When I say production plan, I'm talking about a series of production systems that will execute the work onsite, and these production systems are designed as part of the all encompassing project production plan. In *Built to Fail*, Todd Zabelle goes into extensive detail about the design of a production system and there are three points I would like to emphasize.

Design a production system, not a schedule

Schedules are simply predictions of what should happen, and they do not account for variability. It must be understood that the schedule will change over the course of the project. The schedule is the demand that the production system answers. The production system transforms inputs into reality and determines what will happen, and when it will happen.

Design your production system backwards

The trades execute work in work packages organized by day, located within a zone, and for a specific piece of work. The focus of the system should be to get the resources/materials, and controls to the crew where and when they are needed.

The aim is to design a system where crews have the people, materials, tools, equipment, layout, permissions, and information they need to perform the task in the work package in that zone by day. When we design our system this way, we will achieve **production flow**.

Each work package has its own production system to supply it with resources, comprised of controls, levers, and inventory. Each package is tied to the package that came before it in terms of inventory and preceding operations. You would start with the last item to be completed and then work backwards in construction, from end to beginning.

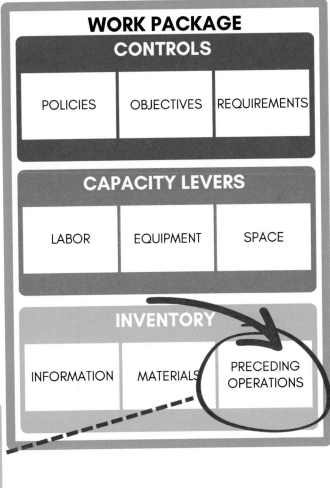

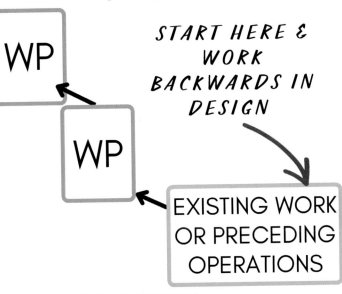

START HERE & WORK BACKWARDS IN DESIGN

WP

WP

EXISTING WORK OR PRECEDING OPERATIONS

CONSTRUCTION WORK WILL BE EXECUTED STARTING HERE & MOVE TO THE RIGHT AND DOWN THROUGH THE ZONES

DESIGN BEGINS AT THE END AND WORKS BACKWARD THROUGH EACH PROCESS

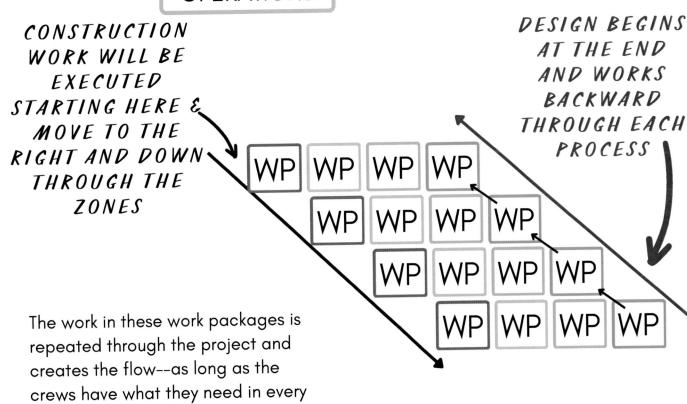

The work in these work packages is repeated through the project and creates the flow--as long as the crews have what they need in every zone the work in for that day.

55

Align all production systems

In order to feed the production system you must align design, fabrication, delivery, and hoisting to get the resources to the place of work on that same flow. This is called project production management.

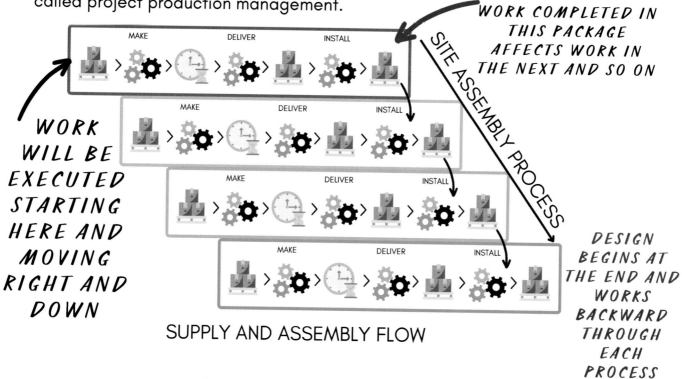

WORK COMPLETED IN THIS PACKAGE AFFECTS WORK IN THE NEXT AND SO ON

SITE ASSEMBLY PROCESS

WORK WILL BE EXECUTED STARTING HERE AND MOVING RIGHT AND DOWN

DESIGN BEGINS AT THE END AND WORKS BACKWARD THROUGH EACH PROCESS

SUPPLY AND ASSEMBLY FLOW

*GRAPHIC CONTAINS SOURCE MATERIAL FROM BUILT TO FAIL

There is so much more to that brilliant book, but again, remember that if you implement the book Takt Planning you will automatically follow the key warnings from *Built to Fail*:

1. Do not rely on schedulers to plan your projects. This creates disconnection from what is possible and hides excessive WIP.
2. Remember that excessive WIP will lengthen cycle times, throughput times, and your overall project duration.
3. Remember that you cannot just add more people or resources and have things go faster.
4. Do not focus more on administration than actually doing work.
5. And, again, create a production system, not a schedule.

There isn't a better or more clear way to create a production plan for your project than the Takt Production System®. You cannot plan your project with Gantt charts, CPM schedules, or any other 2D schedule and win. Planning that way WILL ruin your project. To make your plan you will implement Takt, Last Planner®, and Scrum. We've successfully aligned these three into a seamless system.

Your project production plan will include the following at a minimum:

- **Master Plan** – Your master plan will be a production simulation of the entire project based on how well resources can be obtained and aligned to produced in a flow. This plan will show you your milestones and provide a correct overall total project duration including commissioning and closeout.
- **Pull Plan** – Pull plans are how we verify sequences in phases. Trade Partners collaborate together with the project team to align demand (what the owner wants) with supply (What is possible) into a sequence. These pull plans then become Norm level Takt plans.
- **6 Week Make-ready Look-ahead Plans** – The look-ahead is used to make work ready, align specific dates to supply chains, and see and remove roadblocks ahead of time.
- **Weekly Work Plans** – The work plan is a week look-ahead where fine tune coordination is done with trade partners. Commitments are made according to the Takt flow and work is made ready the week ahead.
- **Day Plans** – Day plans are then filtered from the WWP and work is made ready for the next day in an execution plan for the day of.
- **Crew Plans** – Crew plans are the details of planning needed at a crew level to accomplish their work package on time in their zone.
- **Team Scrum Board** – And the team Scrum board shows roadblocks, constraints, efforts, and tasks needed to create flow in the field. It is the method used to keep the project leadership team focused on creating flow for our amazing trades, foremen, and workers.

To build your **Master Plan**, you will begin with Takt. Macro-level Takt plans are made in pre-construction by the First Planners™ (more on this later) and show target milestones and the general plan for the project.

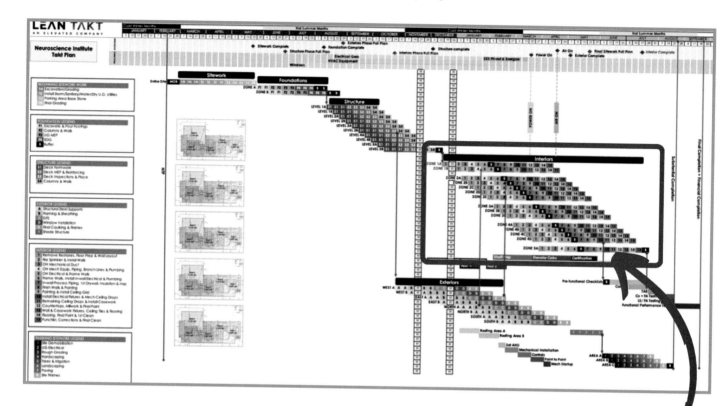

Once we move from pre-con to construction work in a phase (as marked above in red) we will then produce a Norm level production plan with the trades that will target a faster pace and add buffers. To do this we log the number of wagons and zones from the phase into the calculator to find out how many zones we would need for an ideal Norm level plan. Please do not try to run your production system from a Macro level plan because you will find it difficult to stick with a 5-day Takt time between weekends. You will always build from a day-to-day Norm level Takt plan.

If you look at the Takt Calculator on the next page, you will see that the Macro Level production plan uses 15 wagons, 5 zones, and a standard 5 day Takt time. When we optimize to a Norm Level production plan, we have 15 wagons and the option to use a 3, 2 or 1 day Takt time. Together, the team chose to use a 3 day Takt time which meant they could choose 9-12 zones, and the team ultimately chose 11 zones.

Takt Inputs

Takt Wagons	15
Takt Zones	5
Takt Time	5
Duration	95

Area Inputs (m², sqft)

Area / Zone	9,885
Min Zone Size	1,000
Max Zone Size	10,000
Total SQFT of Phase	49,425

Shortest Durations

Best # Zones	Takt Time	Duration
25	1	39
13	2	54
9	3	69
7	4	84
5	5	95
5	6	114
4	7	126
4	8	144
3	9	153
3	10	170

Takt Wagons	Takt Zones	Takt Time	Duration	Trade Time Gained	Area per Zone	Takt Level	Realized Flow Potential	Efficiency Parametric	Value Parametric
15	2	13	208	1	24,713	Bad	19%	7.50	15.00
15	3	9	153	2	16,475	Bad	25%	5.00	7.50
15	4	7	126	3	12,356	Macro	31%	3.75	5.00
15	5	5	95	0	9,885	Macro	41%	3.00	3.75
15	6		100	5	9,038	Macro	30%	2.50	3.00
15	7	4	84	3	7,061	Macro	46%	2.14	2.50
15	8	4	88	7	6,178	Macro	44%	1.88	2.14
15	9	3	69	2	5,492	Norm	57%	1.67	1.88
15	10	3	72	5	4,943	Norm	54%	1.50	1.67
15	11	3	75	8	4,493	Norm	52%	1.36	1.50
15	12	3	78	11	4,119	Norm	50%	1.25	1.36
15	13	2	54	1	3,802	Norm	72%	1.15	1.25
15	14	2	56	3	3,530	Norm	70%	1.07	1.15
15	15	2	58	5	3,295	Norm	67%	1.00	1.07
15	16	2	60	7	3,089	Norm	65%	0.94	1.00
15	17	2	62	9	2,907	Norm	63%	0.88	0.94
15	18	2	64	11	2,746	Norm	61%	0.83	0.88
15	19	2	66	13	2,601	Norm	59%	0.79	0.83
15	20	2	68	15	2,471	Norm	57%	0.75	0.79
15	21	2	70	17	2,354	Norm	56%	0.71	0.75
15	22	2	72	19	2,247	Norm	54%	0.68	0.71
15	23	2	74	21	2,149	Norm	53%	0.65	0.68
15	24	2	76	23	2,059	Norm	51%	0.63	0.65
15	25	1	39	0		Norm	100%	0.60	0.63
15	26	1	40	1	1,901	Norm		0.58	0.60
15	27	1	41	2				0.56	0.58
15	28	1	42	3					
15	29	1	43	4					
15	30	1	44	5					
15	31	1	45	6					
15	32	1	46	7					
15	33	1	47	8					
15	34	1	48	9					
15	35	1	49	10					
15	36	1	50	11					
15	37	1	51	12					

I hope you're excited about this calculator, but don't stress about understanding it yet. Just know that we have ways to see how many zones and wagons you will need for your production plan.

If you now know the ideal number of zones for your Norm level plan, you can make your zone maps reflect your new number of zones according to your work density analysis and start pull planning your first representative zone.

When you **pull plan**, you only pull plan that one zone and then do a stacking comparison according to the rhythm of the Takt time stagger.

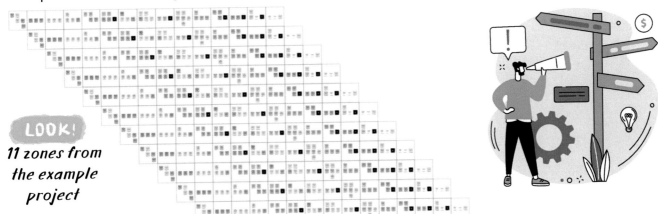

LOOK!
11 zones from the example project

Once you have confirmed you have trade flow, you can transform your stacking comparison into a full blown Norm level Takt plan.

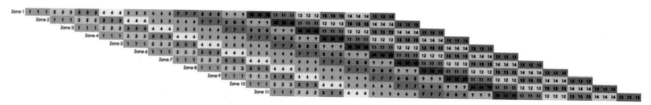

Your Norm level Takt plan is the production level plan that represents the target for you and your trades. You will develop your **look-ahead** and weekly work plans directly from this plan.

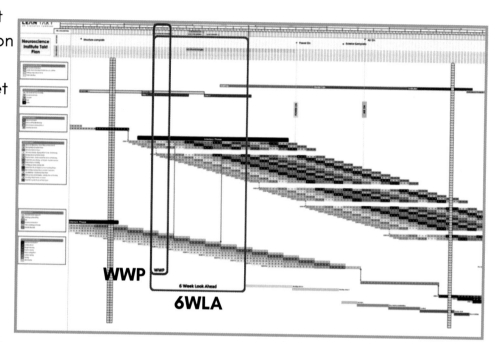

The **Weekly Work Plan** is filtered from the Norm level Takt plan and is complimented with sub-tasks and handoff indicators. It is all in a flow and vertically aligned.

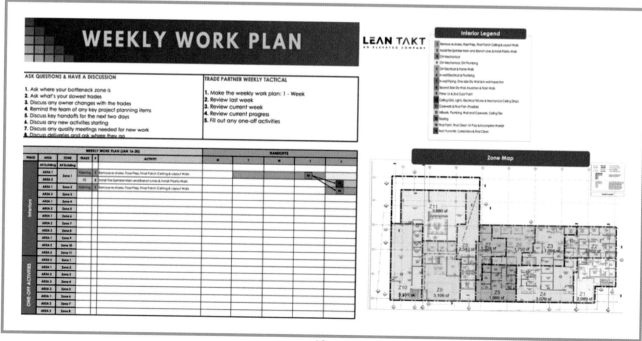

The **Day Plan** is then created from the Weekly Work Plan and formatted in a way that can be easily communicated to workers the next day. This will be the outcome of coordination, collaboration, and commitment among the Last Planners® on your team.

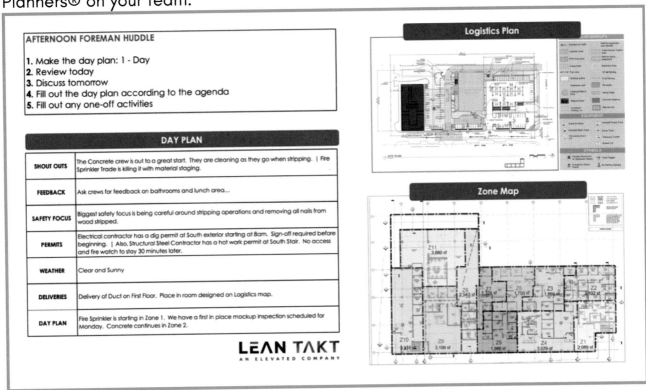

As the trades execute in the field, certain key performance indicators are tracked so the team can see how they are performing.

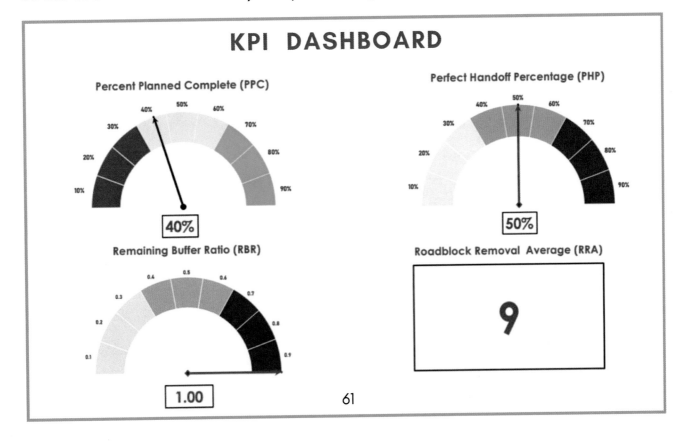

This production system allows us to control the sequences, line of balance, buffers, and milestones at the Macro and Norm Levels. This plan then triggers the need for pull plans, quality pre-con meetings, and material procurement.

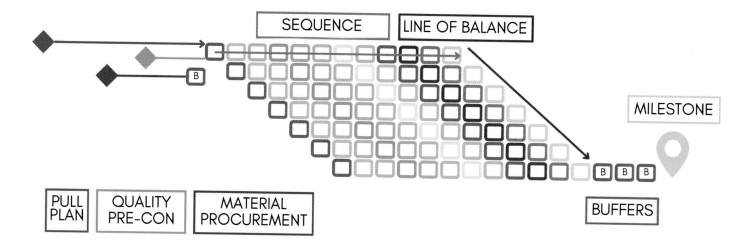

This base then allows you and the team to easily filter the 6-week Make-ready Look-ahead plan for making work ready and removing roadblocks. Additionally the Weekly Work Plan is filtered here and adjusted by trade partners for commitment in the weekly trade meeting.

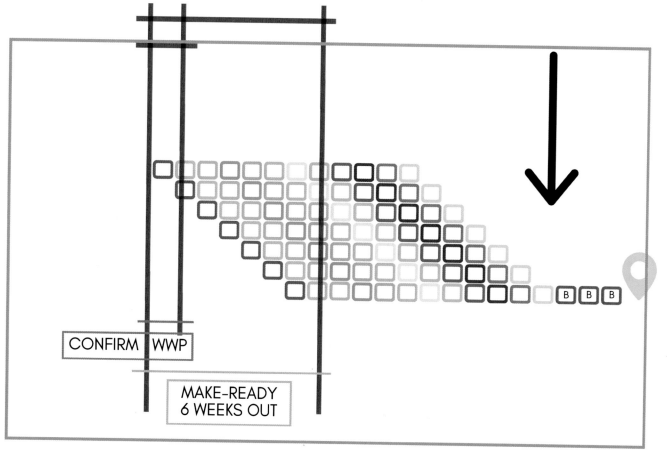

Macro Level Takt Plan: pre-construction effort to visualize the plan, create a project strategy, & verify the overall project duration.

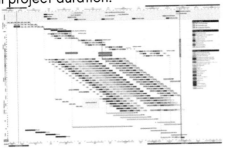

Norm Level Takt Plan: made from pull plans for production on site & for faster target dates. From this you filter your Last Planner® tools.

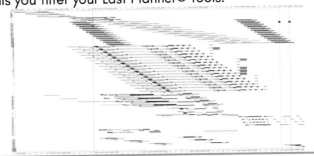

CPM: taken from Norm level production plan, only if required by owner.

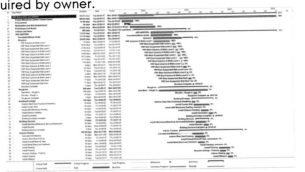

6-week Make-Ready Look-Ahead: auto-filtered from the Norm level Takt plan, trades use to make work ready & remove roadblocks ahead of the work.

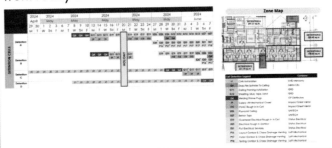

Weekly Work Plan: info is derived from the Norm Takt plan; this is the commitment level plan that trades execute in the field.

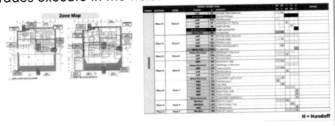

Day Plan: made in the Daily Huddle to provide the foremen & workers with a highly visible plan they can follow in the field.

Pre-Task Plan: With the day plan in hand and well communicated in the Morning Workers Huddle, foremen & workers can now fill out their Safety & Quality Pre-Task Plans.

PPC & Scrum: As work is complete "Percent Planned Complete" is tracked and calculated along with variances that enable improvement. Large problems are taken to the team's Scrum board.

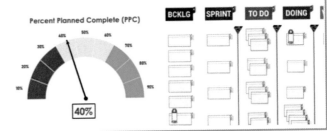

Effective commissioning is crucial for project success. You will need to incorporate commissioning tasks early, understand utility flow, and monitor milestones to ensure system functionality. Clear planning and communication are essential.

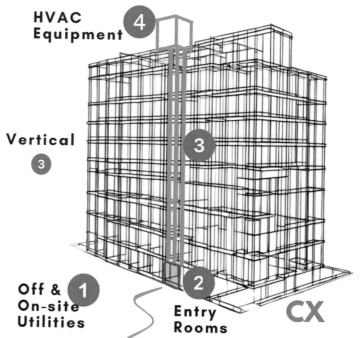

To successfully integrate commissioning into your project production plan, you will go system by system, not zone by zone.

1 **Off- & On-site Utilities**
Utilities reach the building. Start by bringing off-site utilities (water, sewer, power, etc.) to the building, typically within 5 feet of the structure.

2 **Entry Rooms** Utilities are then distributed into entry rooms such as fire pump rooms, mechanical rooms, the SES, and other critical spaces.

3 **Power, communications, internet, duct, and hyd piping** Systems rise through the building to the roof like hydronic piping, HVAC duct, fit-out of electrical rooms and IDF rooms.

4 **AHUs (HVAC SYSTEM)**
- Set up the air handlers.
- Ensure all electrical and control connections are properly made.
- Perform initial startup procedures.
- Prepare to feed the building.

5 **Full Commissioning**
- Begin test & balance
- Perform all life safety inspections
- Finish functional performance testing & building flush

This is a reference for integrating commissioning sequences in a production plan.

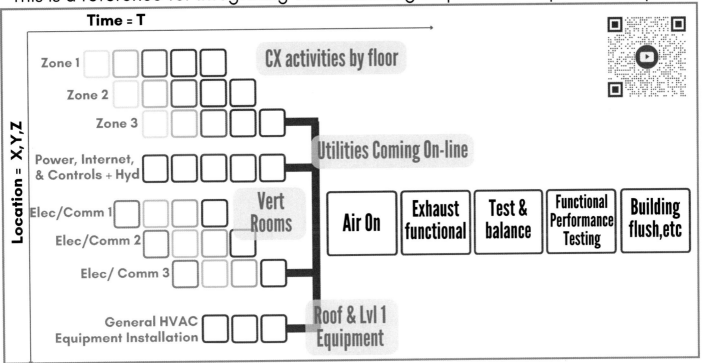

To fully engage these systems on your project, here are crucial references

Takt Planning, by Jason Schroeder

Learn how to design your production system from start to finish in a flow.

*coming Oct '24

Takt Steering & Control, by Jason Schroeder

Learn to control flow in the field in spite of roadblocks, constraints, impacts, and variation.

The Lean Builder, by J. Donarumo & K. Zandy

Turn your subs into trade partners and your foremen into Last Planners®.

Construction Scrum, by Felipe Engineer

Adapt the Scrum system to construction to further enable flow.

We use the following checklists at LeanTakt to develop the Takt plans and implement the production system in the field.

Built to Fail, by Todd R. Zabelle

You'll understand why construction is broken and what we would need to do to fix it.

Takt Development

Takt Requirements

Takt & Last Planner®

MACRO TAKT DEVELOPMENT CHECKLIST

During pre-construction:

1. Identify the target start and end date
2. Study the drawings
3. Identify the general flow of the project
4. Identify phases
5. Do a rough work density analysis
6. Identify initial zones
7. Identify constraints the team must work around
8. Get an idea of the number of Takt wagons in each phase
9. Check zones with the calculator and make sure it is in range
10. Get production rates of all activities
11. Package the sequences for the Macro Takt plan with 5-20% buffers
12. Create overall plan with interdependence ties and other content
13. Do a quick Fresh Eyes Meeting with the internal team
14. Create an initial procurement log to ensure materials support the schedule
15. Create initial logistics drawing
16. Do a Fresh Eyes with the wider project team
17. Verify milestones
18. Verify overall total project duration
19. Add any needed buffers
20. Format beautifully & make any corrections from the Fresh Eyes Meeting
21. Create a basis of schedule

NORM TAKT DEVELOPMENT CHECKLIST

During construction:

1. Create the Norm level format
2. Optimize every phase for optimal production
3. Make sure you have a backup production speed as well
4. Pull plan sequences with trades
5. Work-package phases with updated Takt time and zone configuration with 5-20% buffers
6. Do a work density analysis of zoning
7. Do a risk analysis
8. Add phase buffers
9. Add quality triggers
10. Update logistics drawings
11. Update zone maps
12. Update procurement log
13. Create trailer graphics and signage
14. Create look-ahead format
15. Create weekly work plan format
16. Develop work steps
17. Create meeting schedule
18. Analyze schedule health parametric
19. Create KPI reporting process
20. Create roadblock tracking maps
21. Add a Takt point of no return (TPNR)

YOUR TAKT PLAN MUST HAVE THE FOLLOWING ITEMS INCLUDED FOR IT TO BE PROPERLY FORMATTED.

- Time on the top
- Location on the left
- Trade flow in the middle with colored wagons and a clearly published legend. Wagons are colored. Zones may be colored, but only if it doesn't conflict with wagon colors.
- Weather durations on the top
- Takt zone maps near phases
- Name of project with company logos
- NTP date
- Substantial completion target
- Final completion target
- Financial completion target--when do we run out of general conditions and general requirements.
- Buffers to these targets
- Weather buffers
- Pre-construction Meeting triggers
- Pull planning triggers
- Key milestones
- Long lead and critical procurement with buffers
- The critical three:
    - Permissions
    - Contracting
    - Coordination
- Interdependence ties
- Trade flow of each Wagon
- A TPNR if needed
- You can see the Macro on one vertical page
- You can see the Norm on one horizontal page

1. Get the right Foremen on the bus.
2. Understand your phases and functional areas.
3. Make sure you have Foreman for all functional areas.
4. Decide on a meeting schedule.
5. Implement conference room, trailer, and visuals.
6. Create your look-ahead format and cycle.
7. Create your Weekly Work Plan creation cycle.
8. Set up your Trade Partner Weekly Tactical meeting:
   a. Create your meeting agenda-
      - Look-ahead planning
      - Weekly Work planning
   b. Begin your meetings.
   c. Have them reviewed.
   d. Improve your meetings every week.
9. Set up your Foreman Huddles to take place daily:
   - Day planning
   - Constraint management
   - Roadblock removal
10. Set up your worker huddles to be daily.
11. Implement zone control.
12. Get all trades into their wagons as quickly as possible.
13. Begin reporting on progress.
14. Help client mitigate delays effectively.
15. Implement the **6 Takt Steering & Control Methods**:
    - Leveling work
    - Manage production
    - Foreman & Super control
    - Create stability
    - Quality product
    - Roadblock removal

REFLECTION-CREATE A PRODUCTION PLAN

The purpose of this component in the First Planner System™ is to simulate what is possible with the resources we have and align it to what the the owners want and will accept. I have never seen a project go well without this kind of visual planning of the production system. It aligns all others processes, systems, and supply chains to a rhythm that the project leaders can see, follow, adjust, and win with. Without it you will be lost in a "wish list" CPM schedule that means nothing and negatively impacts everything.

Component Scoring: (1%-100%)
1. Do you have a Macro level Takt plan?____
2. Do you have an optimized Norm level Takt plan with the right no. of zones and the right Takt time?____
3. Are you pull planning every phase?____
4. Are you using 6-week Make-ready Look-ahead plans?____
5. Are you collaborating with Trades in making Weekly Work Plans?____
6. Are you doing day planning with trades?____
7. Do you understand the Takt Production System® well enough to implement it? ____
8. Are you controlling and leveling WIP in a way that you can maintain flow?____

What is your final score, taking the average of all answers? ____

If your score is below 80%, what specific actions do you need to take to elevate your team and leadership?

< NOTE <

You cannot plan the project too early!

70

PLAN
COMPONENT

Lean in Contracts

Hopefully you've taken my advice and you've found our book, *Takt Planning*, a huge help in turning your project into a production system. I'm not trying to sell copies of the book, I'm trying to set you up for success. If we're going to implement lean planning and turn our project into a production system, our trades need to know expectations before they're placed under contract and we need to understand how to build the contract so that Takt production plans are possible. These are the best options for facilitating lean building.

Lean Provisions to Consider in Contracts

Cleanliness

Cleanliness will be real time for all crews onsite. Workers & crews keep their areas clean & swept at all times to support a safe & productive work environment. The focus will be on the habits of the workers, not simply cleanup at the end of the day. Workers & crews will be trained on cleaning as they go, & not allowing things to hit the floor.

Just-In-Time Deliveries

Deliveries of materials shall be coordinated to the right inventory buffer. Too much material inventory will not be allowed, and zero inventory is not productive. Deliveries will be aligned to zones and the project Takt time.

Worker & Foremen Huddles

All foremen will attend a daily foreman huddle to plan work for the next day. Workers will attend a daily worker huddle at the start of the day to communicate safety items and the plan for the day. Attendance is mandatory.

25 Minute Daily Setup

Workers will be expected to spend the first portion of their day preparing the work of the crew. This will include preparing their area, training, 5S, plus safety and quality planning.

QC Checklists & Inspections by Foremen

Each phase of work shall have a checklist or a visual quality board before crews go to work. A representative from each trade will be responsible to research the plans, specs, codes, safety manual, and any other pertinent information before the pre-con meeting, and use the checklist for the installation.

Tablets for Foremen

Foremen will be expected to view the plan for the day, scheduling software, project management software, and other project management applications. Each foreman is to have a tablet for his or her work.

Zero Tolerance Systems

It is said, "The culture of any organization is shaped by the worst behavior the leader is willing to tolerate." On our projects, because of our respect for each person, we will have a respectful and caring "zero tolerance" policy on certain items that are part of, and completely consistent with, our safety program.

Approved Foremen

All foremen must be approved by the onsite team. Foremen must comply with all requirements, or they will be removed from the project.

Foremen by Geographical Area

The project will be broken up into geographical areas for operational control. Each area will be supervised with a superintendent & field engineer. Foremen huddles & morning huddles may be done separately. As such, each trade must provide a dedicated foremen or lead for these areas to communicate, coordinate, & schedule work.

Contractor Grading ★★★★☆

The general contractor and all trade partners will be graded weekly based on non-subjective criteria. The score will be scaled from F to A based on performance. This score will be communicated to the owner, all internal company leaders, all trade leaders and will be posted in the project conference room. The purpose is to elevate together.

Worker & Foremen Safety Training

To be onsite, all workers will be OSHA 10 trained. To be onsite, all foremen will be OSHA 30 trained. If OSHA 10 trained workers are not available, an OSHA 30 trained foremen must be onsite with that crew 100% of the time.

Scheduling & Delivering Materials

Material deliveries will be scheduled on the project delivery software or on the delivery board on a first come first serve basis. Delivery times will be held. If deliveries arrive on the project out of sequence or late, they will be re-routed to a queuing area.

Takt Construction

This project will use Takt construction. It is expected that each contractor participates in pull plan sessions to create the Takt sequences and that each contractor will follow the Takt Production System® explained in the book Takt Planning. This system also requires the participation of trade foremen in the Trade Partner Weekly Tactical meeting and Daily Foremen Huddles. Each contractor shall work within their zone within their Takt time.

You must tell trade partners what you will expect from them. Some in the lean community will say that lean does not need money or contract provisions. I strongly disagree. If we are going to huddle their workers daily, we need to tell them. If we are going to engage foremen in pull plans we need to tell them. The bottom line is that expectations need to be clear for this and included as a part of the contract.

If you do not, you may end up with change orders from Trades asking for compensation for the Foreman's time, or the Worker's time in the huddles. I am happy to share with you that I have never seen one of those COs actually get approved and paid out, but I don't want my record for that tarnished, so please make sure anything we expect from trades is in their contract.

Additionally, this is about respect. To be successful we need the right training, motivation, AND circumstances. The contract provisions I am suggesting will give you the circumstances you need to run a lean project.

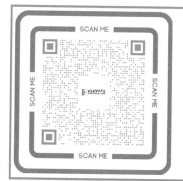

Visit this link to be taken to a blog post with the complete language.

REFLECTION-LEAN IN CONTRACTS

The purpose of this component in the First Planner System™ is to properly onboard trades to project expectations, ensure they have the right scope to accommodate lean systems, and ultimately support your production system in the field with capable trade partners. If you do not have this your trades will be surprised, not be on board, and you will receive change orders for their trouble.

Component Scoring: (1%-100%)
1. Do you have a list of needs for contract inclusions?____
2. Has this list made its way into your Master Subcontract Agreement or inclusions in the contract or work order?____
3. Are you having collaborative sessions with trades throughout the buyout process to onboard them?____

What is your final score, taking the average of all answers? ____

If your score is below 80%, what specific actions do you need to take to elevate your team and leadership? -

NOTE

Risk Management

When you have a production plan and the right contract inclusions to run a lean project, you'll already possess the tools you need to limit your exposure to many potential threats. Catastrophic risks do not account for most projects taking a nosedive; rather it's the compounding effects of many smaller standard risks causing a chain reaction of setbacks which derail the entire project. *How Big Things Get Done* encourages us to take two approaches when evaluating and managing risks.

 1 ANTICIPATE THE RISKS

Your project is special and distinct. There are many things that make your project different from others if only for the unique group of people you've assembled on your team. As you work through the pre-con steps of design/planning and in the various fresh eyes meetings, you will identify many possible risks based on the **known** information at that time.

Find as many **anticipated risks** as possible in pre-construction. Risks are dealt with in the following ways:

- Eliminate the risk through proper planning. You may need to adjust the production plan or how you buy out trades.
- Make provisions for the risk with financial and schedule contingency. Make sure to project those provisions in both.
- Absorb the risk with fee or extra effort. I am not advocating for this option.
- You can ignore the risk, hoping it won't happen on your project. Obviously, I meant you in a rhetorical way, because I know YOU would never read this book if you were the type to get through life with wishful thinking. You came to work. That's why you won't ignore risks.

As you identify risks, place them in the risk and opportunity log to be covered in your Team Weekly Tactical meeting. An OPUR (One Person Ultimately Responsible) is assigned to each risk and they will report weekly what steps are being taken to prevent or mitigate that risk.

RISK & OPPORTUNITY REGISTER

PROJECT NAME
Cost Risk-Opportunity Analysis

Identified Risks/Opportunities	Liquidated Damages Cost per Day	#					
RISK	**Project Impact/consequences**	**Impact in Days**	**Costs**	**Action Plan-Solutions**	**Cost Analysis**	**OPUR**	
					$0.00		
1 Risk 1	Description				$0.00		
2 Risk 2	Description				$0.00		
3 Risk 3	Description				$0.00		
4 Risk 4	Description				$0.00		
5					$0.00		
6					$0.00		
7					$0.00		
8					$0.00		
9					$0.00		
10					$0.00		
11					$0.00		
12					$0.00		
13					$0.00		
14					$0.00		
15					$0.00		
16					$0.00		
17				Total Risk Cost	$0.00		

OPPORTUNITIES	**Project Impact/Consequences**	**Impact in Days**	**Costs**	**Action Plan-Solutions**	**Cost Analysis**	**OPUR**
					$0.00	
1 Opp 1	Description				$0.00	
2 Opp 2	Description				$0.00	
3 Opp 3	Description				$0.00	
4 Opp 4	Description				$0.00	
5					$0.00	
6					$0.00	
7					$0.00	
8					$0.00	
9					$0.00	
10					$0.00	
11					$0.00	
12					$0.00	
13					$0.00	
14					$0.00	
15					$0.00	
16					$0.00	
17					$0.00	
OPUR>One Person Ultimately Responsible				Total opportunity Gain	$0.00	
				Difference in risk vs opportunity	$0.00	

Steps to follow:
1. Identify your risks.
2. Describe them and their consequences.
3. List down the amount of days that risk could impact you.
4. List down the amount of dollars that risk could impact you.
5. Assign an OPUR for each one.
6. Make a plan of attack.
7. Let the days and dollar totals freak you out and motivate you to mitigate the risks and take action daily or weekly.

Download our free template to fight risk today!

2 FORECAST THE FUTURE

Your project isn't special, nor is it distinct. There is nothing that makes your project unique or sets it apart from every other construction project. Did you see what I just did? Are you frustrated right now? Then at least you're not asleep. Stay with me--thinking your project is the exception will give you license to ignore the rules, averages, and historical data, so that you can create your own path to success for your own special project. Thinking your project is different is akin to manifesting a dumpster fire onsite. I promise, even when your project really is special, it's not special. You must take cautious steps to mitigate and manage risks by learning from the past. Simply put, you need to utilize the information available from previous projects to accurately forecast the **unknowns** your own project.

There are too many unknown unknowns to make a complete prediction, but you build a forecast by referencing similar projects that have been completed. Reference class forecasting (RCF), developed by Bent Flyvberg and discussed in *How Big Things Get Done*, is something worth delving into, but we will get you heading in the right direction. When you forecast the numbers for your project, for example cost or duration, the common approach is to use data from an already completed project, and then adjust that anchor based on your project's uniqueness. Don't do this! Instead, take the average from a class or large group of references to get a better anchor and therefore a more accurate estimate; avoid the urge to adjust that number to fit your unique situation. It's safe to assume every project that has ever been completed had unexpected unknowns plague their job site, and the outliers are accounted for by taking the average. Keeping the average as the anchor is a proven safer strategy.

Reference Class: Anchor: Average:

STEPS TO GET A REFERENCE CLASS

- **IDENTIFY A RFC of past similar projects.**
  - *At least 50 projects make up our RCF*
  - *At least 25 projects in the area (state, western region)*
- **Establish PARAMETERS:**
  - *Schedule (duration and sequencing)*
  - *Budget*
  - *Roadblocks & constraints*
  - *Overall variance in each of the above*
- **Deep dive into each of the projects**
  - *Look into Bent Flyvbjerg database if possible*
  - *Call the PM or people involved in the projects to know more about them. (Preferably all of them, but at a minimum the top 10 most similar projects)*
- **Establish the PROBABILITY distribution for our RFC**
  - *Normal distribution*
  - *Fat-tailed distribution*
- **Compare** the specific project with the reference class distribution to establish the most likely outcome.
- **Modify** and adjust as needed
- **Iterate** and fresh eyes as needed
  - *Look for black swans*

	International Benchmark	Cat C estimates	Cat B estimates	Cat A estimates
Average cost overrun	+20%	+11%	+6%	-1%
Frequency of cost overruns	9 out of 10	7 out of 10**	7 out of 10	5 out of 10
Standard deviaton of cost overruns	30%	38%	34%	24%
Average schedule overrun	+38%	+58%†	+30%	+18%
Frequency of schedule overruns	6 out of 10	8 out of 10*	8 out of 10	9 out of 10
Standard deviaton of schedule overrun	85%	103%	39%	29%
Average duration (years)	5.5		8.9***	

Note: Only Cat C estimates are directly comparable to the international benchmark
† $p \leq 0.1$
* $p \leq 0.05$
** $p \leq 0.01$
*** $p \leq 0.001$

It's a wise practice to address the risks the reference class faced. As you research your reference class, ask questions that will help you plan for contingency in your own project. Helpful questions include:

- What risks were realized during that project?
- What were the consequences in time and money?
- Did the project run past the end date? Why?
- Did the project go over budget? Why?
- Did have quality or safety problems? Why?

Forecast these risks to prevent the issues from occurring on your job site but **do not decrease** your anchor numbers because you think your project is different or you're overly confident these issues won't happen to you. If you need to increase the budget or production duration to accommodate for your findings, that is appropriate.

Just remember, you ALWAYS keep the anchor from the reference class in your Macro Level Takt Production Plan as a promise, and you find the anchor risks and concentrate on avoiding them in the Norm target. So, plan on the risks and anchor from the reference class--assume delays will happen on your project, but do your best to prevent them from interfering.

MACRO LEVEL TAKT PLAN

Slowest Speed + Risk Analysis + Reference Class

= *Contractual Promise*

NORM LEVEL TAKT PLAN

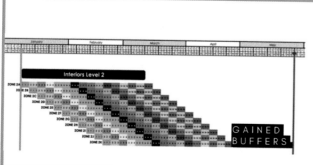

Optimized Speed + Risk Mitigation Strategies +

Reference Class Mitigation Strategies + Buffers

= *Production Target*

REFLECTION-RISK MANAGEMENT

The purpose of this component is to confirm your production plan and contracts include everything needed to prevent risks from happening, and that they are structured to cover them. If you fail in this stage, you'll have an unrealistic plan and trade contract. If you do this properly you and your trades will be able to help each other prevent these risks from ever happening.

Component Scoring: (1%-100%)
1. Did you hold a fresh eyes meeting for this project?____
2. Did you identify as many possible risks for this project as possible?____
3. Did you anchor to past projects?____
4. Have you adjusted (increase) the plan accordingly?____
5. Do you have a risk and opportunity register your team uses weekly to prevent risks?____

What is your final score, taking the average of all answers? ____
If your score is below 80%, what specific actions do you need to take to elevate your team and leadership?

> NOTE

Underpromise, and overdeliver!

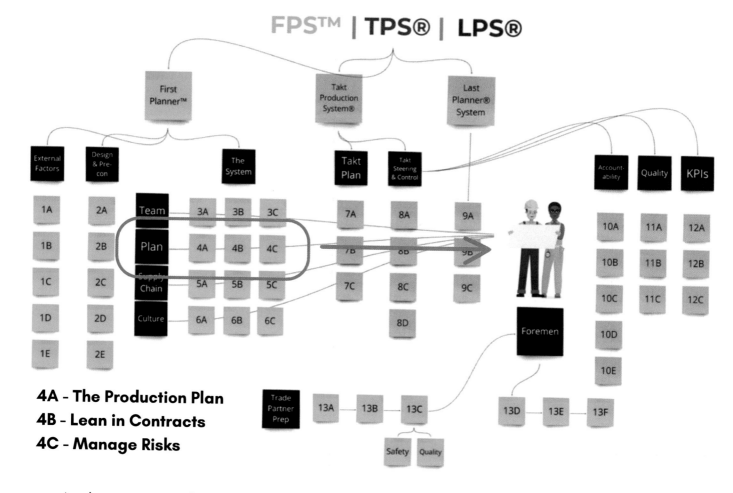

4A - The Production Plan
4B - Lean in Contracts
4C - Manage Risks

At this point you have a plan, collaboratively made with the Last Planners® that each foreman can follow. Everything in this system is engineered to support the foremen installing work with workers in a work package in a zone. They must have a plan they can see and understand to do this.

Now your foremen have a plan they can follow.

SUPPLY CHAIN
COMPONENT

Procurement

Armed with the right people and a good production plan, you are now prepared to align the production demands and the supply chain to provide the crews with the tools, equipment, materials, and information they need to be successful. Trades will execute the work if they have the resources and First Planners™ engineer the system to allow this to happen.

Current trends show that using ChatGPT is more accurate than Google in forming an unbiased, aggregated, and comprehensive definition of most topics. We've added the terms here from ChatGPT to ensure that we are on the same page as we move forward so that we can align on key behaviors.

Supply Chain Management:

Supply chain management (SCM) in construction refers to the management of the flow of materials, equipment, services, and information from suppliers to construction sites, and ultimately to the end-users or clients. It involves coordinating various stakeholders involved in the construction process, including suppliers, contractors, subcontractors, logistics providers, and clients, to ensure that materials and resources are delivered to the right place at the right time, in the right quantity, and at the right quality.

In construction, SCM plays a crucial role in ensuring the smooth and efficient execution of projects, as construction projects typically involve complex supply chains with multiple tiers of suppliers and [trade partners]. Effective supply chain management in construction aims to optimize processes, minimize costs, reduce waste, mitigate risks, and improve overall project performance.

Key aspects of supply chain management in construction include:

- **Sourcing and Procurement**: Identifying and selecting suppliers and subcontractors who can provide the required materials, equipment, and services for construction projects. This involves negotiating contracts, managing relationships with suppliers, and ensuring compliance with project specifications and quality standards.

- **Logistics and Transportation**: Managing the transportation, delivery, and storage of materials and equipment to construction sites. This includes coordinating with logistics providers, scheduling deliveries, optimizing transportation routes, and managing inventory levels to minimize delays and disruptions.
- **Inventory Management**: Managing inventory levels of materials and equipment to ensure that there are adequate supplies available when needed, while also minimizing excess inventory and storage costs. This involves tracking inventory levels, monitoring usage rates, and implementing inventory control measures.

JIT Deliveries:

Just In Time (JIT) delivery in construction refers to a supply chain management strategy where materials, equipment, and components are delivered to the construction site exactly when they are needed for installation or use, minimizing the need for on-site storage and reducing inventory holding costs. The goal of JIT delivery is to streamline the construction process, minimize waste, and improve efficiency by ensuring that materials are delivered in the right quantity, at the right time, and to the right location.

Procurement

Procurement is sometimes misunderstood as only buying what you need without tracking it. That is why supply chain management is a more useful term. It indicates the need to select, purchase, track, and properly receive the resources procured. So, I would advise: don't just procure what you need--manage the supply chain. The supply chain refers to all of the resources of the project.

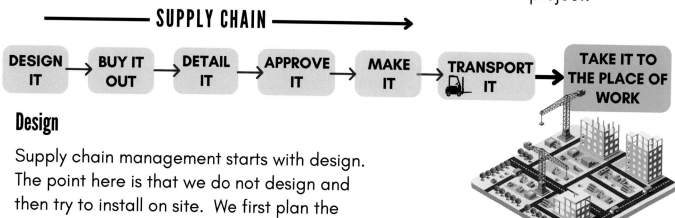

Design

Supply chain management starts with design. The point here is that we do not design and then try to install on site. We first plan the project, break it into its work packages, and then design to that work package.

The process is as follows:

1. We create our production plan early on in design.
2. We understand the **flow** of the project and how it is **phased**.
3. The work packages in zones are clearly defined for the design team.
4. Any needs for that work package are known by design. Examples are:
   a. Testing & inspection requirements.
   b. Placement breaks for concrete.
   c. Structural bracing and fit-up requirements.
   d. Valves for MEP systems.
   e. Design adjustments needed for kitting or prefab.
   f. Adjustments of Cx balancing zones.
   g. Design adjustments to accommodate changes in means and methods.

The key takeaway is that you design to the work package--don't package the work based on design.

| Design Effort | Break Out Design Packages | General Project Strategy | Identify Phases | Pull Plan | Simulate Norm Takt Plan | Package Takt Wagon | Design of Work Package |

Buy-Out

Assuming you have designed your project in a way that supports the work packages you now need to purchase the scope. The key items for this are:

- Sign up the right trade partners.
- Get them to an executed contract on time.
- Release them to begin submittal and procurement efforts.
- Initiate your quality process, complete the pre-mobilization meeting, and schedule the pre-con meeting with them.
- Track their compliance for insurance, bonds, and jobsite requirements as work approaches.

I have not shared any secrets here. The key is to follow your company's process, but do it in a way that enables the procurement of long-lead materials in a timely manner. I recommend reviewing this weekly in your Team Weekly Tactical and using a log of your choice, or the one on the LeanTakt website.

Takt Template

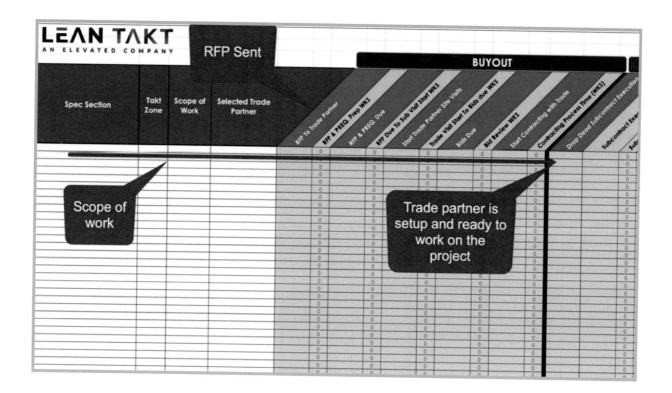

The line item in your buyout log will only trigger the trade for their first work package. Keep in mind that supply needs to feed the successor work packages on a flow and that you need enough time for the entire process to get materials to the place of work when the team needs them.

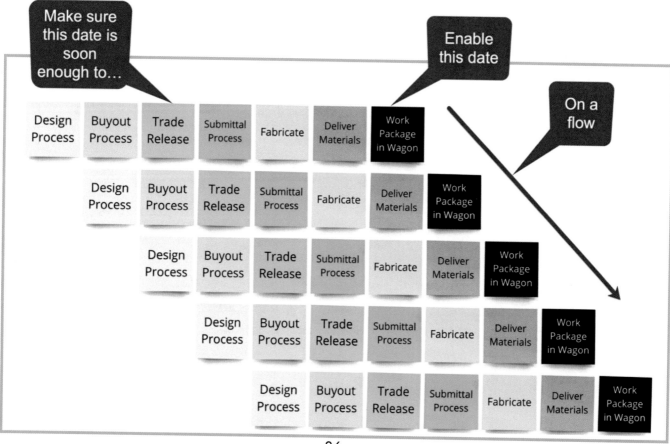

Procurement

Once you have your buyout under control on the project, the next step is your procurement effort. The procurement log or software will confirm that materials, equipment, and information are on track to be delivered on time to the work package. A procurement log or software has two major sections for the submittal process and the fabrication/delivery timeline. Any process or software needs to manage both, not just the submittal portion.

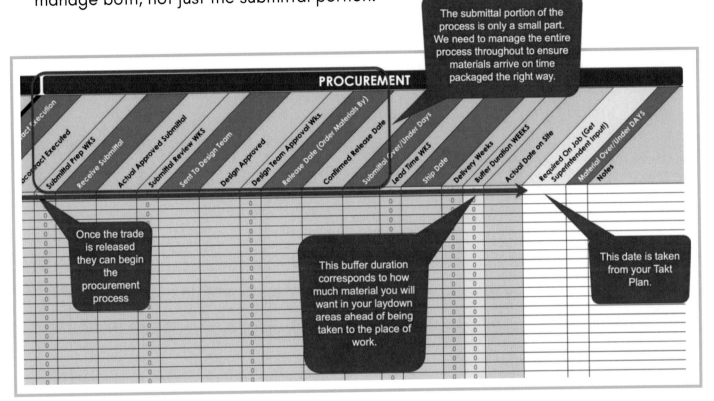

The submittal portion of the process is only a small part. We need to manage the entire process throughout to ensure materials arrive on time packaged the right way.

Once the trade is released they can begin the procurement process

This buffer duration corresponds to how much material you will want in your laydown areas ahead of being taken to the place of work.

This date is taken from your Takt Plan.

Your log or software tool needs to:
- Work dates back from the Required On Job date.
- **Include a Material Inventory Buffer duration in each line.**
- Enable you to see the progress of steps real-time.
- Mark late items red with conditional formatting.
- Mark items within 2 weeks of being late yellow with conditional formatting.
- Enable you and your team to break out items by zone and work package.

The key here is to manage the process throughout and to recover delays real-time. It's not common for people to utilize this process completely, which is interesting and unfortunate as it's a project management 101 tool.

Managing Delays

When you see that there is a delay or problem, there are several options to work through.

- Start sooner.
- Help trades break up submittals.
- Assist trades with team help.
- Swarm the internal review of the submittal.
- Open a Bluebeam session to do concurrent reviews.
- Ask the design team for help expediting.
- Select alternate material types.
- Do an in-person page flip with the designers.
- Negotiate with vendors.
- Visit the fab shop.
- Move the items to a second production site.
- Supplement the contractor.
- Take over shipment.
- Delay into a buffer designed into the supply chain.

Even with all the strategies to manage the supply chain, you may need to use specific buffers to absorb delays. The Material Inventory Buffer is the amount of materials you want onsite to keep workers fed with materials. It cannot be too much, but it cannot be zero. It needs to be right-sized to create flow for the project.

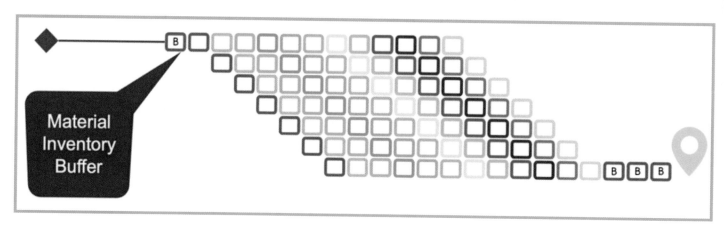

The Supply Chain Buffer is a tool to match and pace project buffers. Meaning, if you have buffers in your phase you need to have them in the supply chain. That way, if you do not need the buffers in the phase you will still have your materials on time.

Supply Chain Buffer

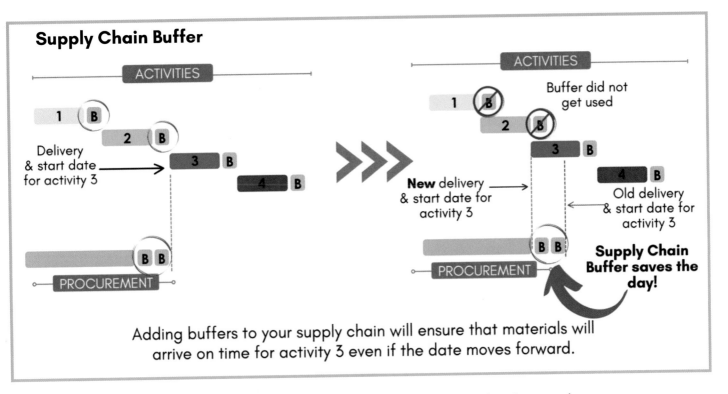

Adding buffers to your supply chain will ensure that materials will arrive on time for activity 3 even if the date moves forward.

If someone has advised you not to use buffers in the supply chain- please disregard that advice. You must have buffers to align resources with the install dates. If you want more information on this, please consider reading *Critical Chain* by Eliyahu M. Goldratt.

And these buffers should be for every delivery. Materials, equipment and information should be packaged in this order:
- Project
- Phase
- Area
- Zone

This means we don't bring out materials all at once. We right size the deliveries to keep the flow of construction and bring them Just-In-Time by zone. If we delivered by building or phase it would create too much inventory onsite and would slow down production.

TARGET: WHEN DO YOU NEED YOUR MATERIAL TO ARRIVE SO YOU HAVE JUST ENOUGH MATERIALS, BUT NOT TOO MUCH?

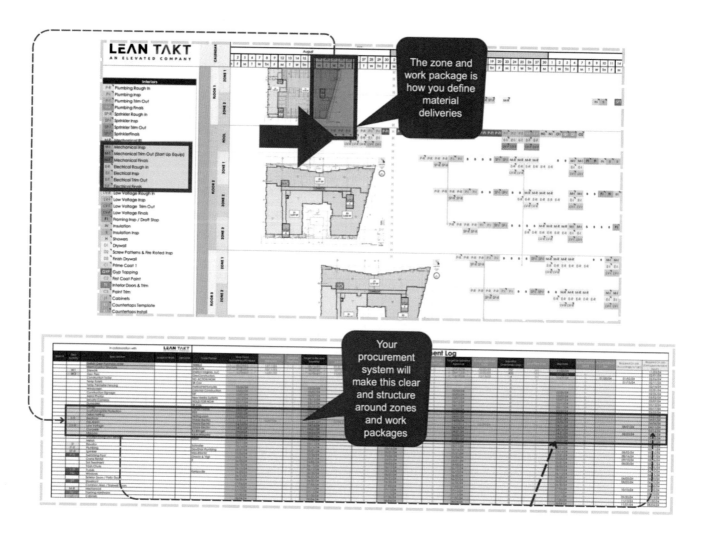

JIT Deliveries

Just-in-time is widely misunderstood and disliked in construction and hopefully I can provide some clarity here. The term JIT, at its root, really means to flow and do, pull, and feed things Just-In-Time according to the production rhythm. We use the term JIT in construction to talk about how we should feed the project with resources, which is different from how it's understood for manufacturing. We are trying to overcome the misperceptions and scale the proper understanding to better utilize the concept.

You bring out materials and other resources to the place of work (zone) for that work package Just-In-Time for that work for that day.

Just-in-Time

- Is not bringing everything straight from the vendor to the jobsite.
- Is not avoiding lay down or staging yards.

You will use lay down/staging yards in a strategic way. If not, you'll have unevenness from waiting on materials. If you bring materials too soon you have excess inventory which causes the 8 wastes in construction. If you bring them too late you will cause delays.

These errors are caused by value stream mapping our deliveries; value stream mapping removes all non-value add activities in the value stream which means that we no longer have a true understanding of the passage of time for certain activities. In supply chain management, the process of using a staging yard would be categorized as such.

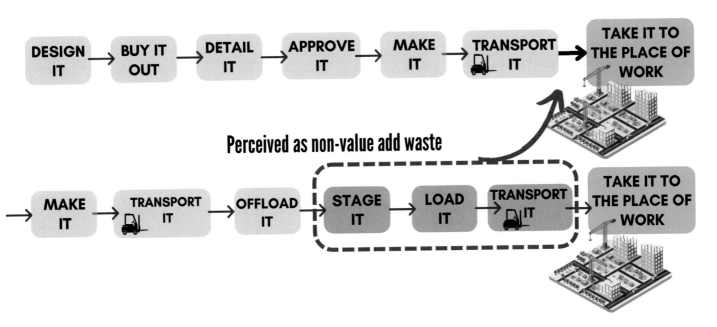

The problem with this thinking is that it does not look at the whole story. The waste from using a laydown or staging yard may be a lot less than the effect of not having the materials when you need them. So, for long-lead items with high amounts of risk, you may want to order them to arrive a period of time before your install. It is all about analyzing risk and dollars.

Possible situations:
- Cost from laydown > Cost from unavailability risk causing delays
- Cost from laydown < Cost from unavailability risk causing delays

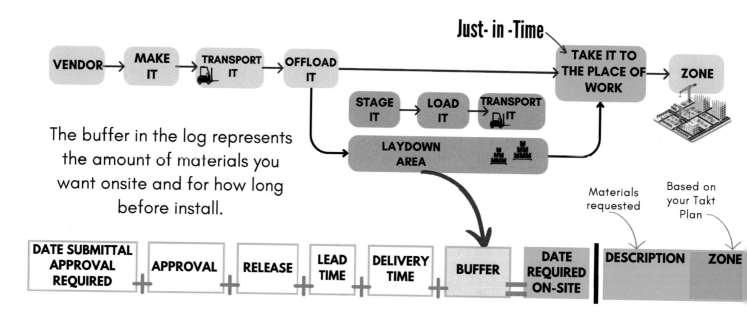

The buffer in the log represents the amount of materials you want onsite and for how long before install.

DATE SUBMITTAL APPROVAL REQUIRED		APPROVAL		RELEASE		LEAD TIME		DELIVERY TIME		BUFFER	DATE REQUIRED ON-SITE	DESCRIPTION	ZONE

Materials requested

Based on your Takt Plan

Warnings

You may have realized this means procurement efforts and order dates need to be moved forward. That is correct as long as you take into consideration the following points:

1. **Don't blindly accept long lead times**. Find out what the actual cycle time is to produce your product pieces and the actual lead time, and take appropriate action to reduce the length of different steps in process. Don't underestimate the power of a phone call and increasing the human connection to understand how the process can be expedited.

2. **Don't overburden the supply chain.** Most of the effects realized from the COVID-19 pandemic were not from the pandemic itself--it was from the panic that ensued that caused over-ordering, ordering incorrect materials, ordering too much, and ordering way too soon as a reaction. As Peter Senge explains in his book The Fifth Discipline, the entire construction market is a complex system, and the variation from pushing, rushing, and panicking will increase lead times.

You will have the vendor deliver some materials such as drywall, screws, lumber, and other readily available materials directly to the zone, and deliver long-lead high-risk items like curtain wall, elevators, and electrical gear to a staging yard-- all in the appropriate amounts. The point with JIT is to bring only the materials you need for that day's work to the zone from the vendor or staging yard. Anything more will mean wasting time with moving it multiple times and possibly damaging it. Ignoring JIT delivery principles means a loss in production.

Procurement Meetings

These discussions will take place in the Strategic Planning & Procurement meeting. You may recognize this from the Takt book. Here is the overview.

① Who attends? Supers, PES, PMS

WEEKLY PROJECT MEETING PLAN

	MONDAY	TUESDAY	WEDNESDAY	THURSDAY	FRIDAY
			NO MEETINGS		NO MEETINGS
5AM / 6AM	WORKER DAILY HUDDLE CREW PREPARATION	WORKER DAILY HUDDLE CREW PREPARATION	WORKER DAILY HUDDLE CREW PREPARATION	WORKER DAILY HUDDLE CREW PREPARATION	WORKER DAILY HUDDLE CREW PREPARATION
7AM	SAFETY ORIENTATIONS			SAFETY ORIENTATIONS	
8AM	TEAM WEEKLY TACTICAL	DAILY HUDDLE	DAILY HUDDLE	DAILY HUDDLE	DAILY HUDDLE
9AM				BIM COORDINATION	
10AM / 11AM		OAC MEETING			
12PM					
1PM	FOREMEN DAILY HUDDLE	FOREMEN DAILY HUDDLE	FOREMEN DAILY HUDDLE	FOREMEN DAILY HUDDLE	FOREMEN DAILY HUDDLE
2PM / 3PM	STRATEGIC PLANNING & PROCUREMENT	TRADE PARTNER WEEKLY TACTICAL		COORDINATION MEETING PLACEHOLDER	
4PM					
5PM					
6PM					

② Details

A First Planner™ Meeting

STRATEGIC PLANNING & PROCUREMENT

OCCURS WEEKLY

Purpose: Long-term planning takes place. Master schedule is updated and work is made ready per the look-ahead schedule. Procurement is intentionally managed.

Agenda:
- **Positive Shout-outs**
- **Review & Update the Takt Plan**
- **Update Procurement Log**
- **Look out 3-12 Weeks**
- **Report out w/ clarity**

The key items to notice when using a Takt Plan:
1. How is production going?
2. Is it on track this week?
3. Is work planned for next week?
4. Do we still have enough buffers?
5. Where are we in relation to the end date?
6. What roadblocks need to be removed or absorbed?
7. Is work being made ready?
8. Are separate phases on track to support each other?
9. Is procurement on track to feed the system?
10. Is work pushing into problematic weather times?
11. Are materials on track to support?
12. Are we on track with pre-construction meetings?

93

3 Visuals needed at location:

- Macro Takt Plan or Norm Takt Plan
- Procurement Log

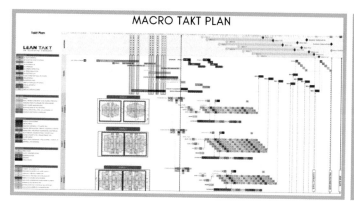

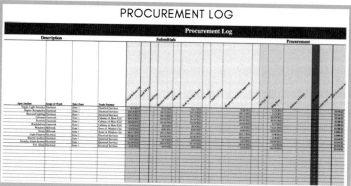

In this meeting the team will discuss procurement at least once a week and artfully manage and engineer the supply chain. This is beyond a review and discussion; this is a deep dive to control the system. You will complete the following steps.

- Review the log.
- Review the production plan.
- Do a page flip.
- Call vendors.
- Map out the supply chain steps.

- Analyze the value stream.
- Pull up the model.
- Use VDC to audit the project materials.
- Dig into large problems.
- Solve problems to recover the supply chain.

Information

Managing procurement extends beyond materials--you need to be procuring the training, tools, equipment, and **information** that accompanies your material. Track and provide the following to ensure that you have designed and understood the entire work package:

- Complete shop drawings.
- Complete submittal packages.
- Lift drawings if necessary.
- A visual quality board from the pre-con meeting.
- Installation instructions/training.
- Distributed and posted RFIs.
- Real-time pricing information and approvals

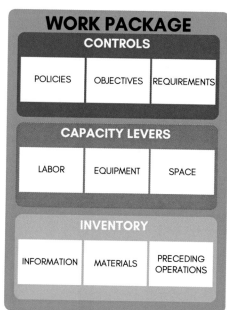

94

REFLECTION-PROCUREMENT

The purpose of this component is to supply your production plan with materials, tools, equipment, and information. If you don't have a supply chain production system in place, you will struggle on site. With a good procurement system you will always have what you need. Without it, you can expect to wait on materials and therefore experience stops, restarts, delays, and an overburdened project. Never leave this component of construction to your trades. It is YOUR job to manage procurement on the project with them.

Component Scoring: (1%-100%)
1. Do you have a procurement system on your project?____
2. Do you have a way to track procurement on a log, software, or visual?____
3. Are you recovering delays in the supply chain proactively as you notice problems real-time?____
4. Have you designed the use of lay down and staging yards with any associated material inventory buffers?____
5. Are you effectively meeting with your team to manage procurement?____
6. Are you using buffers in your procurement efforts?____
7. Are you bringing materials out JIT?____
8. Are you focused on information and materials in your efforts?____
9. Have you leveraged Virtual Design & Construction in your efforts?____

What is your final score, taking the average of all answers? ____

If your score is below 80%, what specific actions do you need to take to elevate your team and leadership? ---

NOTE

SUPPLY CHAIN
COMPONENT

Pre-fabrication

Pre-fabrication should be a major consideration when it comes to procurement and your supply chains. When pre-fab makes sense it can create a safer environment for workers, reduce the chances for impacts and roadblocks on site because many problems are already solved, and can help the project to flow.

Safer environments for crews

Reduces impacts & roadblocks

Increases flow of work

Pre-fabricated options include:
- Pre-cut materials.
- Pre-cut and kitted assemblies.
- Pre-fabricated assemblies like headwalls, exterior panels, overhead MEP, and overhead corridor racks.
- Pre-fabricated pods for bathrooms, rooms, sections of a repetitive building.
- And modular construction.

Consider the following

- Early collaboration with designers & trade partners to ensure pre-fab will meet needs at time of installation
- Designing with the end-user in mind
- Engaging digital design & building information modeling
- Pre-fab transportation & assembly planning
- Coordination with suppliers & contractors
- Worker training that support the install

REFLECTION-- PRE-FABRICATION

The purpose of this component is to supply your production plan with materials, tools, equipment, and information in pre-assembled ways and better enable the flow of construction. If you do not have pre-fabrication on the project you will be forced to stick build everything, will be victim to install bottlenecks, and the site will be riddled with waste and impacts.

Pre-fab should go from an afterthought to a major consideration in construction.

Component Scoring: (1%-100%)
1. Have you planned what you want to pre-fabricate?____
2. Have you engaged the design team early enough to design to what you will be pre-fabricated?____
3. Do you have a good pre-fab plan with your trades that has been coordinated? ____

What is your final score, taking the average of all answers? ____
If your score is below 80%, what specific actions do you need to take to elevate your team and leadership?

NOTE

SUPPLY CHAIN
COMPONENT

Logistics

My good friend John Coffman once told me about a time-lapse that was done on one of his projects. They tracked a particular bunk of plywood that was moved nine times before it was used. It's one thing to get the materials to the jobsite and it's often a different, separate thing to get the materials from that point of receipt to the right location on the jobsite. We need to unify these two to remove excess inventory, motion, transportation, damaging materials, over-processing from having to repair or reorder materials, and time spent waiting for the reorder to arrive--all of it unnecessary waste. The process of managing the logistics of the supply chain is the solution, and we use a series of plans to create success.

Logistics Drawings

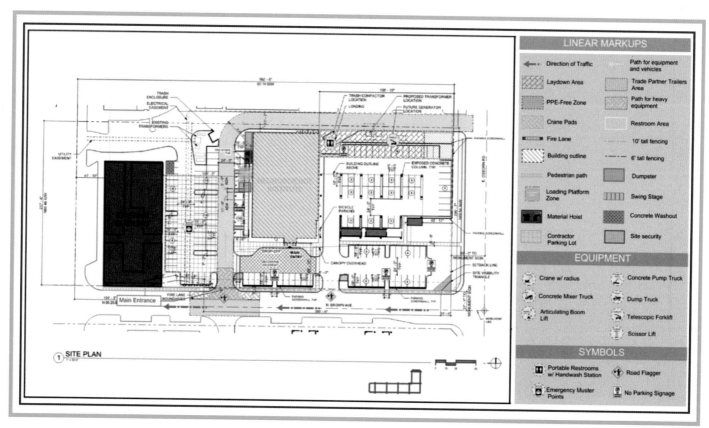

The logistics drawings are used for visually showing:
- The point of receipt for materials and labor.
- How materials and labor are transported on site.
- The staging locations of materials and equipment.
- Access points for bringing materials into the structure.
- The design of human systems on site to create a remarkable experience,
- and much more.

I've included six major plans to illustrate the potential benefits gained from well executed logistics.

PROJECT SAFETY PLAN

This plan has enough details included that it should be its own drawing if possible and will show the plan view of the entire site.
- Defines access and Egress points.
- Shows where your emergency gathering point is.
- Shows the locations of things like:
  - Fire extinguishers
  - AEDs
  - Water
  - Ice
  - Emergency shut-offs
  - Rescue baskets
  - First aid stations, and more.

PROJECT WAYFINDING PLAN

Your project must be intentionally designed and the plan needs to be clear, so that everyone knows where they are going and safety is prioritized.

- Outline how workers and foremen come into the project site.
- Show how deliveries arrive and queue.
- Plan how pedestrians and motorists will interact with your project site.
- Establish clear paths to navigate through the project site with all needed signage, with equipment paths and walkways.

Your project site will evolve as time progresses. Each phase of construction is unique and deserves a Logistics plan to match the current state of operations.

MOBILIZATION, MAKE-READY & FOUNDATION PHASE LOGISTICS PLAN:

In this phase you will need to consider utilities, access, demolition, clearing and grubbing, fence location, trailer setup, the creation of a staging yard, and how you will build your foundations. For foundations you will need to add things like the concrete washout, the access for the pump, and where to stage rebar.

SUPERSTRUCTURE PHASE LOGISTICS PLAN:

You will need a plan to get your workers and foremen to the place of work as a top priority. Receiving materials in and around the structure in addition to accommodating concrete placement and steel erection need to be considered. In this plan you might include cranes, steel, concrete, and form work. You may have a slick line, various pump locations, wall racks for formwork and staging yards for precast.

EXTERIOR PHASE LOGISTICS PLAN:

This phase will likely have a hoist, exterior staging and installation; the focus is moving people and materials into the building while work is happening on the outside.

SITEWORK & CLOSEOUT PHASE LOGISTICS PLAN:

This is when you are exiting the building, finishing things up, and closing areas down. The plan may include access for mobilizing furniture into the building or any other kind of testing or services for the owner.

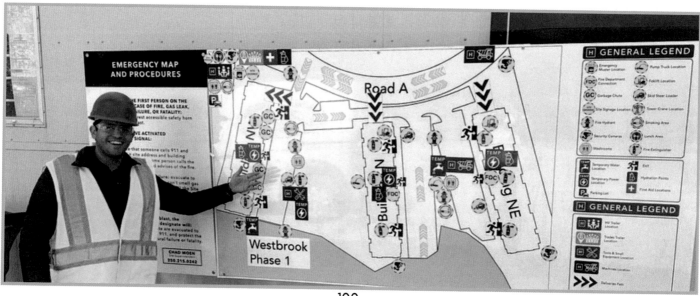

These plans will be the canvas where you do your logistics planning. So, please keep the following in mind:

- Keep them updated. These are living drawings and need to be accurate.
- Use them for actual staging, not just for general information.
- Use them to synchronize deliveries with your points of entry.
- Make sure the hoist, forklift, and crane operators see and know these plans in real-time.
- Use the maps in your huddles to make sure logistics are coordinated.

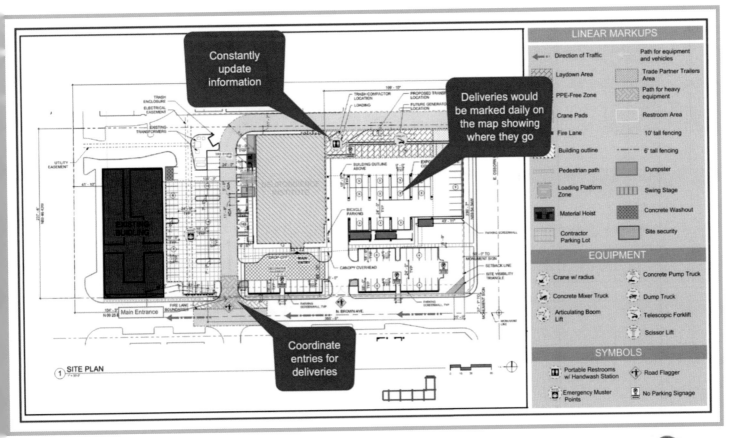

They should be:
- Intelligently designed
- Easy to follow
- Nice to look at
- Current

They are made in:
- BlueBeam
- Canva
- AutoCad, or,
- Revit

Scheduling Deliveries

Logistics drawings are the method you use to communicate the scheduling of project deliveries. The best practice is to schedule all your deliveries either on a software or on your visual Takt Steering & Control boards.

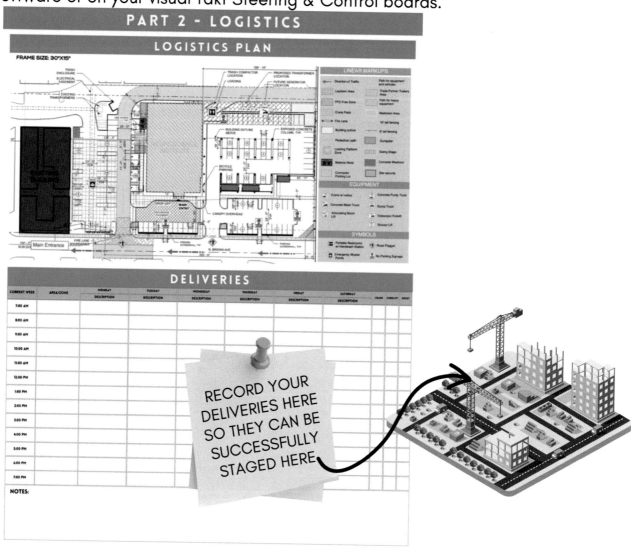

Even if you have plenty of space on your project, you must be disciplined with this practice. Keep in mind the following guidelines:

- Coordinate all deliveries in Foreman Huddles.
- All deliveries are scheduled first come, first served, unless you are prioritizing your bottleneck.
- All deliveries are to be held to the scheduled time.
- All staging is marked on the maps and placed in the proper place the first time.
- This is used as a tool to reduce excess inventory, motion, transportation, defects from moving things, and waste from not having materials when they are needed.

Once deliveries are scheduled, everyone on the site should be able to see the schedule and staging location at a glance either on the software, a distributed link to the plan, or some other way. The key here is that your workers, foremen and especially your hoist, forklift, crane operators and riggers know where to stage things and when.

These operators are the staging guardians on the project site. They make sure everything has a place, that everything goes to its place according to the plan in the Foreman Huddle, and that delivery rules are enforced. If the rules are ignored, the project really will descend into chaos.

RULES *for* DELIVERIES

- Everything staged in the building must be on wheels, color-coded pallets, or dunnage if approved.
- All materials are brought JIT according to the right quantities.
- Staging only happens to the right location, not randomly.
- To use the hoist, forklift, or crane the rigger or company must have the coordinated location shown on the map.
- All staging to be neatly organized, on flat stabilized ground, and in alignment with the grid. No materials in accessways.
- All materials and equipment need to be inspected upon arrival

REMEMBER-Our people will get it built if they have what they need

REFLECTION-LOGISTICS

The purpose of this component is to make sure you receive your procured materials and equipment and get it to the place of install in the right way. Sometimes projects get the materials, fail to inspect them upon arrival, and let them end up anywhere onsite where they get moved, damaged, and put in the way of someone else. It's chaos and will kill your project. If you receive them, inspect them, and move them in an orderly fashion with your operators, you'll set yourself up for massive success.

*Remember, your logistics plans are just as important as your production plan. If you can get workers and materials to the place of work, you can build it.

Component Scoring: (1%-100%)
1. Are you utilizing a site logistics plan that everyone can access?____
2. Are you utilizing all 6 types of maps?____
3. Are deliveries all scheduled?____
4. Are staging locations coordinated daily in Foremen Huddles and distributed to the entire project team?____
5. Are you using your operators as guardians of logistical stability?____
6. Are you inspecting materials when they arrive?____
7. Are you enforcing the rule that things only go where coordinated in the Foreman Huddle?____
8. Are your staging yards beautifully organized?____

What is your final score, taking the average of all answers? ____

If your score is below 80%, what specific actions do you need to take to elevate your team and leadership?

NOTE

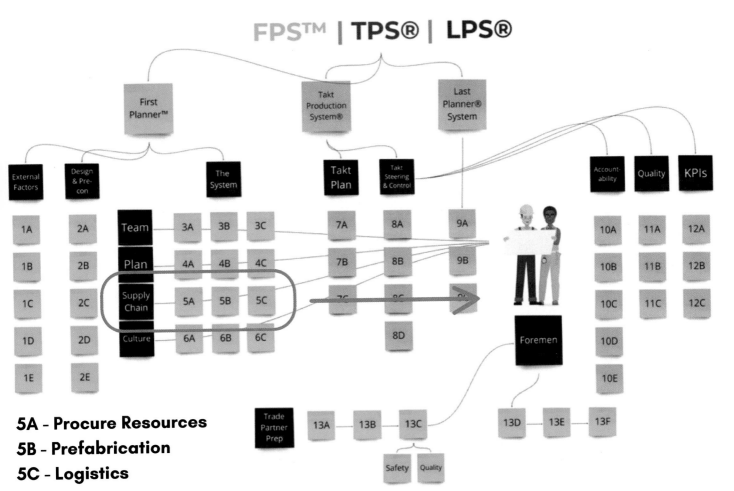

5A - Procure Resources
5B - Prefabrication
5C - Logistics

Now your foremen have the resources they need

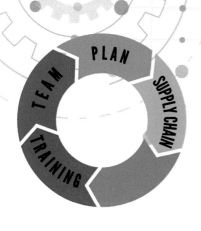

CULTURE
COMPONENT

Culture is the system of learned and shared beliefs, behavioral norms, rituals, values, language and symbols used to provide a framework for the people working on your project. As a leader, you have the responsibility for creating and maintaining your unique culture for your project. Since you've asked my opinion, the best culture is one that has respect at its core--every aspect of your culture should include best practices that respect people and resources. These are the minimum standards of a culture of respect. Improvement comes after these are met.

Open Communication
We listen to people and take feedback for improvement to create a remarkable site.

Support
We train, develop, and support the onsite crews.

Information
We provide a thorough orientation and onboarding to the project, highlighting the big picture & individual roles.

Meet Needs
We care for the physical needs of the project team: parking, ice/water stations, smoking areas and other amenities.

Expectations
We enforce a safe, clean, & organized site. Tolerating less would be dangerous, unproductive & unacceptable.

Connection
We connect with workers often, through job-site huddles, one on one, and we create connection events.

Enjoyment
We try to make work fun with a positive culture, job site lunches, & celebratory events.

Schedule
We create a schedule that flows and prevents burn out and the stress of a crash landing.

Invest
We insist on great lunch areas and bathrooms for the crews. That investment is one of the easiest ways to establish trust.

Protect
We protect our workers and their interests when they are not present or unable to speak for themselves.

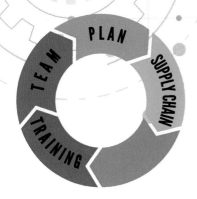

CULTURE
COMPONENT

Win over the Workforce

Winning over the workforce is not just a good idea and a way to respect people, it's also a part of your bottom line. If you don't believe me, try pissing off the workforce and see if they do a good job onsite. Actually don't experiment with this--it's not ethical to treat people badly and still expect excellence. The bottom line is that we shouldn't have to bring it up; everyone should already be doing these things.

OPEN COMMUNICATION

I believe in open communication and cultivating a relationship with the teams you are leading. I want people to give feedback and share their experiences with me. I can't always make things better, but if I am sincerely trying to create a remarkable site, that means that the workers come first. The tool needed to build the lines of communication is the daily Worker Huddle; when you take the time to listen to your workers and trades, you will be better able to facilitate the work they are trying to execute. Do not other them or set yourself apart from them. Listen to them and work for them, rather than treating them like they work for you.

- Gather all workers daily
- Ask for their feedback
- Give positive shoutouts
- Provide training
- Build a culture

1 Who attends? Supers, FES, Foremen, Workers

WEEKLY PROJECT MEETING PLAN

	MONDAY	TUESDAY	WEDNESDAY	THURSDAY	FRIDAY
5AM			NO MEETINGS		NO MEETINGS
6AM	WORKER DAILY HUDDLE	WORKER DAILY HUDDLE	WORKER DAILY HUDDLE	WORKER DAILY HUDDLE	WORKER DAILY HUDDLE
	CREW PREPARATION	CREW PREPARATION	CREW PREPARATION	CREW PREPARATION	CREW PREPARATION
7AM	SAFETY ORIENTATIONS			SAFETY ORIENTATIONS	
8AM		DAILY HUDDLE	DAILY HUDDLE	DAILY HUDDLE	DAILY HUDDLE
9AM	TEAM WEEKLY TACTICAL				
10AM				BIM COORDINATION	
11AM		OAC MEETING			
12PM					
1PM	FOREMEN DAILY HUDDLE	FOREMEN DAILY HUDDLE	FOREMEN DAILY HUDDLE	FOREMEN DAILY HUDDLE	FOREMEN DAILY HUDDLE
2PM	STRATEGIC	TRADE PARTNER		COORDINATION	
3PM	PLANNING & PROCUREMENT	WEEKLY TACTICAL		MEETING	
4PM				PLACEHOLDER	
5PM					
6PM					

2 Details

Agenda:
- Give shout-outs.
- Request feedback from workers.
- Review the plan for the day in an abbreviated format.
- Define safety focus for the day.
- Review safety observations from the previous day's reflection walk.
- Share what was found and ask if the previous day's items are closed out. If not, crews should fix these BEFORE going to work. Drive them to closure.
- Address any owner items.
- Reiterate need for cleanliness and organization.
- Ask if anyone needs permits and then point them to the person/location to get them immediately after the huddle.
- Review deliveries and strategy.
- Review training for the day.
- Address weather conditions for the day.
- Encourage crew preparation huddles.
- Reinforce the need for safety planning.

A Last Planner® Meeting

WORKER HUDDLE

OCCURS DAILY

Purpose: Everyone is brought together into one big social group and the day's plan is communicated to workers. they leave feeling aligned and respected.

108

3 VISUALS NEEDED AT LOCATION

- Day plan
- Day plan board

DAY PLAN PHYSICAL BOARD

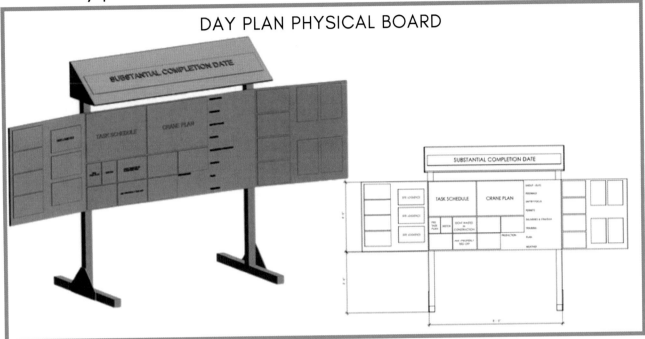

DAY PLAN

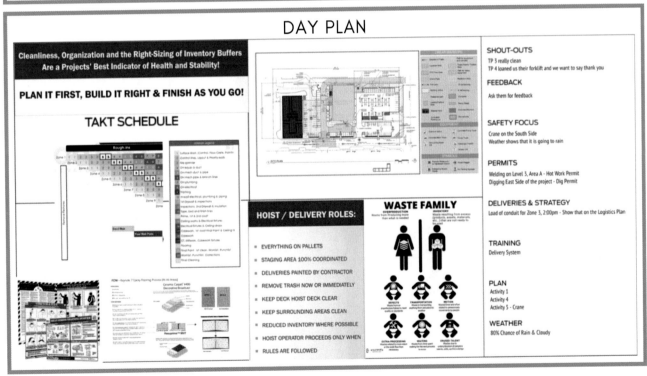

MEETING NEEDS

The less energy the crew spends trying to meet their physical needs on-site, the more quality effort they will spend on value-add tasks. It's not about trying to eek every last bit of them until they drop. It's about treating people as more than just a means to an end. It's about humanizing the team and enabling them to do their job. And it's about stepping back to recognize that buildings exist because crews get their asses out there in all the elements every day to get the job done. If we can help them in any way, it's our obligation. Spend time assessing the culture you are creating in each of these areas and assess how you could improve. The goal is to take care of inherent human needs so that flow can be achieved while executing work, and for the time spent in flow to be as enjoyable as possible.

 Parking-good size and conditions

 Designated Smoking Areas

 Organized Project

 Water Break Stations

 Cooling/Heating Plan

 Wayfinding Signage

SMOKING & BREAK AREAS ARE CRUCIAL

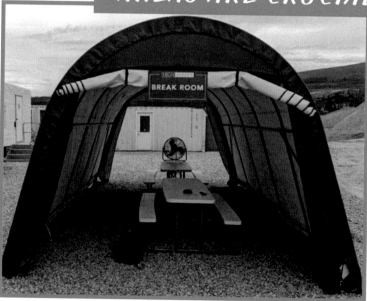

CONNECTION

You are already united with the entire team through the shared goal of finishing the project; the next step is to build that connection into something more meaningful. We want to strengthen these connections because it increases everyone's sense of belonging and emotional safety; we are striving to become a support system for the crew during their time on our project. Here are a few ideas to build connection with people onsite.

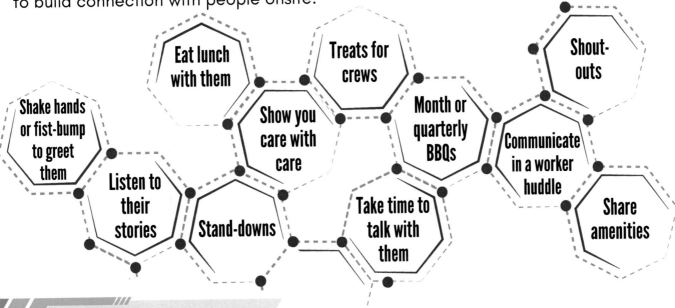

Shake hands or fist-bump to greet them

Eat lunch with them

Treats for crews

Shout-outs

Show you care with care

Month or quarterly BBQs

Communicate in a worker huddle

Listen to their stories

Stand-downs

Take time to talk with them

Share amenities

SCHEDULE

We engineer a project production plan that utilizes workers as the key executors, not as resources to burn through. We create a schedule that protects workers down time and we never expect crews to work faster to make up for our production plan errors.

PROTECTION

We protect our workers and their interests when they are not present or unable to speak for themselves.

ENJOYMENT

Since we spend the majority of our day at work, we do what we can to make the time there enjoyable. You have the power to create a positive and fun culture. Consider monthly or quarterly lunches. Consider contests or competitions with awesome prizes. I insist on decorating at every project I work on; I have carried a Christmas tree through the financial district in Boston to deliver it to the site and wrapped string lights on a crane. A quick Google search tells me that I am out of my league when it come the Christmas Crane Wars but I'll be ready the next time I have the opportunity. I love construction and I want everyone to have as much fun on site as we can have. Now is a good time to mention that at the Schroeder house, we have lights all the trees out front all year–spring colors, patriotic, Halloween... It's always a party because why the hell not?

> LIFE IS NOT A COMPETITION, IT'S A GAME. IT'S NOT ABOUT WINNING OR LOSING, IT'S ABOUT ALL THE FUN WE CAN HAVE BEFORE IT ENDS.
>
> Simon Sinek

INVEST

We insist on providing remarkable bathrooms for the crews. I've been on projects where the executives have the nice bathrooms in the project trailers, and the workers are given porta potties in the sun without wash stations. There is no faster way to tell the crew you don't give a shit about them than that. This is another one of those hills I will die on. Investing in bathrooms that you want to use rather than have to use is money well spent. No one ever regrets the message it sends to the crew--we care about you and your needs. Couple great bathrooms with a lunch area that allows for some peace and relaxation and you will have a legitimate foundation for building trust.

Setup remarkable BATHROOMS –&– LUNCH AREAS *with ...*

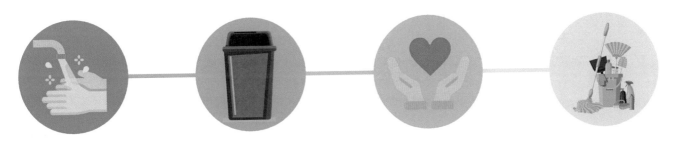

| Handwash Stations | Trash Cans | Comfortable Environment | Frequently Cleaned |

LUNCH AREAS

Lunch areas should be reasonably accessible to the workforce and placed at the right locations on the project with the following components:

- Tables & chairs
- Conditioning if needed & protection from the elements
- Cleaning supplies to sanitize the tables
- Microwaves & refrigeration if possible
- Lunch pail storage
- Charging stations for phones (if possible)
- Signage for lunch-time rotations
- Snacks every now and then to treat the workforce

*This area was set up to accommodate for social distancing during the COVID era.

113

PORTA POTTIES

This is should not be the default option for bathrooms, but if it's necessary here are the requirements:

- Enough units legally required per vendor and OSHA
- Staged at accessible locations around the project
- Cleaned three times a week at a minimum – preferably cleaned every day
- Well stocked with toilet paper – extra paper should be kept in a cabinet near the units
- No graffiti
- Newer units – ask for them to be replaced if they send older ones
- Hand sanitizer in all units
- Separate hand wash stations near the units
- Trash cans near hand wash stations
- An enclosure and heater during cold weather
- A shaded cover during warm weather
- Provide a base or millings at the front so mud is not tracked into stalls
- Well-maintained and professional

THIS TOOK PLACE DURING A MILD AZ WINTER, BUT DURING THE SUMMER THIS WOULD NEED TO BE COVERED.

EXISTING RESTROOMS

When your crew is required to use existing bathrooms, follow these guidelines to provide a remarkable experience:

- Clean stalls
- Good lighting
- Self-replaceable toilet paper and seat covers
- Plunger in every stall
- Place to hang hard hats and vests
- Bathroom stocked with cleaning supplies
- Music for background noise (if possible)
- Signage and instructions Paul Aker's style for using and caring for facility
- A sign encouraging proper use of the facility
- Sinks with running water
- Trash cans
- Air fresheners
- This should be cleaned every day or every other day. The measurement here is not the budget, but the level of cleanliness

Watch Paul Aker's workplace bathroom video

CUSTOM BUILT RESTROOMS

Best! ★★★

When possible, invest in your crew by building restrooms to accommodate the jobsite.

- Urinals, toilets, & sinks with running water
- Clean stalls made with proper separation and privacy
- Wood framed or framed & drywalled walls should be painted with white epoxy paint
- Good lighting in every corner
- Self-replaceable toilet paper and seat covers
- Plunger in every stall
- Place to hang hard hats and vests
- Bathroom stocked with cleaning supplies
- Music for background noise if possible
- Signage and instructions Paul Aker's style for using and caring for facility
- A sign encouraging proper use of the facility
- Trash cans
- Air fresheners
- This should be cleaned every day or every other day. The measurement here is not the budget, but the level of cleanliness
- Conditioned against weather when possible

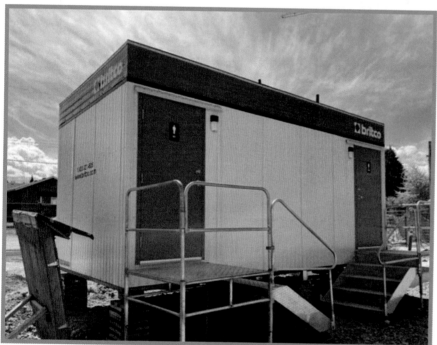

THE MORE RESPECT YOU SHOW THE CREWS, THE MORE RESPECT THE CREW SHOWS THE PROJECT

REFLECTION-WIN OVER THE WORKFORCE

The purpose of this component of winning over the workforce is to ensure the workers and foremen are committed to doing a good job for the team. Again, we cannot piss off the workforce and still build a successful project. The way we win over the workforce will directly affect quality, safety, morale, and engagement among the wider team.

Without this component the people on the project may vandalize the site, do poor work, leave the areas dirty, perform below production targets, or engage in unsafe practices. One key indicator of this is graffiti in the bathrooms. It's an indication that the workforce on the project is disgruntled. Feeling disgruntled or resentful means the crews won't act as a united team. Guardedness and siloing will take over at all levels and the project will spend more time fighting and being defensive than producing actual value-add work.

Component Scoring: (1%-100%)
- Do project leaders fundamentally respect people?____
- Are bathrooms remarkably clean with hand wash stations and trash cans?____
- Are lunch areas provided in good enough condition to win over the craft?____
- Are the workers and foremen so connected to project leaders in the huddles that they collectively want to do a good job for the team?____
- Are site conditions clean, safe, and organized to levels of near perfection?____
- Are celebrations held at least quarterly to celebrate the skilled craft onsite?

____

What is your final score, taking the average of all answers? ____
If your score is below 80%, what specific actions do you need to take to elevate your team and leadership? --

< NOTE

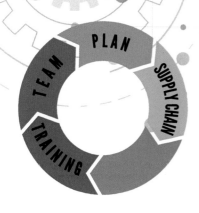

CULTURE
COMPONENT

Orientation & Onboarding

Will Rogers said you never get a second chance to make a first impression, and the science backs him up. Not only will you make judgements about the things you see or experience, but your brain will use thin-slicing to make conclusions about someone's character traits like status and trustworthiness. That means that within 7 seconds, your brain has filled in enough information to create an emotion and a bias that will help you proceed. To override a first impression takes significant thought work, effort, and repeated experience of the opposite being true. I tell you all that to say, you have a responsibility to make a good impression on everyone that you meet and that enters your project. The judgement starts as soon as the project comes into view. If people are open-minded they can forgive a bit of a mess here or there, but even they can't think well of someone who isn't warm, friendly, welcoming, and inviting. Don't blame me-it's science and Will Rogers. So this is my call to action-develop a strong orientation and onboarding strategy to help set the tone for the culture you are trying to create.

INFORMATION

Imagine it's the first day of a carpenter of one of your trades. After a frustrating drive in morning traffic, he's starting to feel anxious about not seeing the parking lot he's supposed to use. Finally finding the lot for workers, he parks and heads to the office. He's been driving for long enough to regret his morning coffee and the fact that there isn't a restroom in site. With no alternative he enters jobsite, skipping the office in search of a porta potty. He asks around but they are fairly new and don't know if there is one on this side. Finally someone knows and he makes it without an accident. Without toilet paper, his anxiety might become panic but I'll let him maintain some dignity. He's carrying his lunch and he has what he needs to keep things fresh, but he's now pretty annoyed at having to open his lunch inside a honey bucket. Now he circles back toward the entrance to check in at the office. He is acknowledged by an admin who treats him like he's a nuisance. He is directed to a conference room to wait. Eventually he is shown a video to introduce him to the project and site. When the video is over, a project engineer gives him a hard hat sticker and tells him to get started. He heads out to find his crew, not entirely sure where he is heading and how to get there. He eventually finds the crew, and decides to put his whole heart into doing the best job he can do. Just kidding. He is as uninspired as he could be and will have to overcome the negative emotions of the morning to be able to focus and do a good job.

Information is a form of respect and when it comes to a construction project, that can look like context, background details, communication, sharing files or documents, and openness from project leaders. It is offering access to the data they need without having to ask or search for it. The target is to share as transparently as possible for the sake of providing safety, clarity, and alignment.

ORIENTATION

Orientation is the process of getting a new person welcomed, acclimated, and situated to their workplace. It includes an introduction to leaders, coworkers, and to the organization's mission, values, policies, and requirements. They will learn the scope of their position and fill out necessary paperwork. This is the best chance you have to form a great impression and the level of care you show here will set the standard for how your employee or guest can expect to be treated throughout their time with you. Orientation tends to be a one day event and prepares the employee to begin the onboarding and training.

Everyone that joins your project team needs to have a certain level of orientation. The first impression that began in the parking lot continues as they enter the gates to the project. What will they see and what will they feel? Take care to make this exciting and energizing for them.
Provide:

- Good parking
- Good way-finding signage
- Great bathrooms
- A kind welcome and introduction
- Overview of policies
- Job walk to orient them to site
- Showcase areas for breaks, huddles, etc.
- Safety stickers and project team merch
- Sincere appreciation that have joined

ONBOARDING

Onboarding is the process of teaching each individual the way to succeed in their role. They need clarity for how they fit within their smaller team or crew, and in the larger picture. Successful onboarding brings employee engagement so they will personally invest in the project success. The more understanding we have, the more empowered we are to integrate and act in ways that benefit our team and our own health. Onboarding can include sharing information about:

- Project systems
- Training and education for tools needed
- Meeting systems
- Logistics systems
- Establish feedback loops

The easiest way to provide meaningful onboarding is to develop a series of trainings that can be delivered in the daily morning huddle. Because project teams fluctuate and new people are joining at different times, you need to be thoughtful and flexible in your approach. A trade joining late in the project deserves just as much information, training, and support as trades that come onsite early.

SUPPORT

We respect construction workers. Full stop. We provide support, training and career development opportunities. The reason we use the Integrated Production Control System™ is because it provides the framework for respect and support at every step. We never have people wondering anything. Everything is planned and provided for, and in place.

We create oppotunites for career growth and we insist on training. All foremen should be be provided with Takt, advanced lean principles and methods, and LPS® training. This can be provided on a quarterly cycle to ensure that all foremen are being properly onboarded.

Providing the plan and the procedures shows respect for people and is the course of action. We can't improve and optimize if we don't have clear standards and expectations.

REFLECTION-ORIENTATION AND ONBOARDING

The purpose of this component is to remarkably orient the workers to your lean systems. When workers arrive on site, we have an opportunity to make an impression, connect, and set the relationship off on the right foot. If we have this in place, then the workers will be engaged with total participation and the entire site can work toward rowing in the same direction as allies.

If you do not have this piece, you will have an entire workforce that feels disconnected, will likely struggle or fail right out of the gate, and you may not ever get the chance to fix your first impression. You will have the system, but not the people's hearts and minds in the system. It will be harder to keep the site clean, maintain operational control, and maintain Takt control within zones.

Component Scoring: (1%-100%)
- Do you have good directions to and signage at the parking lot?____
- Is there great signage and human support systems on the way to the orientation location?____
- Is there a person, process, or visual environment that will warmly welcome the worker?____
- Do you have an interesting and engaging orientation with personal connection?____
- Do you take the workers on a brief tour of the jobsite, orient them, and help them get to their crews?____
- Have you provided a visual indicator of the orientation and ensured they understand the content in a language they understand?____
- Are you onboarding them daily in the morning worker huddle?____
- Do you provide lean training for your foremen?____

What is your final score, taking the average of all answers? ____
If your score is below 80%, what specific actions do you need to take to elevate your team and leadership?

NOTE

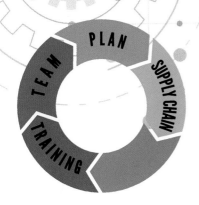

CULTURE
COMPONENT

Clean, Safe & Organized Project

The team, which includes the entire workforce, will be happier and work better in a healthy environment. Creating favorable conditions begins when a project is clean, safe, and organized. I say clean first because without cleanliness you can't properly see well enough to evaluate safety. Knowing that safety is the priority, first and always, we must keep our cleanliness and organization efforts synchronized to provide the safe environment that promotes safe practices. We enforce a clean, safe, and organized project site because tolerating anything less would be dangerous, unproductive, and unacceptable.

EXPECTATIONS

The method we use to ensure that we maintain a remarkable job-site environment is to daily evaluate conditions based on 6S and the 9 Wastes and to adopt a zero tolerance policy when dealing with violations of these standards. Likely you know enough about lean at this point to recognize the 5S methodology developed in Japan to facilitate Just-in-Time manufacturing. We prefer the 6S methodology of workplace organization due to the fact that construction is an inherently dangerous environment and everything we can do to prioritize safety-in daily repeatable and visual ways--is going to improve the environment for the entire team. How many times have you walked the job and seen a minor or major safety violation? We're all adults onsite, and yet safety buy-in is one of the rebellions we constantly experience. Addressing safety as part of the daily standard of behaviors is crucial if we are going to take a zero tolerance policy. Consider the message you send when you don't adopt zero tolerance-"If you don't want to wear your PPE, it's fine because I'll remind you again later. And again. And again. Because I am not a strong enough leader to enforce the policies that will keep us all safe or because I don't actually care if you are maimed or blind the rest of your life." I know the motive is more nuanced than that, but holding the line is black and white. Let's always be in the position to say I did everything I could to keep you safe.

6S to success

 ① **SORT** seiri 整理 ② ③ ④ ⑤ ⑥

>>> **Goal:**

Remove everything that isn't needed, and maintain only what is needed for the day's work. When you remove trash or scrap, ensure nothing hits the floor, and have gondolas at cut stations, you will reduce waste in your work. Materials should arrive Just-in-Time and nothing is stored at the work zone "just in case". Workers don't need to search for their materials or tools, or be distracted by extras. Eliminate obstacles to flow.

>>> **Methods:**

- Check the kit for the work package--ensure that there are no extra or unnecessary items to manage and that kit is complete with all items needed for the day.
- Keep the floor clear of everything that is not being installed that day.
- Confirm that deliveries are JIT each day, and that materials arrive from the staging area or lay down yard on time and in the proper amounts.

Sort through what is absolutely needed at the site of installation and what should be stored elsewhere.

Goal:

Straighten and organize all tools and material to make the work flow. Reduce the amount of time workers need to hunt for materials and resources.

Methods:

- Lay-down yards should have clear labels for material, and materials should be stacked and arranged in sequence according to need.
- Ensure deliveries go to the right place the first time where they will be sorted, assembled, or picked.
- Organize everything logically; eliminate the need to search for things deep in tool bags/boxes.
- Determine that workers have a full kit before they begin their work.
- Consider recycling bins and color-coded dumpsters.
- Every work station should be highly organized.

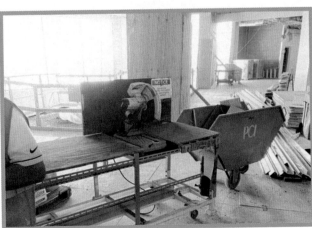

 SHINE seiso 清掃

Goal:

Entire work site is clean and organized at all times. Environment is free of problems and issues are easily detected.

Methods:

- Every morning, work and crew areas are swept up and wiped down.
- Before lunch and at the end of each day, all areas are tidied and trash is removed.

keep areas beautiful and clean as you go.

Goal:

Set standards for daily implementation to ensure the site is clean, safe and organized. Procedures are clear, visual, and repeatable.

 Methods:

- Visuals are used to manage daily tasks and organization.
- Cleaning and storage methods become standards project-wide.
- Maintenance on equipment takes place on a weekly/monthly routine.
- Consider shadow-boarding, standard hooks, or customized bins.
- Ensure tools and equipment are stored, organized, accessible, and easy to use in the right bins or carts.
- Make it easy for everyone to get power to their work with organized cords, power boxes, and well organized temp power stations.

SELF DISCIPLINE shitsuke 躾

Goal:

Build repeatable systems that the workers are easily able to sustain, because the systems are visual, clear, and promote a positive environment. Problems are seen and corrected immediately.

Methods:

- Mine for issues at all levels and fix problems as they arise. When you are slow to correct, workers are not able to sustain the daily habits. Prioritize maintaining these standards.
- Huddles should include training to reinforce project standards.
- Make 6S a daily habit in morning huddles and specifically the Crew Preparation Huddle.

Sustain your habits daily and use huddles to teach, reinforce, and maintain habits.

128

SAFETY

 ## Goal:

Build a culture of safety where accountability is site wide and care and concern for workers is prioritized every single day.

Methods:

- PPE is provided to all, free of charge and at all times. Remove all excuses from all workers. You can hold people to remarkably high standards when you provide a remarkably high level of care.
- Develop maintenance and safety checklists for all equipment.
- Safety logistics maps should be updated weekly; protocol for all first aid and safety equipment should be established and maintained.
- Every high risk area of work should have safety standards visibly communicated. Ensure that language translations are available as needed.
- Safety training should take place at a regular cadence. A daily reminder, a monthly course, etc.

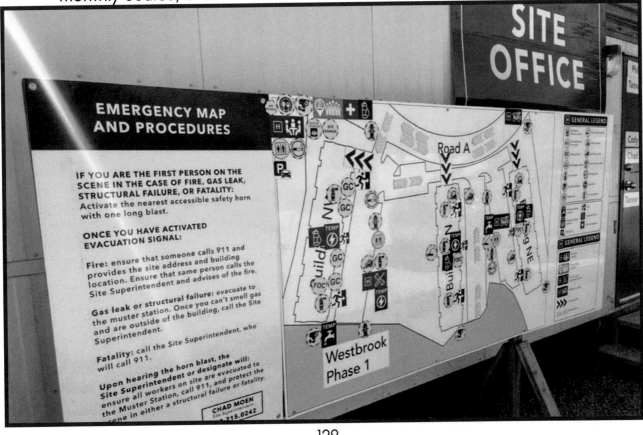

- Everyone knows how to **be safe** in their task

- Everyone knows **what they are installing**

- Everyone makes **improvements daily**

- Keep bathrooms **clean**

- **Be good neighbors** & take care of customer needs

- **Nothing hits the floor**-No materials, trash, nor any other items hit the floor

- **Just-in-Time** deliveries & scheduled deliveries: create correctly sized inventory buffers for all material & coordination daily

- **All cords off the floor** & managed in a remarkable way

- **Everything on wheels**, greenies, or painted pallets

- All **access ways clear** at all times

- Organize workspaces--**everything clean & organized**. A place for everything; everything in its place

- **Pull work** behind you--Nothing left behind, clear & sweep your areas, & leave the area complete

9 Wastes in CONSTRUCTION

Taiichi Ohno recognized things that were not value-add and developed the seven wastes as part of the Toyota Production System. The eighth and ninth wastes were added as the world began to adopt lean practices and recognize the way that teams are not utilizing the social and emotional intelligence of their people. The practice of doing 6S daily allows problems to be seen immediately and provides the framework for taking corrective and lasting action. Having set procedures allows you to easily implement additional steps by tying-in or piggybacking on existing structures. As leaders walk the job and watch the work, they need to be constantly aware of the many ways waste negatively impacts the flow.

Waste occurs with quality, quantity, and with people. The idea isn't to simply point out every little thing that could possibly go wrong- we leave that to Murphy. The point is to try to train yourself to recognize the categories of waste and develop an easy and visual way to address the inefficiencies.

Set up the work area for success by eliminating the nine wastes. Remember, you 6S daily so you can see and remove these...

OVER-PRODUCTION

QUANTITY

Making more than is immediately required. This happens when we make too many materials before they're needed, pre-fabricate assemblies in massive quantities out of rhythm, bring too many materials onsite or by finishing areas of work too soon so they get damaged in the wait time.

EXCESS INVENTORY

QUANTITY

Storing parts, pieces, documentation and overproduced work ahead of when it is required. This manifests itself when materials are stored in the way of other crews, when lay-down yards are overburdened, and when finished product is sitting around getting damaged before the next step or final use.

TRANSPORTATION

QUANTITY

Moving people, products, and information because you have excess inventory. This happens when we move materials around onsite because it was not staged properly, when workers are forced to go on treasure hunts because material is not organized, or when logistics are setup to sub-optimize travel onsite.

MOTION

PEOPLE: WORK

Bending, turning, reaching, and lifting while transporting excess inventory. Not having things staged properly, being on treasure hunts, and moving materials/equipment because of bad planning causes workers to move and strain their bodies. We prevent this because we respect the bodies of our people and reduce wear and tear.

DEFECTS

QUALITY

Reworking things that have been moved multiple times or defects created by the team being distracted with other wastes. You get defects when you unnecessarily move things and when you're distracted. Either way you end up with damaged items or work and problems with quality.

OVER-PROCESSING

Having to fix defects is over-processing. Anytime you have to do something twice when you could have done it once, is over-processing. Moving things, fixing defects, performing rework, and reacting all lead to over-processing which takes time.

PEOPLE: WORK

WAITING

PEOPLE: WORK

Time spent waiting for parts, information, instructions, and equipment because of over-processing or improper scheduling. When we have rework, defects to fix, and staging to correct it ends up making work wait on workers or workers wait on work to be done.

NOT USING THE GENIUS OF THE TEAM

This looks like not utilizing Last Planners® early in the planning process. Builders have skills and knowledge crucial to design stages and it is overlooked. It's also manifested when people are undertrained, micromanaged, or not properly incentivized. The entire team of people adding value daily is using the genius of the entire team.

PEOPLE: MINDSET

ALIGNMENT

PEOPLE: MINDSET

It's a waste when the entire team is not aligned toward the same goal. You'll find this when people don't buy in when it comes to culture or systems. The rogues drain the time and energy of the team and leaders as they have to fight to keep everyone aligned.

Steps to a SAFE SITE

We've all heard the horror stories. Some of us have witnessed tragedies on site, or been personally affected by onsite accidents and injuries. It's heartbreaking that so many of these incidents are preventable. You must adopt a zero tolerance safety policy to avoid this. Life is so precious and everyone deserves to be safe while they are in your care.

I'm going to go high level for a few minutes so that I can bring you back with a good framework for my approach to safety. Our actions and behaviors are based on the values and beliefs that we hold. We have beliefs and values based on our experiences and at the root of it all is our mindset. All of these are influenced by our environment and our emotional state.

To have a safe site, we need to understand that behavior is the tip of the iceberg, and all the other influences are not always seen or understood. Some people may just "do as they are told," but most will not. So we apply safety to many layers to have the greatest possible impact.

ENVIRONMENT -the surroundings & conditions

ACTIONS & BEHAVIOR- the way you move and think

VALUES & BELIEFS- values are how we attribute worth to something, beliefs are our assumptions about the world

EXPERIENCES- direct observation of or participation in events, includes education

below surface level

MINDSET-how we see people, problems, challenges, circumstances, opportunities

MINDSET- There are two mindsets that we are dealing with when it comes to safety-outward and inward. An outward mindset means that we see others comparable to how we see ourselves; we recognize that others have needs and are autonomous. The inward mindset is when we tend to see others for the value they provide for us, or as obstacles to reaching our desires. To reach people with an inward mindset, safety might be **gamified** or **rewarded**. There needs to be **collaboration** and **teaming** to help shift to an outward mindset, where one desires safety for one's self and those around us.

 EXPERIENCES- This means that we push to experience safety onsite through **training**, clear **logistics** with visual reminders, and a **zero tolerance policy**.

 VALUES & BELIEFS- When we value safety, it the common thread running through every choice that is made. It is **never sacrificed** for profit or speed. Priorities will change based on the situation, but when safety is the value, **every decision is weighed with safety**. When we believe that everyone has a right to be safe, we will not act outside of that belief consistently. Of course there are times when our actions betray our beliefs and values, and that is something that we seek to minimize as we mature emotionally.

 ACTIONS & BEHAVIORS- We remind and support safe behavior. We never tolerate unsafe behavior. There are **consequences** in place and agreed to by the team to help everyone have buy in. This might look like a contract signed where everyone pledges to wear their **PPE** and to help hold each other **accountable**. There might be a **reward** for no safety violations.

 MOOD & EMOTIONS- Our mood and emotions affect our behavior as well. When we are down or depressed, going through a daily habit or routine can be overwhelming. I'm not asking you to try to regulate everyone's emotions, I'm asking you to be aware that if someone is struggling, compassion should temper interactions, but there is no excuse for being unsafe onsite. People will use all sorts of reasons why they can't send someone home for unsafe behavior. "I don't want to piss them off," or "I don't feel comfortable sending someone home," or "I think they need a few more days to adjust." These are **fear based responses** that have **no place on a safe site**.

ENVIRONMENT- We react to the things around us and in order to help create a **culture of safety**, we need to establish a safe environment. This is reinforced in daily **6S** practices, well designed and maintained **logistics plans** for safety, daily and monthly **training** and through **zero tolerance** for violations. Clean and organized enviroments allow you to see where safety can be improved.

Steps *to a* SAFE SITE

- ✓ **Standards common to group**
- ✓ **Consequences established**
- ✓ **Orientation and training**
- ✓ **Visual reminders**
- ✓ **Accountability**
- ✓ **No unsafe behavior tolerated**

SAFETY FIRST

Building a safe project culture is only possible when every member of the team is **committed** to implementing and enforcing the rules.

SAFETY IS A MINDSET NOT JUST A TASK

STANDARDS COMMON TO GROUP

| OSHA REGULATIONS | LOCAL REGULATIONS | COMPANY RULES | TASK SPECIFIC REQUIREMENTS | PROJECT SPECIFIC REQUIREMENTS |

There are common standards on every project. These include OSHA regulations in the USA, local government regulations, company rules, task specific approaches to safety, and project requirements. Not following these means there is a resource, environment, training, or mindset problem at play. So, when we say consequences, we mean there must be consequences to not following these standards--not punishment.

 # CONSEQUENCES ESTABLISHED

The culture of any organization is shaped by the worst behavior it will tolerate. It's frustrating to look at life this way, but negative behavior ignored, tolerated, or condoned speaks louder than any pep talk or training speech. When it comes to safety, there are many ways to hold the line without making things personal or about someone's character. Simply put, zero tolerance on safety is a black and white issue where you can confidently hold the line and the project to high standards.

ZERO TOLERANCE

Any violation of safety that is contrary to the company standards, orientation, and OSHA 10 training.

Anything that is indicative of **bad behavior**, bad attitudes, not paying attention, or not being trained for the task.

Anything that is **high risk** like ladder use, electrical, fall protection, confined space, excavations, etc.

✓ ORIENTATION AND TRAINING

When you orient a trade partner to the project, they will sign a safety agreement to hold the standards you have set as a project team. You can take that to individual levels if you have the bandwidth. This can be terms of the project. Morning huddles should include a safety moment that isn't boring or redundant. Saftey workers or emergency response system?

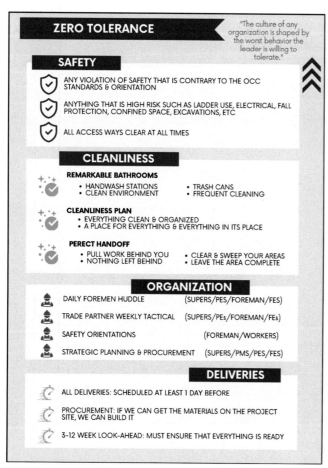

✓ VISUAL REMINDERS

All safety information should be available at a glance and posted in common areas. The safety logistics plan should be kept current. signs for walkways and vehicle traffic, fall dangers, etc flaggers.

 ACCOUNTABILITY

Because all of the systems are interwoven, you are able to achieve desired results throughout the entire project immediately. Do not try to roll out the structured processes one trade or area at a time. Unify the team and act as a team. We should hold each team member accountable for the following things specifically.

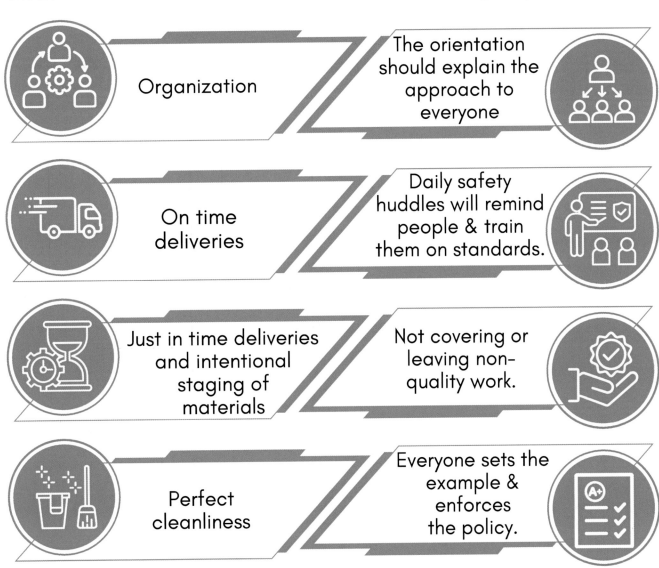

Organization — The orientation should explain the approach to everyone

On time deliveries — Daily safety huddles will remind people & train them on standards.

Just in time deliveries and intentional staging of materials — Not covering or leaving non-quality work.

Perfect cleanliness — Everyone sets the example & enforces the policy.

If someone is not being safe, they cannot work on the project.

The superintendent is ultimately responsible for the safety of their project. They never delegate safety. It is one of their fundamental responsibilities.

NO UNSAFE BEHAVIOR TOLERATED

If you implement Zero Tolerance on-site, you can have a remarkably well-run project with fewer safety incidents. Once everyone has agreed to the safety standards, you can follow these steps if a violation occurs.

Is this a minor violation?

 YES

 NO

Stop them and tell them, "Because I care about your safety, we need to give you time to focus, re-train, or plan the work. So, let's have you go home for the day, and **you can come back tomorrow for orientation.**"

If it is a serious violation that could have resulted in death, they cannot come back.

This means that the individual has been properly trained and oriented to policies and has flagrantly ignored safe site practices. You don't have the time and energy to spend trying to fight their rebellion.

Send an email to that person's company explaining why that person was allowed to go home for their own safety and the benefit of their family. Ask that the person is **re-trained and offer for them to come back through orientation.**

Log the name and violation on a log to track repeat offenders or people who cannot come back.

HOLD THE LINE ⫶ *BE STRICT* ⫶ *BE CALM*

Within 3 weeks the site will uphold the standard without a lot of oversight. Every new wave of contractors will have to be trained and agree to holding the site standards. This will only work if everyone on the team holds the line.

REFLECTION-CLEAN, SAFE, AND ORGANIZED

The purpose of this component is to provide operational stability that will enable all other success. Cleanliness and safety are not only good ideas, they are required in order you to make any further progress. Your flow, problem solving, the morale of your project, and the flow of materials all depend on cleanliness, safety, and organization. If you do not have this piece, you will have chaos that will slow down production, clutter the minds of people onsite, and prohibit you from seeing what you need to see. No other lean system can be implemented successfully without this component coming first.

Component Scoring: (1%-100%)
1. Is your project clean?____
2. Is your project safe?____
3. Is your project organized?____
4. Do you have a 6S system in place that people will remember and use?____
5. Does your workforce know the 9 wastes and have reminder cards?____
6. Do you have a zero tolerance system for cleanliness and organization?____
7. Do you have a zero tolerance system for safety?____

What is your final score, taking the average of all answers? ____
If your score is below 80%, what specific actions do you need to take to elevate your team and leadership? --

< NOTE <

141

At this point you have a culture onsite for your amazing foremen and workers that they can use to install work.

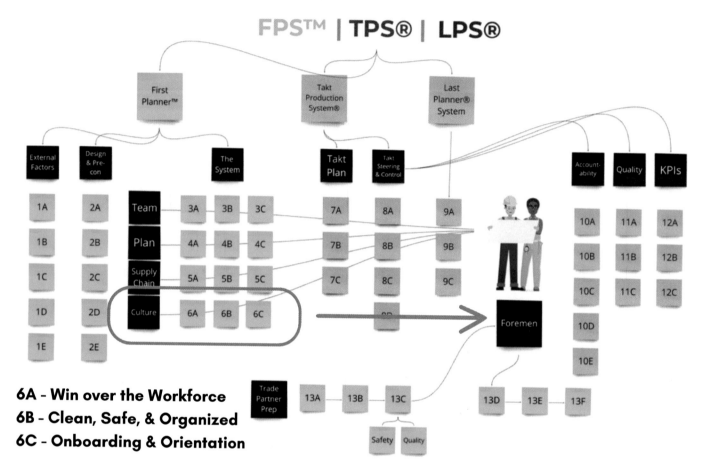

6A - Win over the Workforce
6B - Clean, Safe, & Organized
6C - Onboarding & Orientation

Now your foremen have the culture they need

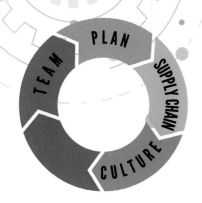

TRAINING
COMPONENT

For the fifth part of the system, we recommend you get training. While we obviously recommend training with Elevate Construction, I can tell you we provide those at a sacrifice--meaning we are not getting rich over here. We are trying to help teach a better way of building and executing with production systems. Here are a few things I recommend for your onsite teams.

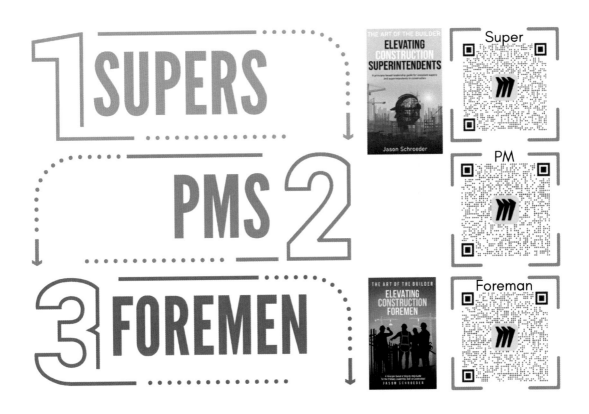

You can access the books through Amazon, the Miro boards have position specific content, and training events are found on our website, www.elevateconstructionevents.com.

REFLECTION-TRAINING

Without training on these systems as a team you run the risk of reverting back to old habits. The key here is to help people to know what is expected, motivate them to do it, and clear the path for them. Training will cover the first two.

Component Scoring: (1%-100%)
1. Has your team been trained on the Takt Production System®?____
2. Have your supers and foremen read the Art Of The Builder book for their roles? ____
3. Have they attended their role's boot camp?____

What is your final score, taking the average of all answers? ____

If your score is below 80%, what specific actions do you need to take to elevate your team and leadership? --------------------------------------

> NOTE

Now that we have covered the five component categories of team, plan, supply chain, culture, and training, my hope is that it is clear these are all intended to get the foremen and crews what they need so they can install their work package in their zone within their Takt time. But what brings it all together? What pulls this into a package or plan for the crew specifically? The answer is Takt Planning, Takt Steering & Control, and Last Planner®. These systems provide the Rhythm, Flow, and Collaboration needed to bring it all together.

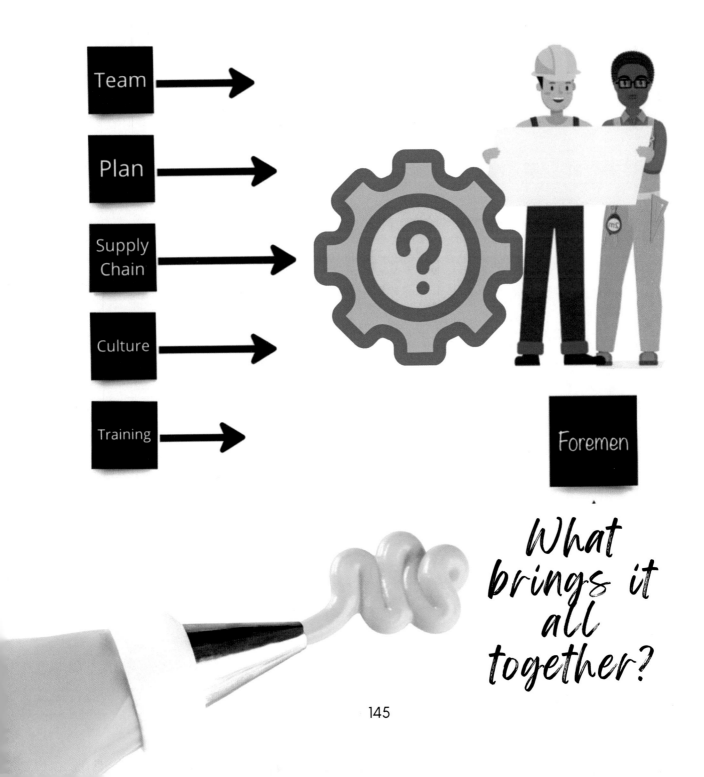

What brings it all together?

The First Planner™ System, covered in this book, provides the framework of system components that need to be in place to run a lean project as a production system in addition to how it is made in pre-construction (Second Part of Book). The team, plan, supply chain, culture, and training need to be provided for the system to work.

It enables the design, fabrication, transportation and preparation of activities that will occur in your production system. It aligns them together into one continuous flow.

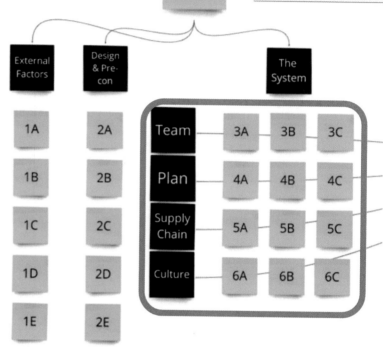

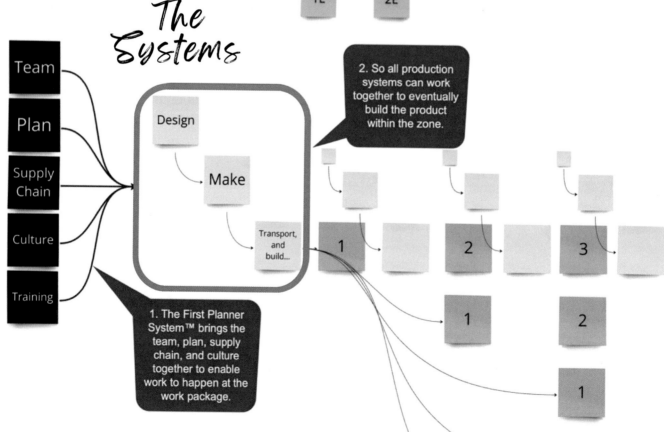

The Systems

2. So all production systems can work together to eventually build the product within the zone.

1. The First Planner System™ brings the team, plan, supply chain, and culture together to enable work to happen at the work package.

146

The Takt Production System® creates the rhythm of your production system. Not only is it able to put your trades on a rhythm, it does it without overburdening resources and increasing WIP above the capacity of the system. You make the plan, review it, manage it, and use it to enable Last Planners®. It is your master schedule.

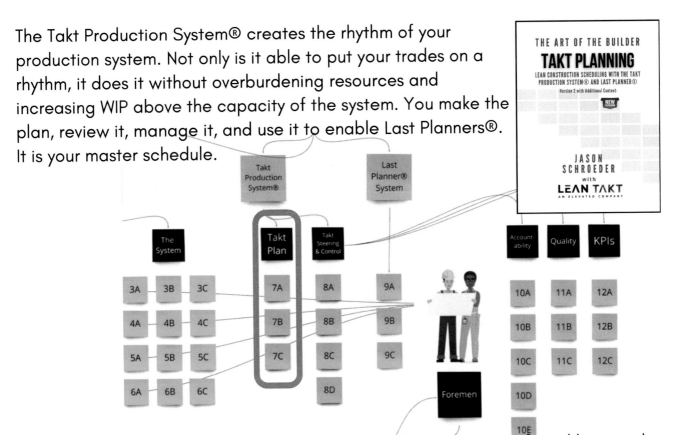

It creates a system that has workflow, trade flow [most important], and logistical flow. Through the Little's Law (Dlouhy & Binninger's Law) formula we are able to identify the right no. of zones, wagons, and the right Takt time to get the best possible duration and end date. Then everything in the First Planner System™ is aligned to it. It aligns your other production systems and simulates your best scenario onsite.

The Rhythm

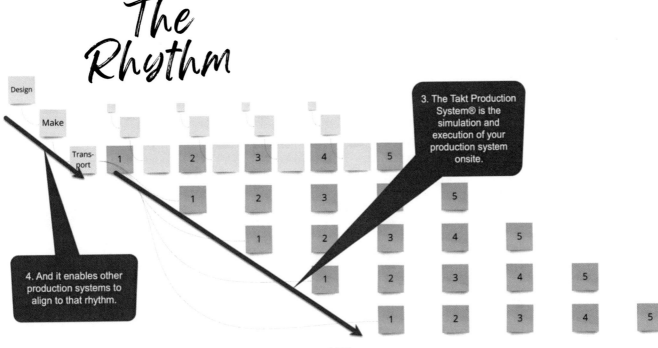

3. The Takt Production System® is the simulation and execution of your production system onsite.

4. And it enables other production systems to align to that rhythm.

Takt Steering & Control enables you to take your brilliant production plan into the field, steer around constraints, and control the removal of roadblocks in your environment. It is the strategy that keeps the flow going when the plan experiences impacts.

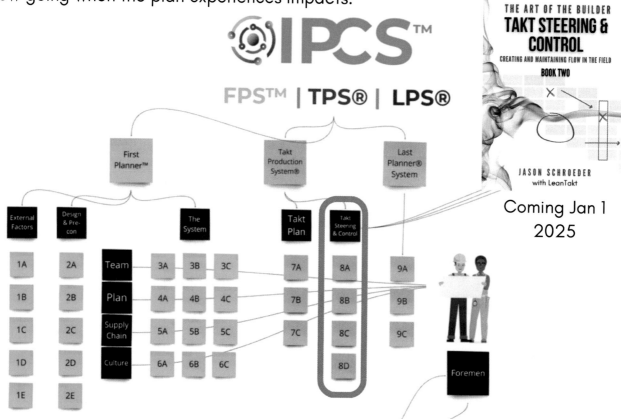

Projects will always experience impacts, delays, and problems. That is a historical fact. The key is not to hope or wish they go away, but rather to have an effective way to deal with them. That is called Takt Steering & Control. The approach enables the team to deal with delays, steer around constraints (permanent or semi-permanent), and remove roadblocks (temporary).

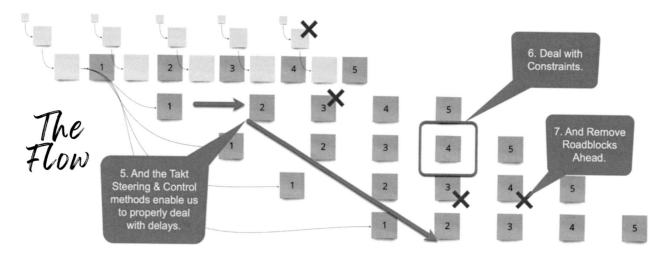

The Last Planner® System then provides the framework for our foremen or Last Planners® to collaborate, weigh-in to, and commit to the plan in the short-interval. The book The Lean Builder explains this culture perfectly. Additionally all this integration will be explained in detail in the book Takt Steering & Control.

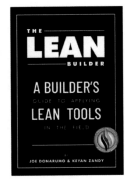

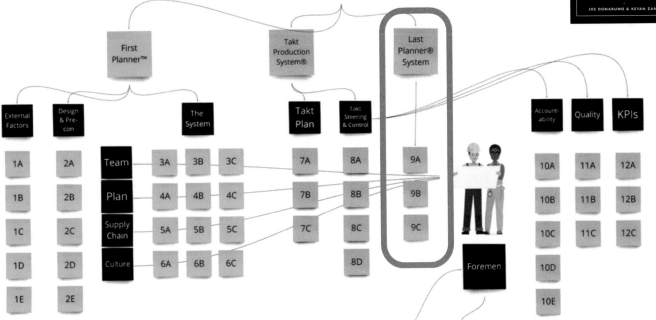

It provides a pattern for the trades to participate in the pull plan, collaborate, commit to, and execute a weekly work plan, and remove roadblocks out ahead in the look-ahead while they make work ready.

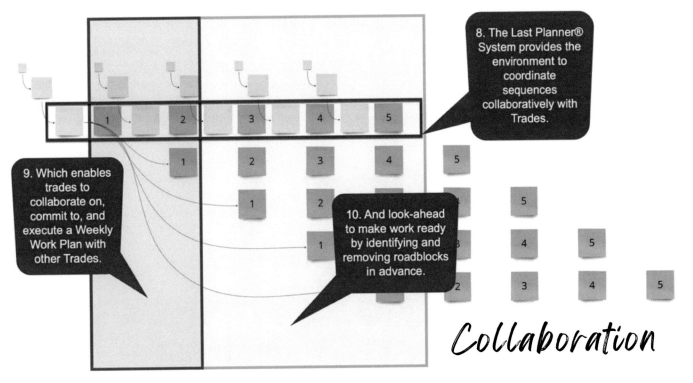

Collaboration

Each component fits together so foremen get what they need for their crew.

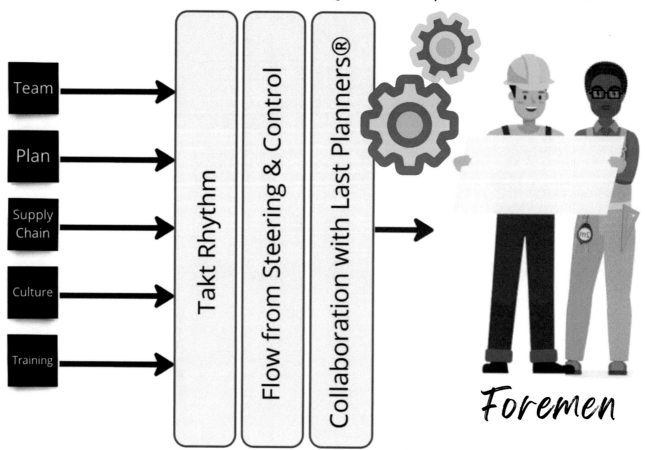

Foremen

Remember this image from page 12? I've checked off the components we have up to this point. The only things I'm missing are the quality expectations. That is picked up in the Trade Partner Preparation Process. So, let's cover that right now!

- QUALITY/SAFETY EXPECTATIONS
- ✓ MATERIALS
- ✓ LAYOUT
- ✓ INFORMATION
- ✓ PLAN
- ✓ STABILITY
- ✓ RESPECT

- TRAINING ✓
- LABOR ✓
- TOOLS ✓
- EQUIPMENT ✓

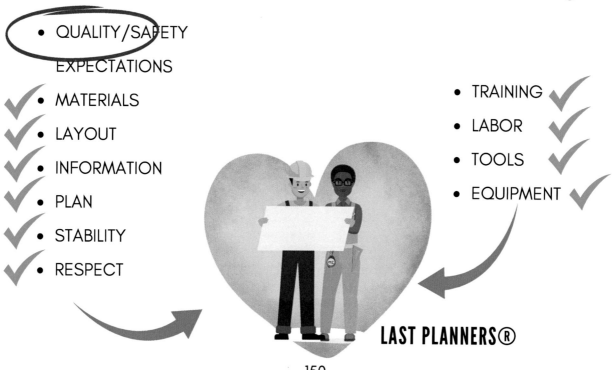

LAST PLANNERS®

Let them eat cake.

Marie Antoinette never said that, and we're just kidding. The Trade Partner Preparation Process is how you implement and convert trades to the IPCS™ and First Planner System™. This is the moment where you have a beautiful cake, and you are attempting to convince the trades to eat the cake. We can't force people to enjoy the cake, but we can make it beneficial, profitable, and remarkable.

THE *Who*
Part 2– Trade Partner Preparation Process

This is a 6-part process to prepare contractors to build well on projects. Others have called this a quality process or QC plan, but we use Trade Partner Preparation Process because it prepares trade partners to plan their work, build their work right, and finish as they go. It includes the necessary meeting system to prepare and support the trades working safely and installing quality work.

Trade Partner Preparation Process

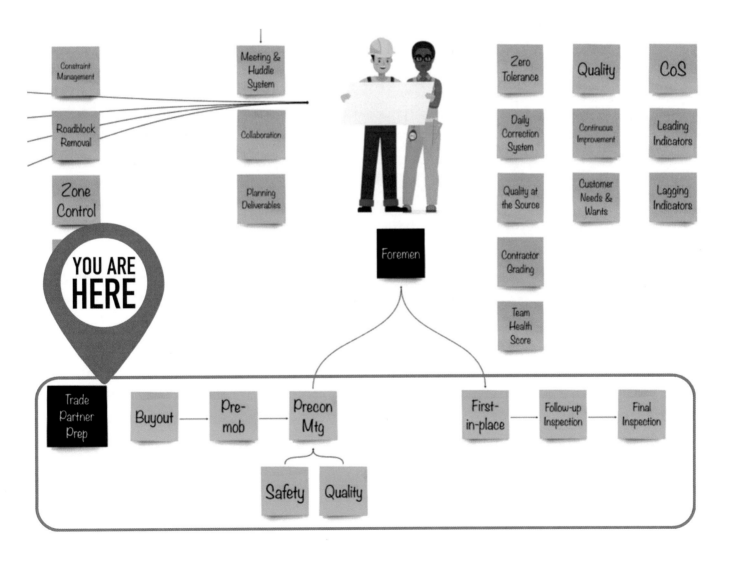

Constraint Management

Roadblock Removal

Zone Control

Meeting & Huddle System

Collaboration

Planning Deliverables

Foremen

Zero Tolerance

Quality

CoS

Daily Correction System

Continuous Improvement

Leading Indicators

Quality at the Source

Customer Needs & Wants

Lagging Indicators

Contractor Grading

Team Health Score

YOU ARE HERE

Trade Partner Prep

Buyout

Pre-mob

Precon Mtg

Safety

Quality

First-in-place

Follow-up Inspection

Final Inspection

Trade Partner Preparation Process

The Trade Partner Preparation Process, if followed, will prepare your trade partners to be successful when it is time to execute their scope. You have the opportunity to help your trades early on in the process, which promotes flow throughout.

MEANS AND METHODS:

1. **Buyout Meeting:** The buyout meeting is to ensure we have purchased the right scope
2. **Pre-mobilization Meeting:** The pre-mob is to notify the trade what the general contractor wants and expects before the pre-con meeting to set them up for success.
3. **Pre-construction Meeting:** The pre-con meeting is to orient the trade foreman, super, and PM to jobsite requirements and create checklists and visuals that will be used to install the work.
4. **First-in-Place Inspection:** The FIP is to inspect the first portion of work to confirm it is compliant with the expectations of the pre-con.
5. **Follow-up Inspection:** The follow-up is to continue controlling quality throughout the remainder of the install.
6. **Final Inspection:** And the final inspection is to properly inspect the work before the trade demobilizes for the purpose of finishing all work and finalizing everything.

TOOLS:

1. **Meeting Agendas** – Used to trigger communication in meetings.
2. **Meeting Minutes** – Used to develop the end installation checklist and visual.
3. **Quality Checklist or Visual** – Used to install work in the work package.
4. **Inspections** – Used to verify installation.

PURPOSE:

1. A focus on one process flow.
2. A commitment to alignment.
3. Communication of expectations.
4. Determination to execute according to expectations.

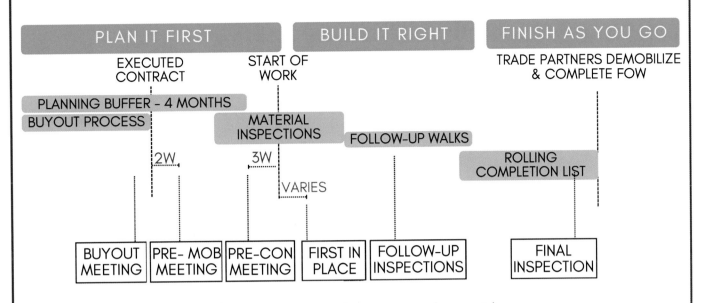

- The buyout meeting happens according to your buyout log.
- The pre-mob should be within 2 weeks of having an executed contract.
- The pre-con meeting happens 3 weeks before the work begins. That leaves you some buffer if you need to re-schedule or have a follow-up.
- Your first in place happens once the first work package is ready to inspect.
- Follow-up inspections happen in zone control walks (To be discussed in next book) or when the crew encounters newer work or the foreman changes.
- The final should happen in enough time to finalize any punchlist and reconcile any change orders. --DO NOT WAIT until the Trade leaves site--

We'll walk you through them.

BUYOUT MEETING

1 Who attends? Trade representative & GC PM

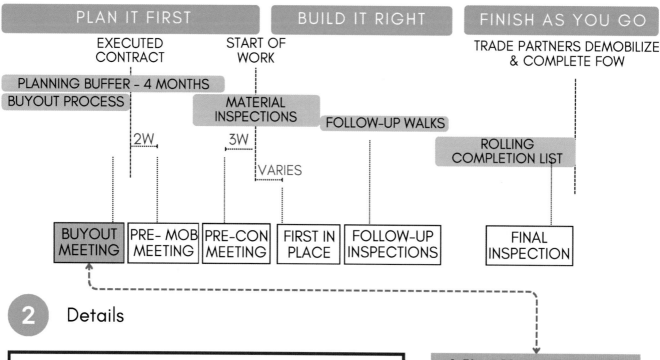

| PLAN IT FIRST | | BUILD IT RIGHT | FINISH AS YOU GO |

- EXECUTED CONTRACT
- START OF WORK
- TRADE PARTNERS DEMOBILIZE & COMPLETE FOW

PLANNING BUFFER – 4 MONTHS
BUYOUT PROCESS
MATERIAL INSPECTIONS
FOLLOW-UP WALKS
ROLLING COMPLETION LIST

2W — 3W — VARIES

| BUYOUT MEETING | PRE- MOB MEETING | PRE-CON MEETING | FIRST IN PLACE | FOLLOW-UP INSPECTIONS | FINAL INSPECTION |

2 Details

AGENDA ITEMS:

- Review Owner's Top 10
- Review work package checklist
- Obtain commitments to comply with:
  - Project-specific plans (Safety / QC)
  - Schedule
  - Project-specific requirements
- Review Procurement log
- Identify need for mock-ups
- Schedule all other meetings
- Review permitting
- Verify testing & inspections
- Update buyout logs

A First Planner™ Meeting

BUYOUT MEETING

AS NEEDED

Purpose: Verify contractor scope; ensure the contractor is legally obligated to perform

PRE-MOBILIZATION MEETING

1 Who attends? Trade PM & GC PM

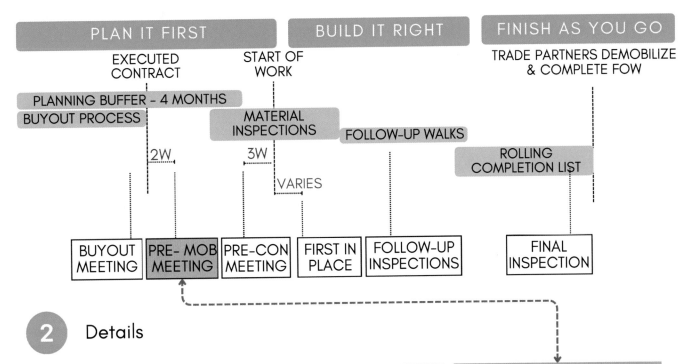

2 Details

AGENDA ITEMS:
- Review Owner's Top 10
- Review work package checklist
- Confirm commitments:
  - Project-specific plans (Safety / QC)
  - Schedule
  - FOW Project-specific requirements
- Develop Feature of Work breakout for contractor
- Define project office/admin requirements
- Get buy-in for scope of submittals and commit to schedule
- Follow-up on permitting action items
- Identify special / source inspections

A First Planner™ Meeting

PRE-MOBILIZATION MEETING

2 WEEKS AFTER CONTRACT

Purpose: Explain to contractor deliverable needs. Commit contractor to deliver by pre-construction meeting

PRE-CONSTRUCTION MEETING

1 Who attends? Trade PM, Super, Foremen + Onsite Team

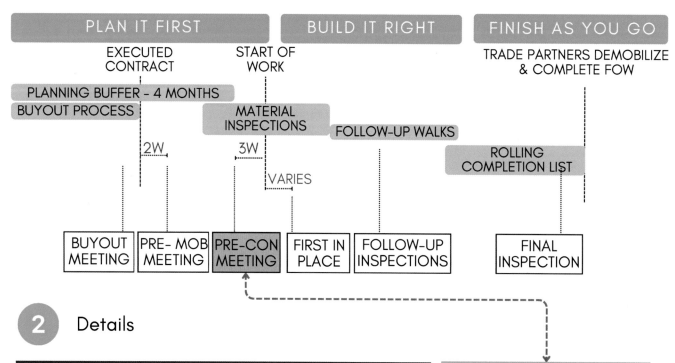

PLAN IT FIRST	BUILD IT RIGHT	FINISH AS YOU GO

EXECUTED CONTRACT — START OF WORK — TRADE PARTNERS DEMOBILIZE & COMPLETE FOW

PLANNING BUFFER - 4 MONTHS

BUYOUT PROCESS

MATERIAL INSPECTIONS

FOLLOW-UP WALKS

ROLLING COMPLETION LIST

2W — 3W — VARIES

BUYOUT MEETING	PRE-MOB MEETING	PRE-CON MEETING	FIRST IN PLACE	FOLLOW-UP INSPECTIONS	FINAL INSPECTION

2 Details

AGENDA ITEMS:

- Review Owner's Top 10
- Review work package checklist
- Collect and review pre-mobilization deliverables
- Set safety and quality expectations
- Set-up the first in place inspection
- Coordinate with all applicable trades
- Review schedule for work
- Complete testing expectations
- Review current project plans
- Follow-up on source/special inspections
- Finish inspections requirements
- Review all drawings
- Review all specifications
- Review site logistics
- Review Pre-con Safety Quality Form
- Detail the checklist or visual

A First Planner™ Meeting

PRE-CONSTRUCTION MEETING

3 WEEKS BEFORE FIRST WAGON

Purpose: Collect and explain deliverables; enable the foreman and superintendent. Develop the quality checklist or visual.

158

FIRST IN PLACE INSPECTION

1 Who attends? GC Super & FE + Trade (Super, Foreman, & Crew)

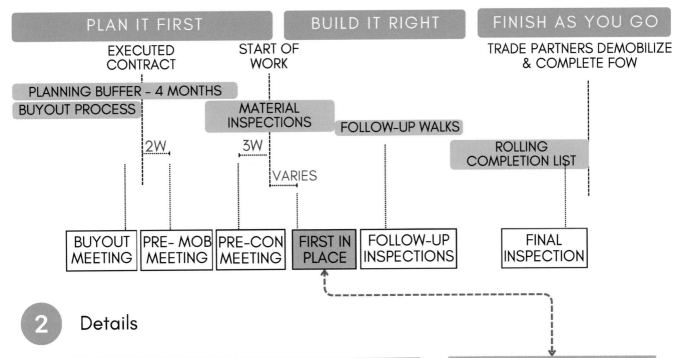

PLAN IT FIRST	BUILD IT RIGHT	FINISH AS YOU GO

EXECUTED CONTRACT — START OF WORK — TRADE PARTNERS DEMOBILIZE & COMPLETE FOW

PLANNING BUFFER - 4 MONTHS
BUYOUT PROCESS

MATERIAL INSPECTIONS

FOLLOW-UP WALKS

ROLLING COMPLETION LIST

2W · 3W · VARIES

BUYOUT MEETING | PRE- MOB MEETING | PRE-CON MEETING | FIRST IN PLACE | FOLLOW-UP INSPECTIONS | FINAL INSPECTION

2 Details

AGENDA ITEMS:
- Review Owner's Top 10
- Review work package checklist
- Review quality checklist and visual
- Review installation
- Confirm crew knowledge
- Congratulate the team
- Educate, educate, educate
- Are the checklists being used?
- Substrate accepted?
- Spec and drawings being reviewed?

A First & Last Planner™ Inspection

FIRST IN PLACE

ONCE FIRST PROCESS/WAGON IS DONE

Purpose: Get the crews off on the right foot; set the expectation and make sure it is followed.

FOLLOW-UP INSPECTION

1 Who attends? GC Super & FE + Trade (Super, Foreman, & Crew)

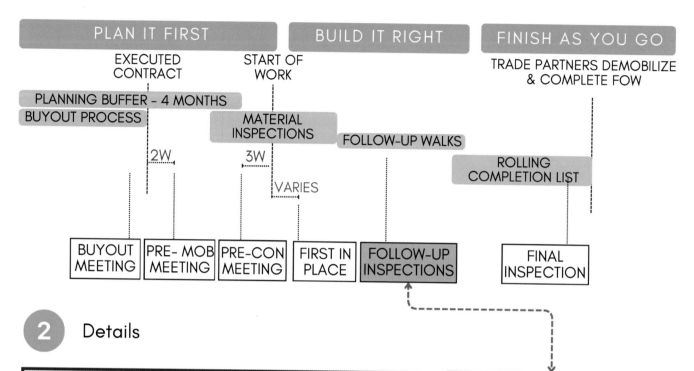

2 Details

AGENDA ITEMS:

- Review Owner's Top 10
- Review work package checklist
- Use tablet to inspect work
- Do we have the same foremen?
- Are the crews up-to-date?
- Are the correct materials being used?
- Educate, educate, educate

A First & Last Planner™ Inspection

FOLLOW-UP
INSPECTION

AS NEEDED

Purpose: Keep an eye on the work; check requirements on an ongoing basis.

FINAL INSPECTION

1 Who attends? GC Super & FE + Trade Super & Foreman

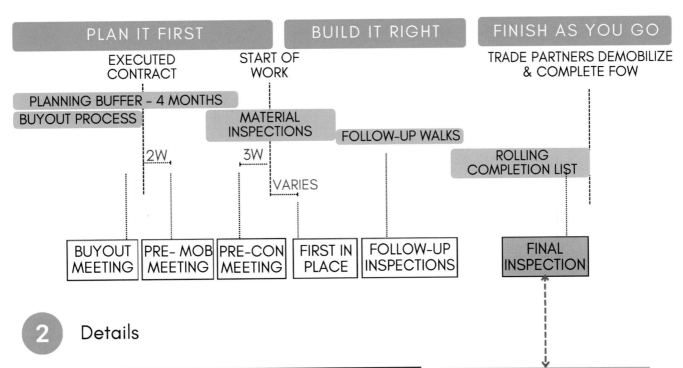

| PLAN IT FIRST | BUILD IT RIGHT | FINISH AS YOU GO |

- EXECUTED CONTRACT
- START OF WORK
- TRADE PARTNERS DEMOBILIZE & COMPLETE FOW
- PLANNING BUFFER - 4 MONTHS
- BUYOUT PROCESS
- MATERIAL INSPECTIONS
- FOLLOW-UP WALKS
- ROLLING COMPLETION LIST

2W · 3W · VARIES

| BUYOUT MEETING | PRE- MOB MEETING | PRE-CON MEETING | FIRST IN PLACE | FOLLOW-UP INSPECTIONS | | FINAL INSPECTION |

2 Details

AGENDA ITEMS:

- Review owner's Top 10
- Review checklist
- Perform a final inspection
- Log all items on rolling completion list
- Complete requirements before de-mob

A First & Last Planner™ Inspection

FINAL INSPECTION

BEFORE DEMOBILIZATION

Purpose: Finish the contractor's scope before they leave.

Some of these terms may be new to you, so here is an explanation of the ones that may not be common:

- Review **Owner's Top 10** – It is important to know the Owner's hot buttons. Top 10 refers to our knowing the Owner's most important focuses. We do owe a great install per the drawings and specs, but the Owner may really care about specific details throughout like how stairs are installed, or the alignment in the lobby, or the waterproofing in the courtyard. If we care about what they care about, we are on track to build a great project with great relationships.
- Review **work package checklist** – Some companies maintain a database of checklists by scope for specific work packages. If this is the case, please bring them up in the meetings.
- Obtain commitments to comply with:
  - **Project-specific plans** (Safety / QC) – Throughout this process we are getting buy-in to install safely and in a quality manner.
  - **Schedule** – Always confirm the Trade's idea of durations and overall sequence and flow align with what is planned.
  - **Project-specific requirements** – Orient the Trade throughout to any job specific requirements they may not already know.
- **Quality checklist** or visual – The purpose of this process is to make sure the Trade knows the expectations for the work and can follow them. We must collect all relevant information onto a checklist or preferably a visual so they can use it to install in the field.

Remember that throughout the process, you are ensuring that safety and quality are the mindsets that anchor everyone. Speed and budget are prioritized as you are able to, and after safety and quality have been satisfied.

REFLECTION-TRADE PARTNER PREPARATION PROCESS

The purpose of this part of the system is to select the right Trade, orient them, set them up for success, and then ensure patterns are being followed. If you do not have this you will install defective work and be riddled with rework and delays. The trade will not be ready and you will be stuck fighting fires.

Component Scoring: (1%-100%)
- Do you have a remarkable buyout process that is followed?____
- Do you have a way to communicate expectations to Trades before they mobilize? ____
- Are you holding a pre-construction meeting that is effective? ____
- Are you distilling all needed information into a checklist or visual for the crews to use while installing? ____
- Are you inspecting the first piece of work to make sure the Trade is off to a good start? ____
- Are you facilitating follow-up inspections and final inspections to keep the quality going? ____

If your score is below 80%, what specific actions do you need to take to elevate your team and leadership?

NOTE

The Trade Partner Preparation Process also has weekly meetings. These are First Planner™ meetings and a continuation of the process to prepare trades for their work.

MEETINGS

1. **Team Weekly Tactical:** This is the meeting where the team comes together and ensures they have coverage which will lead to a balance for each member. Then, as a united and balanced team they tackle the project needs.
2. **Strategic Planning & Procurement:** This meeting enables the team to strategically plan the project and align the supply chain. Without this the Last Planner® system cannot be successful.

TOOLS

1. **Meeting Agendas** – Used to trigger communication in meetings.
2. **Team Board** – Used to install work in the work package.
3. **Macro Takt Plan** – Used to verify the plan is solid.
4. **Procurement Log** – Used to verify the team is feeding the production system.

PURPOSE

1. Balance the team.
2. Ensure coverage.
3. Confirm & Communication the Strategic Plan.
4. Ensure all Production Systems are aligned.

Let me provide you with the meeting structure and then I'll provide some explanation.

1 Who attends? Supers, PEs, FEs, PMs,

WEEKLY MEETING PLAN

	MONDAY	TUESDAY	WEDNESDAY	THURSDAY	FRIDAY
5AM			NO MEETINGS		NO MEETINGS
	WORKER DAILY HUDDLE	WORKER DAILY HUDDLE CREW	WORKER DAILY HUDDLE CREW	WORKER DAILY HUDDLE CREW	WORKER DAILY HUDDLE CREW
6AM	CREW PREPARATION	PREPARATION	PREPARATION	PREPARATION	PREPARATION
7AM	SAFETY ORIENTATIONS			SAFETY ORIENTATIONS	
8AM	TEAM WEEKLY	DAILY HUDDLE	DAILY HUDDLE	DAILY HUDDLE	DAILY HUDDLE
9AM	TACTICAL			BIM COORDINATION	
10AM		OAC MEETING			
11AM					
12PM					
1PM	FOREMEN DAILY HUDDLE	FOREMEN DAILY HUDDLE	FOREMEN DAILY HUDDLE	FOREMEN DAILY HUDDLE	FOREMEN DAILY HUDDLE
2PM	STRATEGIC	TRADE PARTNER		COORDINATION	
3PM	PLANNING & PROCUREMENT	WEEKLY TACTICAL		MEETING	
4PM				PLACEHOLDER	
5PM					
6PM					

2 Details

AGENDA ITEMS:

- Lightning round
- PTO coverage, Saturday coverage
- Review weekly coverage schedule
- Reminder about, "no meeting days."
- Customer experience review
- TP3 management (if not covered in sppm)
- Contracting needs
- Submittal needs
- Pre-con mtg meeting setup
- First-in-place inspections
- Final inspections
- Schedule management
- Safety management
- Cost & budgeting
- Teaming moment from P. Lencioni books
- Communicate a team message
- Other topics as needed

A First Planner™ Meeting

TEAM WEEKLY TACTICAL

WEEKLY

Purpose: Team reviews current workload, coverage for the week, & everyone's individual outstanding or open items.

TEAMING MEETING

165

When you run the Team Weekly Tactical you can use these boards that have been formatted for that purpose. I will take you through each component one by one. This is the Team board.

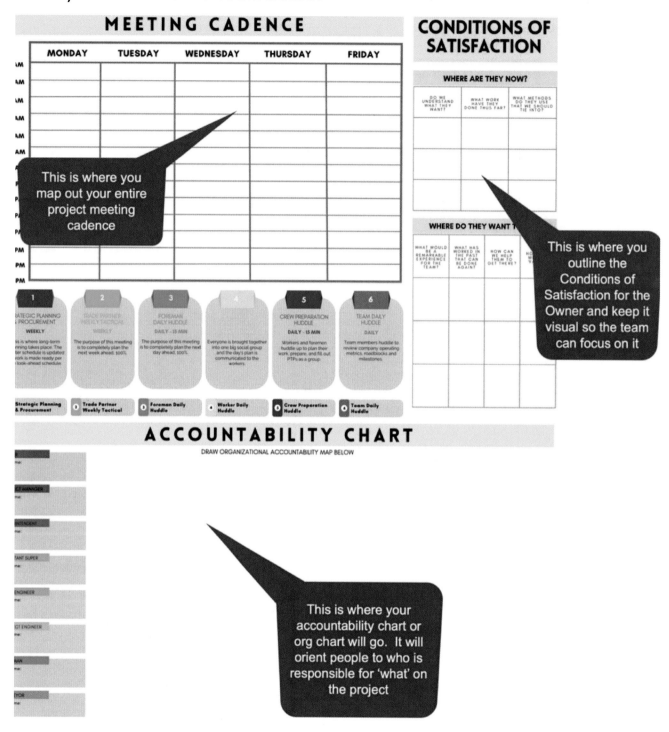

*Contact Jason for the template.

MEETING CADENCE

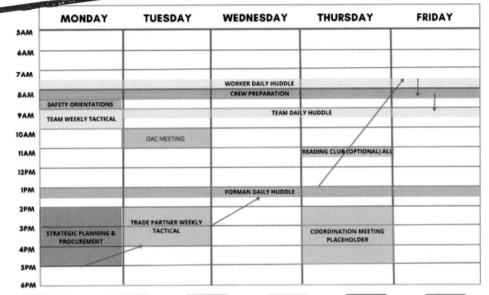

	MONDAY	TUESDAY	WEDNESDAY	THURSDAY	FRIDAY
5AM					
6AM					
7AM					
8AM			WORKER DAILY HUDDLE		
			CREW PREPARATION		
9AM	SAFETY ORIENTATIONS		TEAM DAILY HUDDLE		
	TEAM WEEKLY TACTICAL				
10AM		OAC MEETING			
11AM				READING CLUB (OPTIONAL) ALL	
12PM					
1PM			FORMAN DAILY HUDDLE		
2PM					
3PM	STRATEGIC PLANNING & PROCUREMENT	TRADE PARTNER WEEKLY TACTICAL		COORDINATION MEETING PLACEHOLDER	
4PM					
5PM					
6PM					

CONDITIONS OF SATISFACTION

WHERE ARE WE?

UNDERSTAND WHAT THEY WANT?	WHAT WORK HAVE THEY DONE THUS FAR?	WHAT METHODS DO THEY USE THAT WE SHOULD TIE INTO?
HIGH QUALITY FINISHES	WEEKLY MEETING SYSTEM	LPS
FINISH ON TIME OR BEFORE	ROADBLOCK TRACKING LOG	TAKT
NO ACCIDENTS	PROCUREMENT	BIM

WHERE DO WE WANT TO GO?

WHAT WOULD BE A REMARKABLE EXPERIENCE FOR THE TEAM?	WHAT HAS WORKED IN THE PAST THAT CAN BE DONE AGAIN?	HOW CAN WE HELP THEM TO GET THERE?	HOW CAN WE ADD VALUE?
TRAINING	TAKT	SITE VISITS	INTEGRATED SYSTEM
	LPS	ZONE CONTROLS	

1	2	3	4	5	6
STRATEGIC PLANNING & PROCUREMENT	TRADE PARTNER WEEKLY TACTICAL	FOREMAN DAILY HUDDLE		CREW PREPARATION HUDDLE	TEAM DAILY HUDDLE
WEEKLY	WEEKLY	DAILY - 15 MIN		DAILY - 15 MIN	DAILY
This is where long-term planning takes place. The master schedule is updated & work is made ready per the look-ahead schedule	The purpose of this meeting is to completely plan the next week ahead, 100%.	The purpose of this meeting is to completely plan the next day ahead, 100%.	Everyone is brought together into one big social group and the day's plan is communicated to the workers.	Workers and foremen huddle up to plan their work, prepare, and fill out PTPs as a group.	Team members huddle to review company operating metrics, roadblocks and milestones.

 1 Strategic Planning & Procurement
 2 Trade Partner Weekly Tactical
 3 Foreman Daily Huddle
4 Worker Daily Huddle
 **5** Crew Preparation Huddle
 6 Team Daily Huddle

ACCOUNTABILITY CHART

DRAW ORGANIZATIONAL ACCOUNTABILITY MAP BELOW

OWNER	Name: HOMER
PROJECT MANAGER	Name: SPONGE BOB
SUPERINTENDENT	Name: ARIEL
ASSISTANT SUPER	Name: MALEFICENT
FIELD ENGINEER	Name: MR. INCREDIBLE
PROJECT ENGINEER	Name: PERCY JACKSON
FOREMAN	Name: MEGAMIND
SURVEYOR	Name: SHREK
WORKERS	Name: HARRY POTTER AND PERCY JACKSON

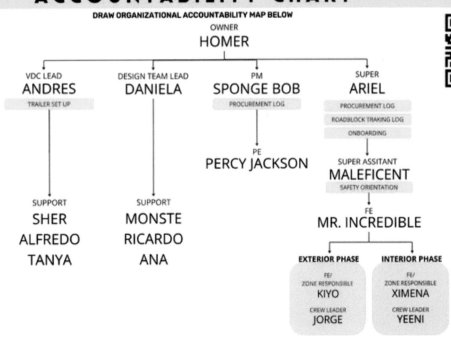

OWNER
HOMER

VDC LEAD
ANDRES
TRAILER SET UP

DESIGN TEAM LEAD
DANIELA

PM
SPONGE BOB
PROCUREMENT LOG

SUPER
ARIEL
PROCUREMENT LOG
ROADBLOCK TRAKING LOG
ONBOARDING

PE
PERCY JACKSON

SUPER ASSITANT
MALEFICENT
SAFETY ORIENTATION

FE
MR. INCREDIBLE

SUPPORT
SHER
ALFREDO
TANYA

SUPPORT
MONSTE
RICARDO
ANA

EXTERIOR PHASE
FE/ ZONE RESPONSIBLE
KIYO
CREW LEADER
JORGE

INTERIOR PHASE
FE/ ZONE RESPONSIBLE
XIMENA
CREW LEADER
YEENI

LEAN TAKT
AN ELEVATED COMPANY

The second board you may use is the coverage board. This is where you take the team, the meetings, and the focus from the first board and make sure those people in that system have the right balance & coverage.

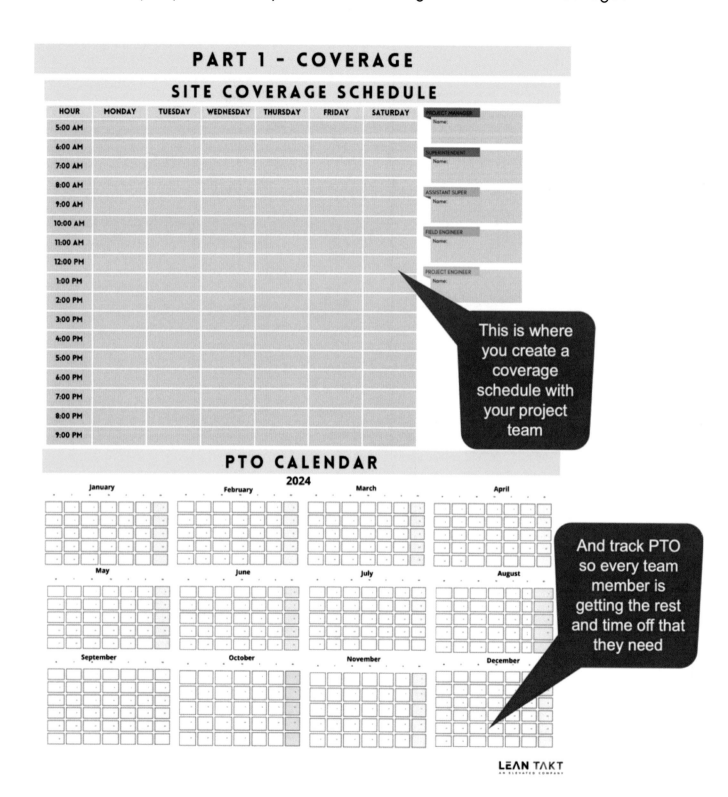

PART 1 - COVERAGE

SITE COVERAGE SCHEDULE

HOUR	MONDAY	TUESDAY	WEDNESDAY	THURSDAY	FRIDAY	SATURDAY
5:00 AM	☆	☆	☆	☆	☆	
6:00 AM						
7:00 AM						
8:00 AM						
9:00 AM						
10:00 AM						
11:00 AM						
12:00 PM						
1:00 PM						
2:00 PM						
3:00 PM						
4:00 PM						
5:00 PM						
6:00 PM		☆	☆	☆	☆	
7:00 PM	☆					
8:00 PM						
9:00 PM						

PROJECT MANAGER
Name:
Spongebob

SUPERINTENDENT
Name:
Ariel the Mermaid

ASSISTANT SUPER
Name:
Malificent

FIELD ENGINEER
Name:
Mr. Incredible

PROJECT ENGINEER
Name:
Percy Jackson

☆ Open/ Close

PTO CALENDAR

2024

January
H
H

February
Malificent
H | Spongebob

March
PJ

April
PJ
Mr Incredible

May
Percy Jackson
H

June
Ariel
Malificent

July
Ariel | H
Ariel
PJ

August
Spongebob

September
H
Ariel
Malificent

October
Percy Jackson
H

November
H | Spongebob
H

December
Mr Incredible
H | Ariel

169

And the third board for this is the focus board. In this board you will keep the team focused on the most important items and track those to the successful completion of Key Performance Indicators.

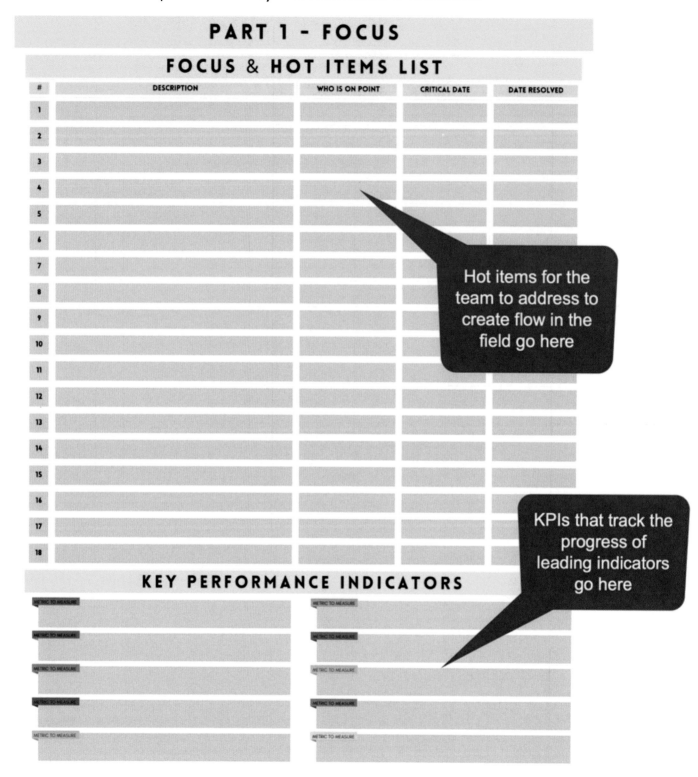

PART 1 - FOCUS

FOCUS & HOT ITEMS LIST

#	DESCRIPTION	WHO IS ON POINT	CRITICAL DATE	DATE RESOLVED
1	LOGISTIC BETWEEN INT AND EXT (MOVE LAYDOWN AREA)	KIYO & XIMENA	20-JAN	19-JAN
2	FLOORING TRADE (MISSING CREW)	LUCÍA	22-FEB	
3	SITE PERMIT DELAY (3 DAYS)	ANA LUISA	02-JAN	01-JAN
4	RESTROOMS NEED MORE FREQUENT CLEANING	ARIEL	13-MAR	
5	RAIN (STRATEGY AND CLAIM DAYS)	SPONGE BOB	20-JAN	18-JAN
6				
7				
8				
9				
10				
11				
12				
13				
14				
15				
16				
17				
18				

KPI'S

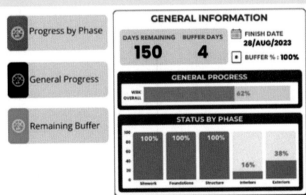

WEEKLY STRATEGIC PLANNING & PROCUREMENT

1 Who attends? Supers, PEs, PMs,

WEEKLY MEETING PLAN

	MONDAY	TUESDAY	WEDNESDAY	THURSDAY	FRIDAY
5AM			NO MEETINGS		NO MEETINGS
6AM	WORKER DAILY HUDDLE CREW PREPARATION	WORKER DAILY HUDDLE CREW PREPARATION	WORKER DAILY HUDDLE CREW PREPARATION	WORKER DAILY HUDDLE CREW PREPARATION	WORKER DAILY HUDDLE CREW PREPARATION
7AM	SAFETY ORIENTATIONS			SAFETY ORIENTATIONS	
8AM	TEAM WEEKLY TACTICAL	DAILY HUDDLE	DAILY HUDDLE	DAILY HUDDLE	DAILY HUDDLE
9AM				BIM COORDINATION	
10AM		OAC MEETING			
11AM					
12PM					
1PM	FOREMEN DAILY HUDDLE	FOREMEN DAILY HUDDLE	FOREMEN DAILY HUDDLE	FOREMEN DAILY HUDDLE	FOREMEN DAILY HUDDLE
2PM	STRATEGIC PLANNING & PROCUREMENT	TRADE PARTNER WEEKLY TACTICAL		COORDINATION MEETING	
3PM					
4PM				PLACEHOLDER	
5PM					
6PM					

2 Details

AGENDA ITEMS:
- Positive Shout-outs
- Review & Update the Takt Plan
- Update Procurement Log
- Look out 3-12 Weeks
- Report out w/ Clarity
- Manage the TP3

Key questions when using a Takt Plan:
1. How is production going?
2. Is it on track this week and planned for next week?
3. Do we still have enough buffers?
4. Where are we in relation to the end date?
5. What roadblocks need to be removed or absorbed?
6. Is work being made ready?
7. Are separate phases on track to support each other?
8. Is the production plan networked to create a complete plan?
9. Is work pushing into problematic weather times?
10. Are materials on track to support?
11. Are we on track with pre-construction meetings?

A First Planner™ Meeting

STRATEGIC PLANNING & PROCUREMENT

WEEKLY

Purpose: Long term planning takes place. Master schedule is updated and work is made ready per the look-ahead schedule. Procurement is intentionally managed.

TEAMING MEETING

In this meeting you will use the Macro or Norm level Takt plans and review the following:

1. How is production tracking?
2. Do we have enough end buffers?
3. Are milestones and inchstones on track?
4. Do we have any upcoming risks to manage?
5. Is procurement aligned to the plan?
6. What things do project leadership need to do to support the work?

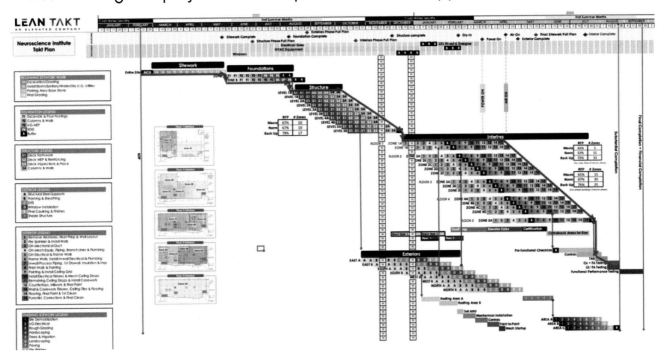

To do this you will confirm that your procurement in the production plan or log match the Required on Job dates per the plan.

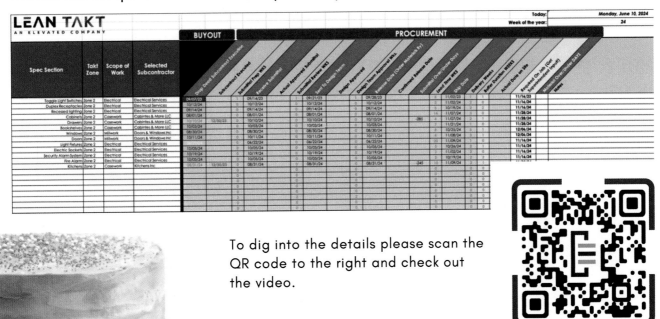

To dig into the details please scan the QR code to the right and check out the video.

The keys here are to make sure you do the following in these meetings:

1. Make sure that **PTO** and coverage are coordinated so the team has the balance and capacity to carry out the needs of your project operations and support the Foremen in the field.
2. **Validate the master schedule**-which should also be a production plan-and confirm the overall structure is complete and up to date.
3. Confirm **resources** on on track to support the overall plan in the long and short-term by tracking and managing the procurement process in detail.
4. **Manage** the Trade Partner Preparation Process and ensure Trades are ready to begin their scopes on time the right way.

But please remember to not get too hung up on the utility of the meeting. The focus is the outcome. And again, I want to say that the Foremen are the most important here. Do they have what they need? That is always the question.

- You will create team balance so you have the capacity to give the Trades support.
- You will review the Macro or Norm master schedule and plan to provide planning support.
- You will manage the procurement log to make sure resources are on their way on time and the right way.
- And you will always ask what your Trades need from a training and environment standpoint.

THE PURPOSE OF FIRST PLANNERS™ IS TO SUPPORT LAST PLANNERS®

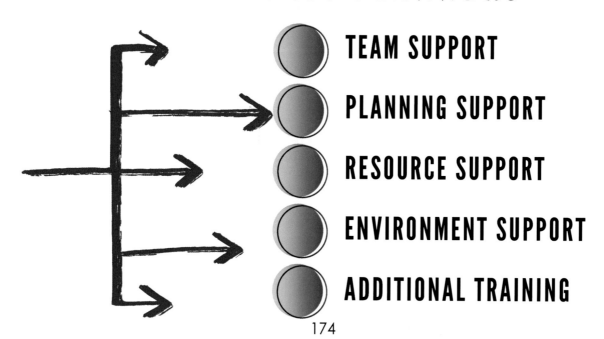

TEAM SUPPORT

PLANNING SUPPORT

RESOURCE SUPPORT

ENVIRONMENT SUPPORT

ADDITIONAL TRAINING

Once the Team Weekly Tactical and Strategic Planning & Procurement Meetings are done, the Last Planner® System can be implemented with Takt Steering & Control.

- Pull Plans can validate phases in the master schedule.
- Look-ahead planning can be done 6 weeks out.
- Executable Weekly Work Plans can be coordinated in the short interval.
- Day planning can target the right work every day.

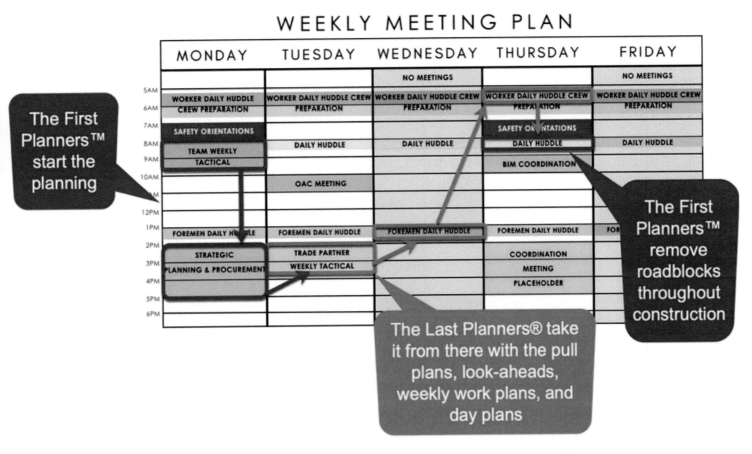

The only thing that still needs to be done by the First Planners™ in this cycle is to remove roadblocks for the field on a daily basis in the Team Daily Huddle.

This meeting typically uses the Scrum framework and focuses on prioritizing tasks that:

- Remove roadblocks.
- Optimize constraints.
- Get materials to workers.
- Provide needed information.
- Solve any design conflicts.
- Get the right financial or jurisdictional permissions.

175

1 Who attends? Supers, PEs, FEs, PMs,

WEEKLY MEETING PLAN

	MONDAY	TUESDAY	WEDNESDAY	THURSDAY	FRIDAY
5AM			NO MEETINGS		NO MEETINGS
6AM	WORKER DAILY HUDDLE CREW PREPARATION	WORKER DAILY HUDDLE CREW PREPARATION	WORKER DAILY HUDDLE CREW PREPARATION	WORKER DAILY HUDDLE CREW PREPARATION	WORKER DAILY HUDDLE CREW PREPARATION
7AM	SAFETY ORIENTATIONS			SAFETY ORIENTATIONS	
8AM	TEAM WEEKLY TACTICAL	DAILY HUDDLE	DAILY HUDDLE	DAILY HUDDLE	DAILY HUDDLE
9AM				BIM COORDINATION	
10AM		OAC MEETING			
11AM					
12PM					
1PM	FOREMEN DAILY HUDDLE	FOREMEN DAILY HUDDLE	FOREMEN DAILY HUDDLE	FOREMEN DAILY HUDDLE	FOREMEN DAILY HUDDLE
2PM	STRATEGIC PLANNING & PROCUREMENT	TRADE PARTNER WEEKLY TACTICAL		COORDINATION MEETING	
3PM					
4PM				PLACEHOLDER	
5PM					
6PM					

2 Details

AGENDA ITEMS:

- What did you do yesterday?
- What will you do today? What does the field need?
- Anything blocking your progress?
- The team gets a clear picture of if they're on track to complete the sprint goal.
- Teammates get a chance to help each other by removing blockers/impediments.
- tasks are prioritized for the field on a scrum board.
- Everyone leaves with a clear picture of how the management team can enable the craft with no duplication or gaps.

A First Planner™ Meeting

TEAM DAILY HUDDLE

DAILY

Purpose: The team gets on the same page, organizes specific tasks, reviews the plan for the day, and covers anything blocking the progress. This is how the office team supports flow for the field.

TEAMING MEETING

LEAN TAKT
AN ELEVATED COMPANY

TEAM HUDDLE-DAILY

3 Visuals needed at location:

- SCRUM BOARD

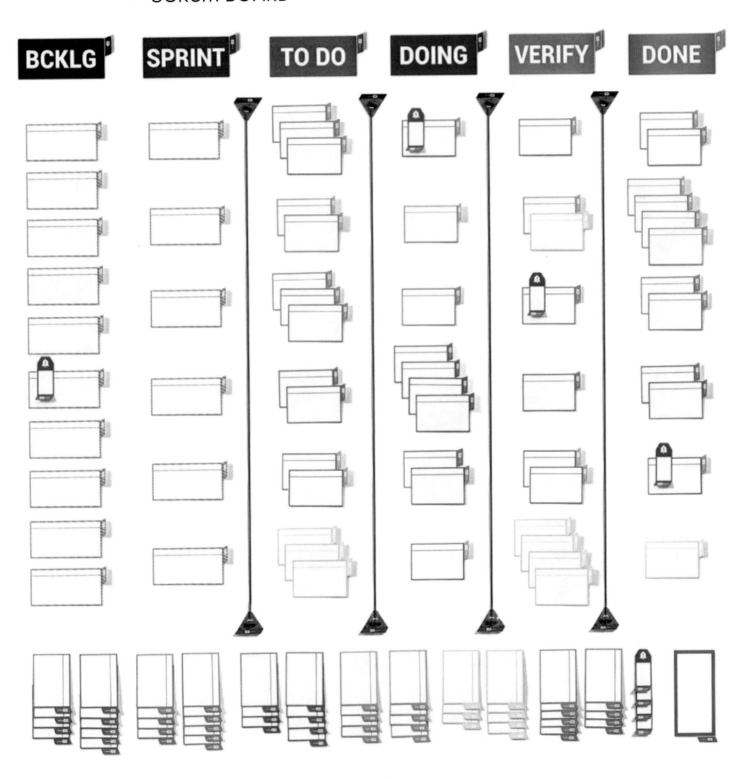

BCKLG SPRINT TO DO DOING VERIFY DONE

REFLECTION-WEEKLY MEETINGS

This component ensures that you not only have the pre-construction meetings and the ad-hoc meetings to prepare contractors, but also a weekly meeting cadence to enable the Trades on a continual basis. If you have this you will keep creating flow for the field. If you do not, they will be held up at almost every turn.

Component Scoring: (1%-100%)
- Do you have a Team Weekly Tactical where you ensure your team has balance and coverage? ____
- Do you have a Strategic Planning & Procurement Meeting where you ensure your master schedule is correct and that procurement is on track? ____
- Do you have a Daily Huddle where you continuously clear the path for the field? ____

If your score is below 80%, what specific actions do you need to take to elevate your team and leadership? --

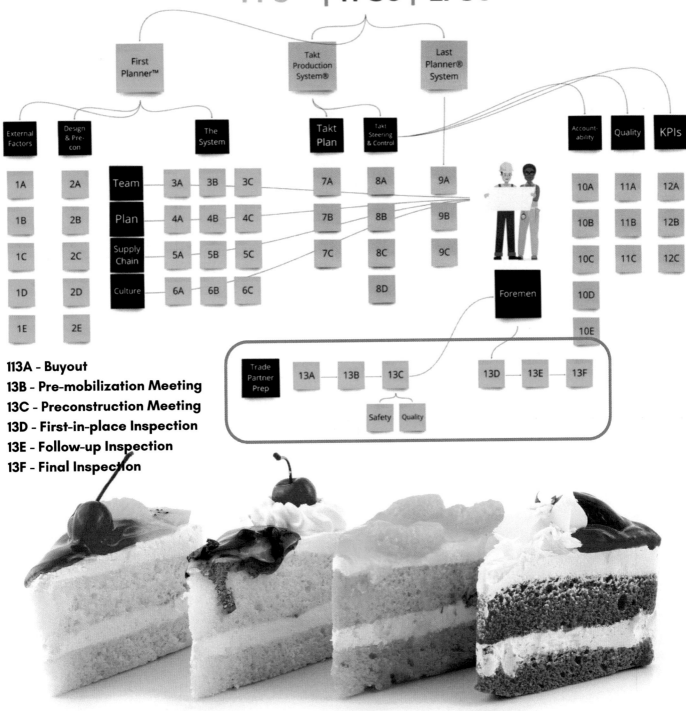

113A - Buyout
13B - Pre-mobilization Meeting
13C - Preconstruction Meeting
13D - First-in-place Inspection
13E - Follow-up Inspection
13F - Final Inspection

Now your foremen have the preparation, support, and systems they need.

The rest of the IPCS™overall system will be described in our next book Takt Steering & Control. It will cover in detail Takt Steering & Control, Last Planner® implementation, and these remaining components:

- Holding the Trades accountable in a positive way.
- Ensuring Quality.
- Continuous Improvement.
- Tracking Key Performance Indicators.

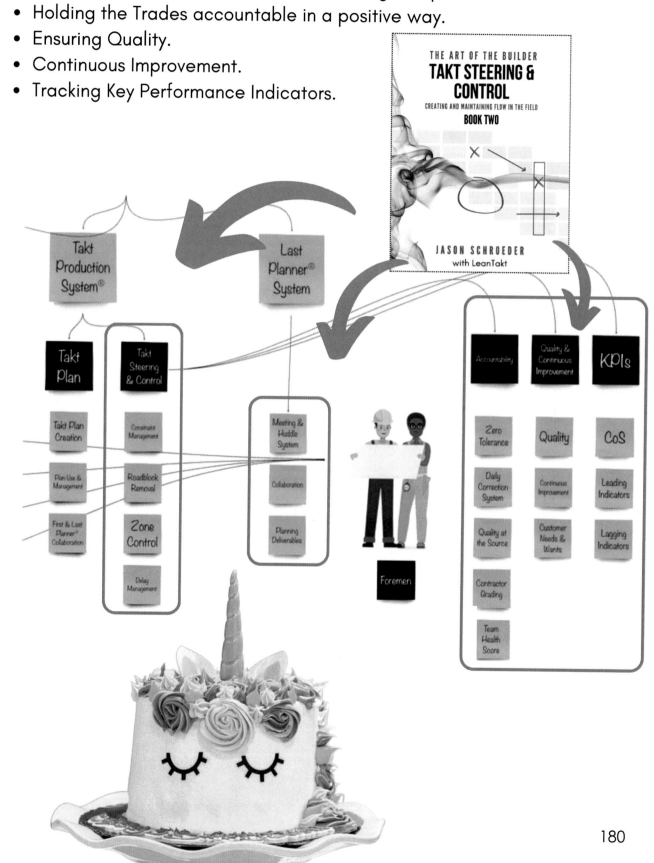

At this point I hope you are able to understand the system we encourage you to implement. It works every time and everywhere we implement it with results that increase profit, decrease project durations, and improve the experience of people. That is not an exaggeration. This production system has worked every time we have ever implemented it fully. The challenge is to average all final component scores and see where your score lands. If you are above 80% you will reap the rewards. If you are below 80% then you know exactly where to focus. Remember, lean is implemented as a system and not as isolated components and should be implemented as holistically as possible.

IF YOU HAVE ANY QUESTIONS PLEASE REACH OUT AT JASONS@ELEVATECONSTRUCTIONIST.COM OR AT +1.602.571.8987.

THE *How*
Part 3-
Design &
Pre-construction

This is how to plan the project. This is how to make the cake--the recipe and the ingredients. So it's preheating the oven, gathering and measuring ingredients, mixing them properly and baking the cake. Then the cakes come out and have to be cooled, then assembled and decorated. This is all done in pre-construction.

Designing & Implementing Your Production System

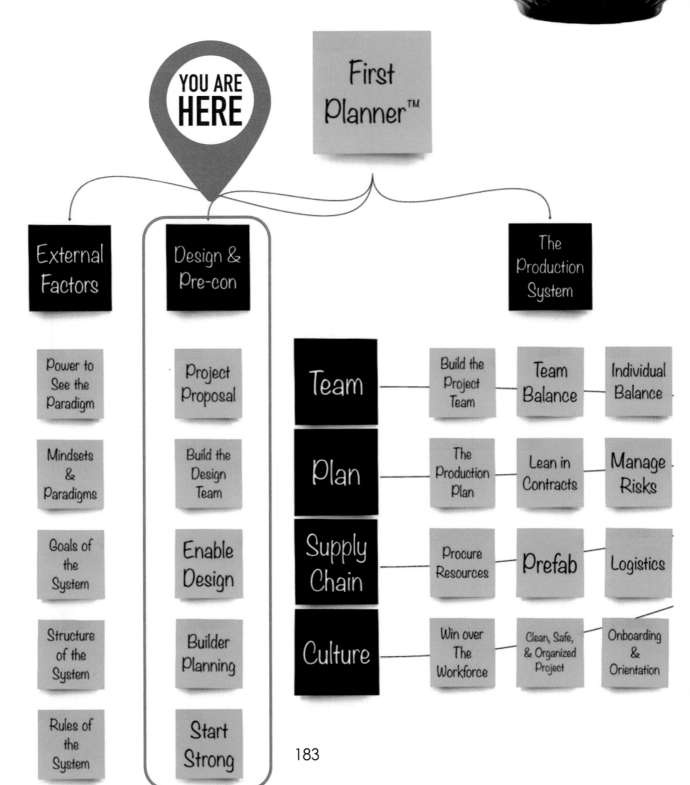

YOU ARE HERE

First Planner™

External Factors
- Power to See the Paradigm
- Mindsets & Paradigms
- Goals of the System
- Structure of the System
- Rules of the System

Design & Pre-con
- Project Proposal
- Build the Design Team
- Enable Design
- Builder Planning
- Start Strong

The Production System

Team	Build the Project Team	Team Balance	Individual Balance
Plan	The Production Plan	Lean in Contracts	Manage Risks
Supply Chain	Procure Resources	Prefab	Logistics
Culture	Win over The Workforce	Clean, Safe, & Organized Project	Onboarding & Orientation

183

Will you work with me?

PROJECT
PROPOSAL

BUILD TEAM → ADAPT & ENABLE DESIGN → PLAN WITH BUILDERS → PREPARE & START STRONG

This book is about planning a project so it can finish well according to these measurements.

Measuring Success
in construction

The project was safe with a remarkable culture.

 The Owners & Designers are raving fans.

 The team was high-functioning & happy.

 The project was built with high quality.

Trade Partners were successful.

 The project met or exceeded original profit targets.

People on the team met their career goals while there, & had a well rounded experience.

This is success. When we understand what the goals are, we simply need to reverse engineer the process to find the standards and actions we should use. So we begin planning on the right by understanding the goal. Thinking right to left is not natural, so it forces you to think more creatively.

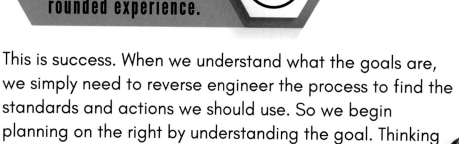

184

are completed.

Determine the best people & plan for the job.

4

previous steps

Propose options for assembling the team & plans.

3

until the

Understand the timelines. Do as much research & planning as possible.

2

Don't build

Learn what success looks like. You have the goals & can measure what each means.

1

Thinking right to left is beginning with the end in mind. As a First Planner™, you will bring this mindset to the proposal and interview processes. Here is an example of the proposal and interview steps that should be taken, with a few notes to reference.

Think of what you want here...

when you are still way back here!

PROPOSAL

SCHEMATIC DESIGN

CONSTRUCTION DOCUMENTS

SUBSTANTIAL COMPLETION

CONCEPT DESIGN

DESIGN DEVELOPMENT

NTP

END OF WARRANTY

There is typically a process we fit into, as planners, when beginning our planning in the proposal phase. On the following pages are common outlines for both the written proposal and interview preparation and notes concerning where you'll focus.

PROPOSAL PROCESSES

PROPOSAL
RFQ
RFP

Want

GO/NO GO

Work with Leadership & Business Development on a Go/No Go Analysis

Text and/or email group decision

EMAIL RFP/RFQ DOCUMENTS TO MARKETING TEAM

SET KICK-OFF MEETING ON CALENDAR

Use Schedule Assistant function in Outlook to host a Kick-off Meeting with proposed group

Immediately identify Lead (responsible contact) for effort

1

2

MARKETING DIRECTIVE

VISION- Form a single message

30 Minutes

Outline Needs- Every team member should know their topics

Make Assignments- The team should know which topics/ questions are assigned to them, where documents are located, and where to send content

3

ASAP

KICK-OFF MEETING

VISION

30 Minutes

Outline assignments and deploy, including directive and timeline in email

Set up Outlook Meetings

BIM Sketches- Send vision to VDC

4

5

BREAKOUT 1- Use Bluebeam session and/or folder

HUDDLE 1- Remind and hold people accountable

HUDDLE 2- Remind and hold people accountable

BREAKOUT 2- Use Bluebeam session and/or folder

In

8 HOURS

Print & Bind

4 HOURS

Email or Drive

Win!

NO OVERTIME

186

INTERVIEW PROCESSES

INTERVIEW

RFQ
RFP

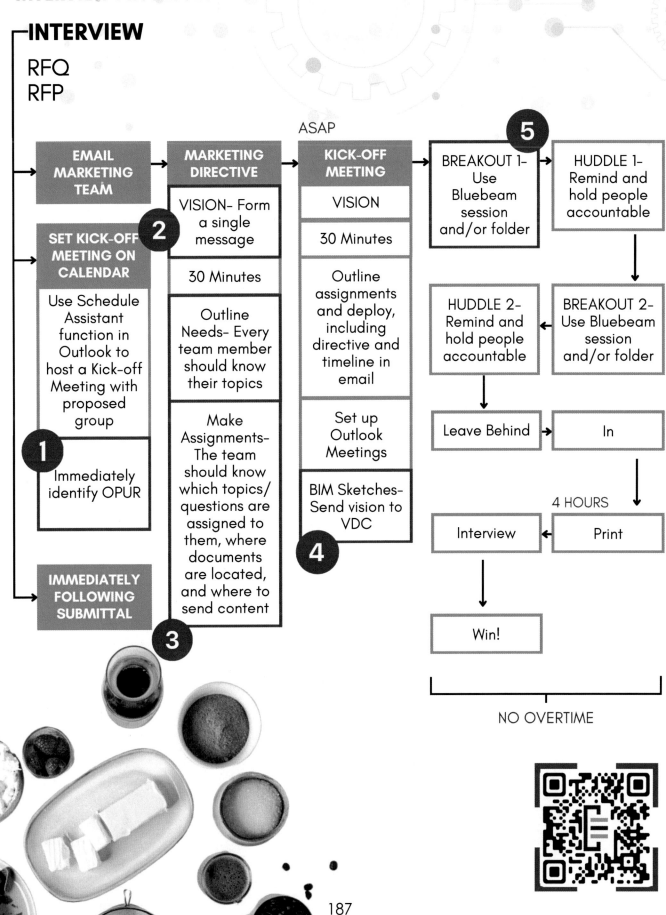

ASAP

EMAIL MARKETING TEAM → **MARKETING DIRECTIVE** → **KICK-OFF MEETING**

MARKETING DIRECTIVE

VISION- Form a single message

30 Minutes

Outline Needs- Every team member should know their topics

Make Assignments- The team should know which topics/questions are assigned to them, where documents are located, and where to send content

SET KICK-OFF MEETING ON CALENDAR

Use Schedule Assistant function in Outlook to host a Kick-off Meeting with proposed group

Immediately identify OPUR

IMMEDIATELY FOLLOWING SUBMITTAL

KICK-OFF MEETING

VISION

30 Minutes

Outline assignments and deploy, including directive and timeline in email

Set up Outlook Meetings

BIM Sketches- Send vision to VDC

5

BREAKOUT 1- Use Bluebeam session and/or folder → HUDDLE 1- Remind and hold people accountable

HUDDLE 2- Remind and hold people accountable ← BREAKOUT 2- Use Bluebeam session and/or folder

Leave Behind → In

4 HOURS

Interview ← Print

Win!

NO OVERTIME

1

2

3

4

187

NOTES ON THE PROPOSAL & INTERVIEW PROCESSES...

1 These proposal and interview prep efforts always go best when there is a **OPUR**--One Person Ultimately Responsible--otherwise it will be a nightmare. You, the builder-planner, need to know who this is so you can align with him or her. Always stay aligned and in good communication with that person. This will give you more time to plan and prepare to be awarded the project.

2 The proposal and interview team need to have a **vision** for the proposal. You cannot just slam together different slides and stories into a PPT and win the job. It needs to have a theme. For example, take the client through the hero's journey. The client is the hero with a problem, and meets a guide (you), who has a solution, and the hero then wins. The plan you make needs to address this hero's journey and help the client anticipate and solve real problems. The problems, solutions, and finished project are what you need to research and address in your portion of the proposal. There are lots of ways to generate interest in the proposal; a hero's journey theme is only a suggestion. Be unique and be thorough. We've walked you through an example just to help you see it visually.

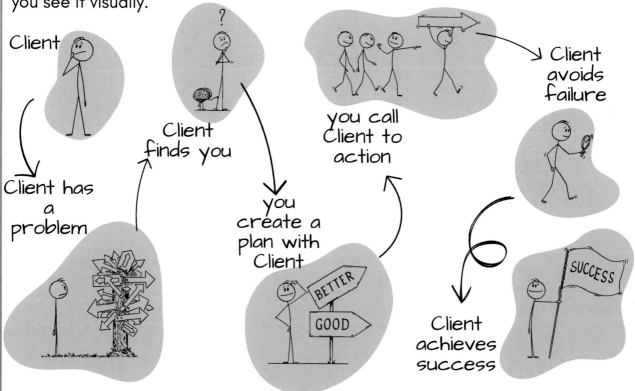

Client

Client has a problem

Client finds you

you create a plan with Client

you call Client to action

Client avoids failure

Client achieves success

3 Once you have the overall vision of the proposal and interview, and as the guide with the plan, you need to know:
- What questions you will answer?
- What pages or slides you are responsible for?
- What content you need to make?

Once you understand the **assignment**, you'll work to create the Macro Takt Plan. This is an example, and we will walk you through the steps.

a. create your Macro Level Takt plan

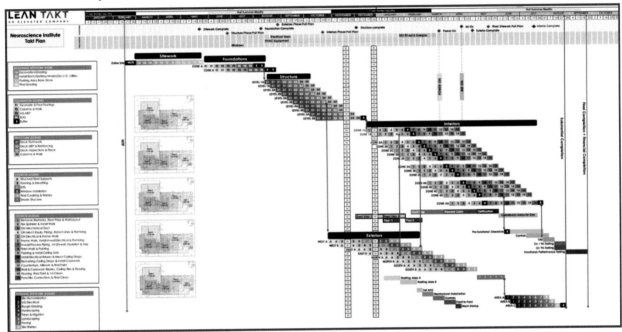

b. map out your zoning

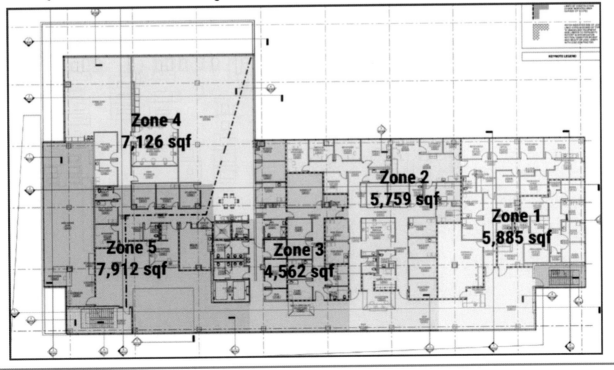

c. strategically design your logistics for the project

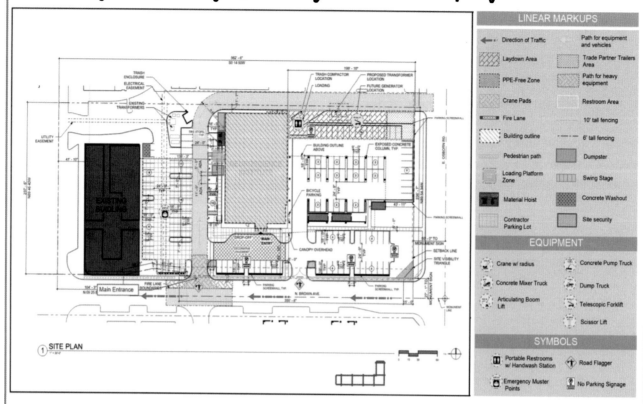

d. showcase the right plan through 3- and 4D modeling

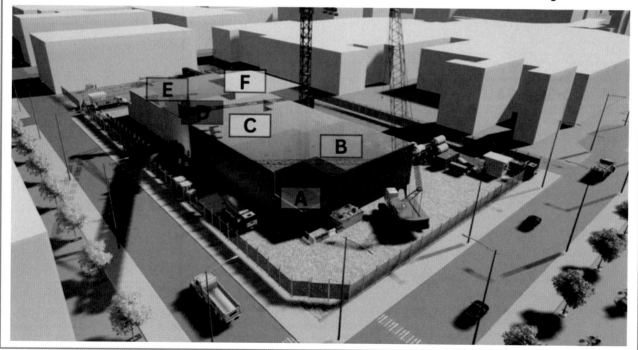

4 You won't get the model, 4D schedule, or images you need if you don't send your vision to the VDC team right away. Once you know your outline, get it to them asap. Don't assume modeling is quick and easy. I'm a Revit and AutoCAD certified professional and I've created many models and 4D schedules--trust me when I say it's not as simple as it seems. Please get the request out immediately so you have what you need for the proposal and interview and don't overburden your VDC peeps.

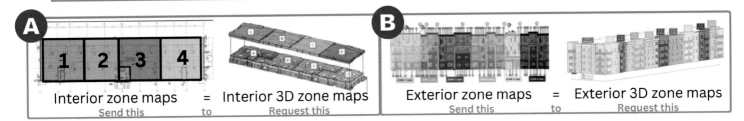

A
Interior zone maps = Interior 3D zone maps
Send this   to   Request this

B
Exterior zone maps = Exterior 3D zone maps
Send this   to   Request this

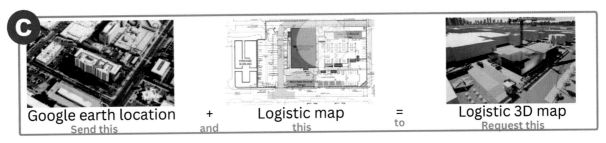

C
Google earth location + Logistic map = Logistic 3D map
Send this   and   this   to   Request this

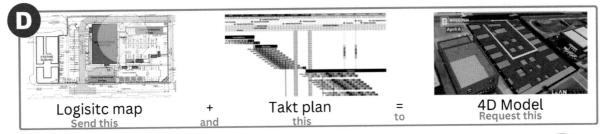

D
Logisitc map + Takt plan = 4D Model
Send this   and   this   to   Request this

5 Encourage the team to use a synchronized collaborative platform to create the proposal or interview prep. You will add your content as you develop the plan, and align with the vision and efforts as you go.

As a First Planner™, the proposal process is where your planning begins. You have the opportunity to use your Macro-level Takt Plan, Zone Maps, Logistics Plans, and Models in the presentation as a builder to showcase how you will help the client solve their problems. Let's break these down, one-by-one. We'll give you the overview, and you can refer to our Takt Planning book to dig deeper.

IDENTIFY YOUR CONDITIONS OF SATISFACTION

Before you begin making the proposal schedule you need to know the Conditions Of Satisfaction. Conditions of satisfaction (COS) in construction refers to the specific criteria or requirements that must be met for a construction project to be considered complete and satisfactory. These conditions are typically outlined in the contract documents and serve as benchmarks against which the project's progress and quality are assessed.

For this phase of pre-construction, we are mainly discussing client satisfaction, meaning meeting the expectations and requirements of the client as outlined in the RFP, RFQ, verbal instructions, project specifications and contract agreements. Conditions of Satisfaction provide a clear framework for evaluating the progress and success of a construction project and serve as a basis for determining if it is going the way the client expected. It's important information to know here so you can tailor your planning to their needs, rather than offering them a pre-packaged or generic solution that doesn't fit the situation.

Since this is a proposal or interview you may not be able to directly ask them. You may need to perform research to answer these questions before you begin. At a minimum make sure your proposal team is aligned on the assumed information so you can all head in the right direction.

We're not in manufacturing - we're service providers. We're in the customer service business, and as such, we need to know what our customer wants and what they think success means.

 Assignment 1 - Fill out your known COS for this proposal

192

On the next page you will find a complete worksheet you can use to understand your client's needs. Ask each of the questions and come up with all reasonably possible answers. Write your answers in the boxes below the corresponding questions.

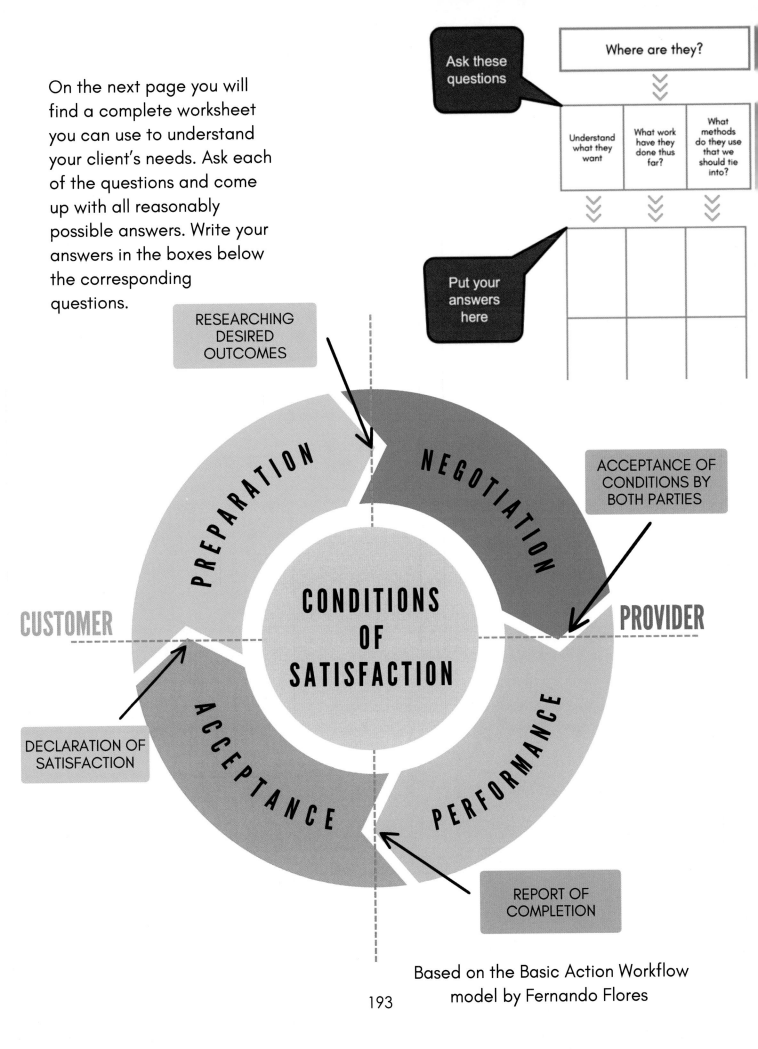

Based on the Basic Action Workflow model by Fernando Flores

CONDITIONS OF SATISFACTION

Where are they?

Where do they want to go?

Understand what they want	What work have they done thus far?	What methods do they use that we should tie into?

What would be a remarkable experience for the team?	What has worked in the past that can be done again?	How can we help them to get there?	How can we add value?

2 RESEARCH THE PROJECT

Second, we will research as much as we can about the project. You may have limited information about the project, but at this point you will dive right in and really get to know whatever you have.

Assignment 2 - Go through the drawings and note items like the following:
- Important features of the building or site
- Direction of work
- Limiting constraints - Constraints are permanent or semi-permanent
- One-off or complicated areas that need attention
- Different phases and possible zoning strategies
- Opportunities to accelerate
- Possible problem areas
- Logistical considerations
- any other thing that can help you schedule it or find problems that you can help the client solve

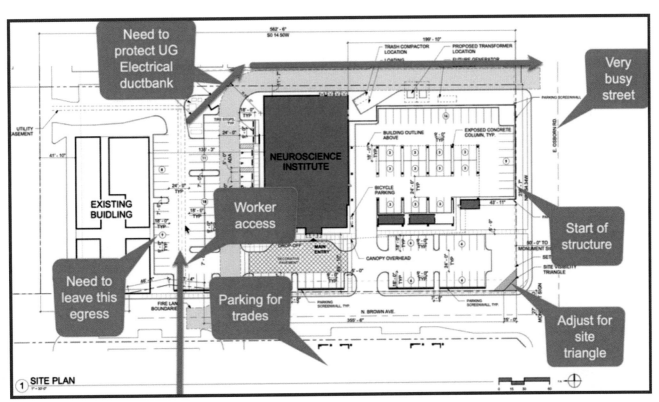

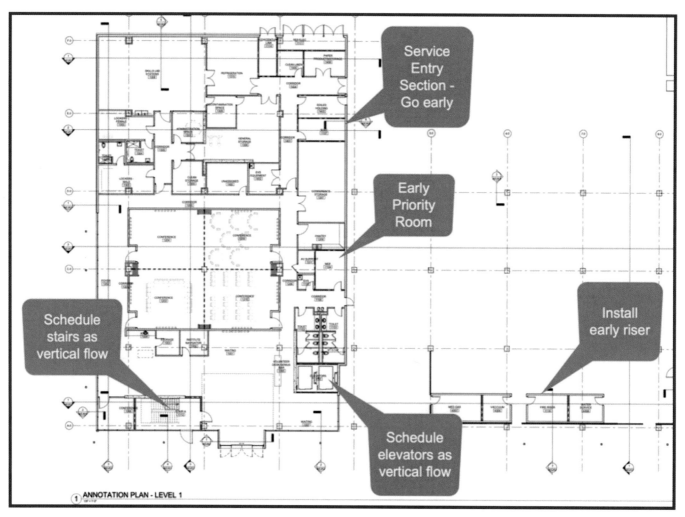

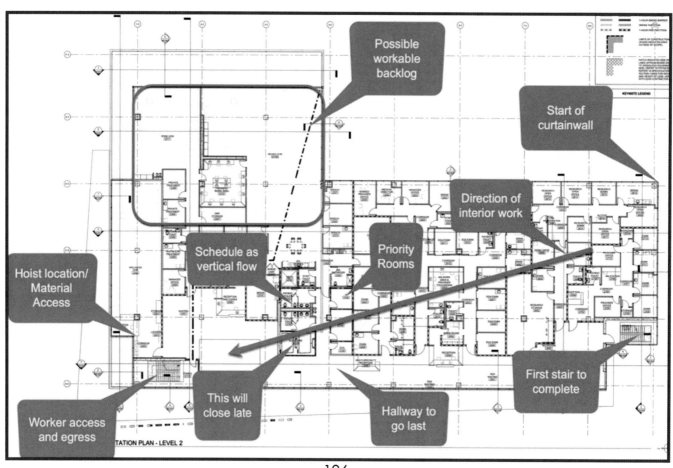

3 PERFORM A WORK DENSITY ANALYSIS

Next you will do a work density analysis on the project if there is enough information. If you have drawings, you will need to dig into the information to the greatest extent possible so you can identify preliminary zones. These zones will be shown on your production plan, in your proposal, and will be needed in the future.

When you begin the process of creating zones from a work density analysis, you will want to identify the general flow of the project. Let's begin with the example we will use in this book, and in our book, *Takt Planning*. We are using a medical office building that is a part of a larger campus, and for simplicity we will show how to do zoning for level 2.

The building features:
- Mild-reinforced Concrete Decks
- HVAC System, Air Handlers, VAVs, FCUs
- Half of walls are full height
- Normal interior finishes
- No med gas, vacuum, or air
- Normal utilities feeding the building
- Exterior Unitized Curtain Wall

Based on the observable constraints on the floor, the builder believes the flow through this floor will run in the direction of the purple arrow.

LEVEL 2

CHASE, RESTROOMS & ELEVATORS TO CLOSE LATE

LEVEL 2

START OF CURTAINWALL

HOIST LOCATION

WORKERS ACCESS & EGRESS

FIRST STAIR TO COMPLETE

Before we pick preliminary zones for this floor, we need to do a work density analysis. This is a method to identify the level of effort of the work to be done within areas for the purpose of leveling zone sizes. To start, we need to break up our floor into grid segments. We've used red grid lines to demonstrate. After you've created the smaller area segments, begin the analysis process.

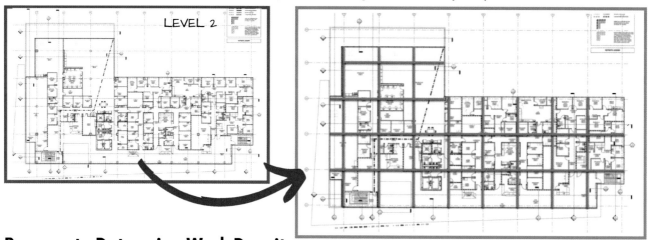

LEVEL 2

Process to Determine Work Density

1. Study the drawings & understand the level of effort of each area.
2. Create your density scale and example. WE HAVE ANCHORED THE NUMBERS 1, 3, 8, AND 10 THAT WAY THE LEVEL OF EFFORT FOR ALL AREAS CAN BE COMPARED TO THESE ANCHORS AS THEY ARE SCALED FROM 1-10. Make notes by the column square on your plans.
3. Identify any one-off scopes of work that do not represent the average and note them
4. Aggregate your scores from your plans
5. Create work densities by column square
6. Adjust if needed

WORK DENSITY SCALE:
1 - EMPTY
2
3 - HALLWAY
4
5
6
7
8 - EXAM ROOM
9
10 - HIGH MEP & HIGH ARCH

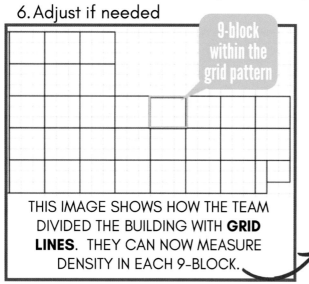

9-block within the grid pattern

THIS IMAGE SHOWS HOW THE TEAM DIVIDED THE BUILDING WITH **GRID LINES**. THEY CAN NOW MEASURE DENSITY IN EACH 9-BLOCK.

Areas with low work density

Areas with high work density

```
0 0 0 0 0 0 0 0 0 0 0
0 0 0 0 0 0 0 0 0 0 0
0 3 3 3 3 3 3 3 3 3 3
0 3 3 3 3 3 3 3 3 3 3
0 3 3 3 3 3 3 3 3 3 3
0 3 6 6 3 6 6 6 3 3 3
3 3 6 6 4 6 6 6 3 3 3 8 8 8 8 8 8 8 8 8 8 8 8 8 8 8
3 3 6 6 4 6 6 6 3 3 3 8 8 8 8 8 8 8 8 8 8 8 8 8 8 8
3 3 6 6 4 7 7 7 9 9 9 8 8 8 8 8 8 8 8 8 8 8 8 8 8 8
3 3 6 6 4 7 7 7 9 9 9 8 8 8 8 8 8 8 8 8 8 8 8 8 8 8
3 3 3 4 4 7 7 7 9 9 9 8 8 8 8 8 8 8 8 8 7 7 8 8 8 8
3 3 3 4 4 7 7 7 9 9 9 8 8 8 8 8 8 8 8 8 7 7 8 8 8 8
3 3 4 4 4 4 4 4 9 9 9 8 8 8 8 8 8 8 8 8 7 7 8 8 8 8
2 2 8 8 8 4 4 4 8 8 8 8 8 8 8 8 8 8 8 8 8 8 8 8 8 8
2 2 8 8 8 4 4 4 4 4 4 4 4 4 4 4 4 4 4 4 4 4 4 4 4 4
```

THIS IMAGE SHOWS THE RESULTS OF THE ANALYSIS OF THE DRAWINGS BY THE SUPER.

The work density now allows you and your team to take a stab at initial zoning. The team in the example below chose **three zones to start with**. Based on work density they ended up with the shapes below.

These are some questions the team considered:
1. How many zones do we want to create, knowing that we want to keep them on the larger side to start with?
2. What are the zone types?
   a. **Horizontal**
   b. **Vertical**
   c. **Workable backlog**
3. What is the SF of each area?
4. What is the SF of the entire floor?
5. In what direction will work flow?

Zone is larger because the work is less dense

14,998 sf   7,264 sf   7,395 sf

SF is not equal because zones were analyzed by density, not area

ZONE DENSITY RESULTS FROM 3 ZONES:

ZONE:	SF:	DENSITY TOTAL:
ZONE 1 –	7,395SF	#494
ZONE 2 –	7,264SF	#512
ZONE 3 –	14,998SF	#493

Assignment 3 - Go through the drawings to do a work density analysis. While you are there, you may want to take a stab at identifying your first pass at how you will zone your phases:

We always schedule with this level of detail:
- **Program** - A group of multiple projects.
- **Project Phase** - Larger areas with their own unique zones.
- **Area** - Groupings between phases and zones that are primarily used for context and print areas.
- **Zones** - production areas that break-up the phase into production areas that will set the pace of your trades
- **Micro-zone** - Smaller breakdowns within the zones.

For this exercise you will simply identify projects, phases, and zones

Examples:

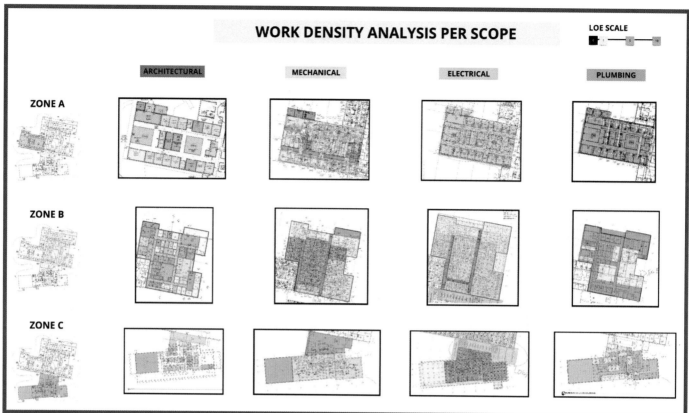

WORK DENSITY ANALYSIS PER SCOPE

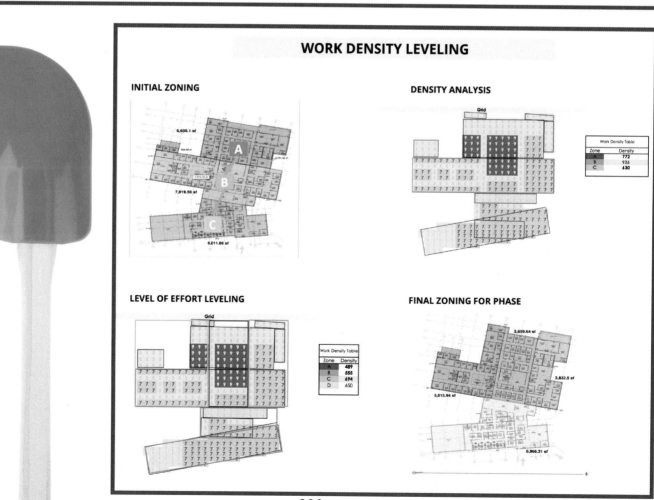

WORK DENSITY LEVELING

4 SKETCH OUT YOUR MACRO PHASES

Now that you are familiar with your project and know how many zones you want, it's important to get an idea of what your plan will look like. This is an important step in the shaping of your plan. Every phase, as a part of your Takt plan, will have four components:

1. **Sequence** – the sequence for a single zone.
2. **Line Of Balance** – the speed of the train of trades in the phase
3. **Buffer** – the buffer for the phase that is designed to absorb delays
4. **Tie** – the tie from one phase to other phases; phases grouped together are what will make your plan.

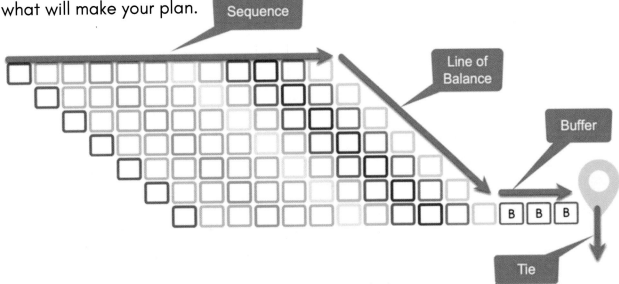

In order to properly sketch these phases you must check the wagon and zone counts to make sure they are correct. In order to do that you need to know how many wagons you will have. Take your list of activities with their duration and translate that into a wagon count.

Activity List:	Duration per Floor:
Remove re-shores	5
Final patch ceiling	10
Sweep floor	3
Refresh control lines	3
Layout walls	5
Install fire sprinkler main and branch lines	15
Install priority walls including elec and comm rooms	9
Install overhead mechanical duct	25
Install overhead mechanical equipment	10
Install overhead mechanical piping	10
Install overhead mechanical branch lines	10
Install overhead plumbing	9
Install overhead electrical	15
Frame all walls	15
Install in-wall electrical	15
Install in-wall plumbing	15
Install in-wall process piping	8
One-side drywall	12

The calculator will tell you if you have the right number of zones to be competitive as a Macro level Takt plan. For our example here, we know we would want to switch to 5 zones to be in the right range.

Optimize the Takt Phase

Takt Inputs

Takt Wagons	25
Takt Zones	3
Takt Time	5
Duration	135

Area Inputs (m², sqft)

Area / Zone	9,885
Min Zone Size	1,000
Max Zone Size	10,000
Total SQFT of Phase	29,655

Macro Level Zoning

Takt Wagons	Takt Zones	Takt Time	Duration	Trade Time Gained		Level	Realized Flow Potential
25	2	8	208		14,820	Bad	19%
25	3	5	135	0	9,885	Bad	29%
25	4	4	112	1	7,414	Macro	35%
25	5	3	87	0	5,931	Macro	45%
25	6	3	90	3	4,943	Macro	43%
25	7	3	93	6	4,236	Macro	42%
25	8	2	64	1	3,707	Norm	61%
25	9	2	66	3	3,295	Norm	59%
25	10	2	68	5	2,966	Norm	57%
25	11	2	70	7	2,696	Norm	56%
25	12	2	72	9	2,471	Norm	54%
25	13	2	74	11	2,281	Norm	53%
25	14	2	76	13	2,118	Norm	51%
25	15	1	39	0	1,977	Norm	100%
25	16	1	40	1	1,853	Norm	98%
25	17	1	41	2	1,744	Norm	95%
25	18	1	42	3	1,648	Norm	93%
25	19	1	43	4	1,561	Norm	91%
25	20	1	44	5	1,483	Norm	89%
25	21	1	45	6	1,412	Norm	87%
25	22	1	46	7	1,348	Norm	85%
25	23	1	47	8	1,289	Norm	83%

For more details you can reference our book about Takt Planning. For now, I'll simply say that you need to do a decent job of identifying a reasonable sequence from the list of activities you derive from the drawings so you can use the calculator above. Once you know the shape you can begin your Macro Phase Sketching.

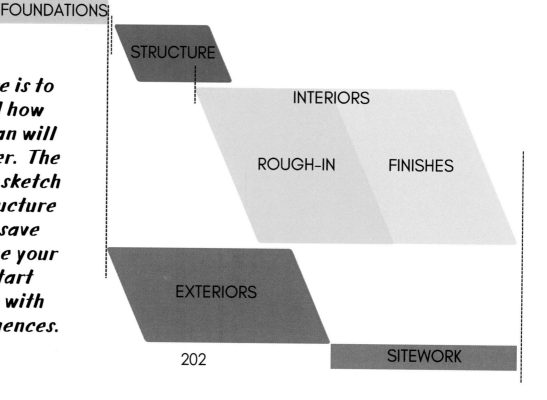

The idea here is to understand how your Takt plan will come together. The purpose is to sketch the basic structure so you can save time, visualize your ties, and start confidently with creating sequences.

202

Now that you know your sequence, your number of wagons, and the right number of zones, and you know how the phases fit together, you can enter the colored wagons into your template.

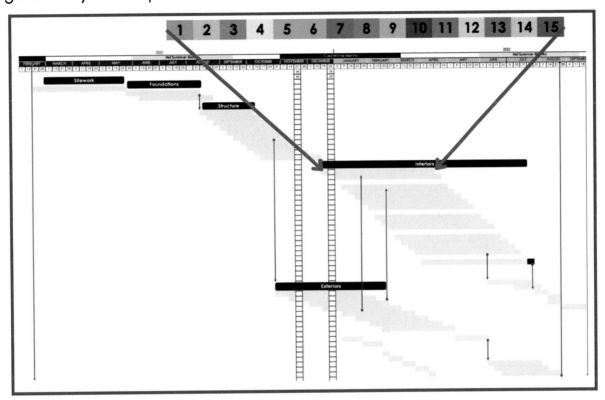

When you're finished, you'll be ready to make a Takt plan you can review with the team for the proposal.

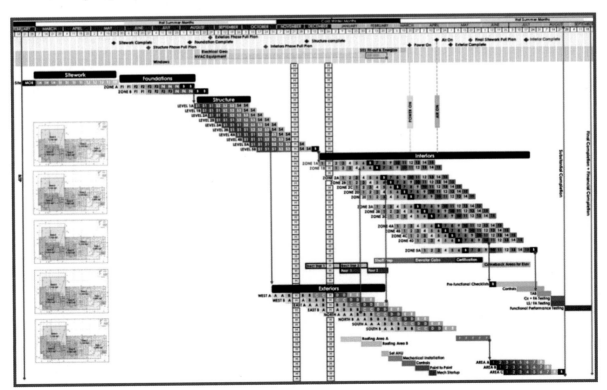

 Assignment 4 - Sketch out your Macro phase and take a picture.

Sketching this out will enable you to envision how the project goes together. It will also save you quite a bit of time when you begin making your schedule. Keep in mind the following:

1. Sketch the start and end dates
2. Sketch out the phases to the best of your ability. Do not be too worried about having the perfect shape yet
3. Draw critical ties between phases and give thought behind how the building will come together
4. Identify your sequence
5. Check it with the calculator
6. Enter in the highlighted cells into Excel

5 CREATE A MACRO LEVEL TAKT

Once you have your base for your Macro level Takt plan, you can finalize the format and get it ready for review.

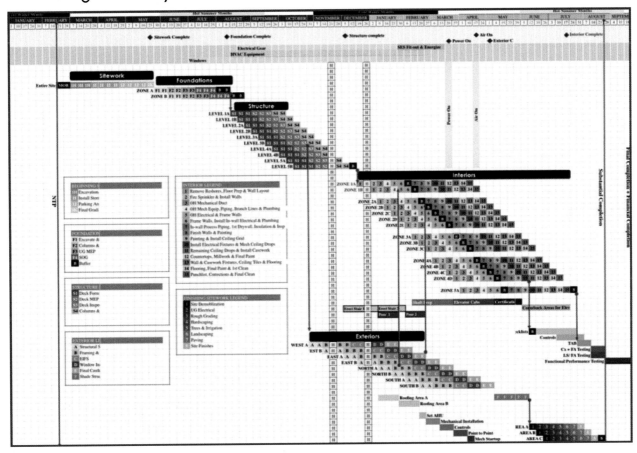

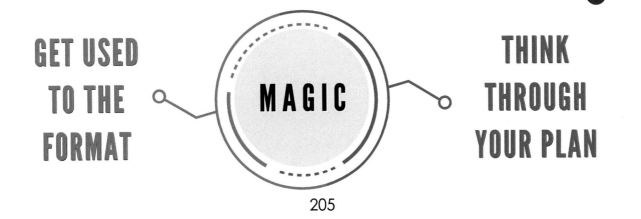

Assignment 5 - Create your Macro level Takt plan using the next three pages of checklist.

GET USED TO THE FORMAT

MAGIC

THINK THROUGH YOUR PLAN

- ☐ Identify the target start and end date
- ☐ Study the drawings
- ☐ Identify the general flow the project
- ☐ Identify phases
- ☐ Do a rough work density analysis
- ☐ Identify initial zones
- ☐ Identify constraints the team must work around
- ☐ Get an idea of the no. or Takt wagons in each phase
- ☐ Check zones with the calculator and make sure it is in range
- ☐ Get production rates for all activities
- ☐ Package the sequences for the Macro Takt plan - 5-20%
- ☐ Create overall plan with interdependence ties and other content
- ☐ Do a quick fresh eyes meeting with the internal team
- ☐ Create an initial procurement log to ensure materials support the production plan
- ☐ Create initial logistics drawing
- ☐ Do a fresh eyes with the wider project team
- ☐ Verify milestones
- ☐ Verify overall total project duration
- ☐ Add any needed buffers
- ☐ Format beautifully & make any corrections from the fresh eyes meeting
- ☐ Create a basis of schedule

MACRO TAKT PLAN GUIDE

LEGEND

DATE & WEATHER DURATIONS

MILESTONES

COMPLETION DATES

LONG LEAD PROCUREMENT

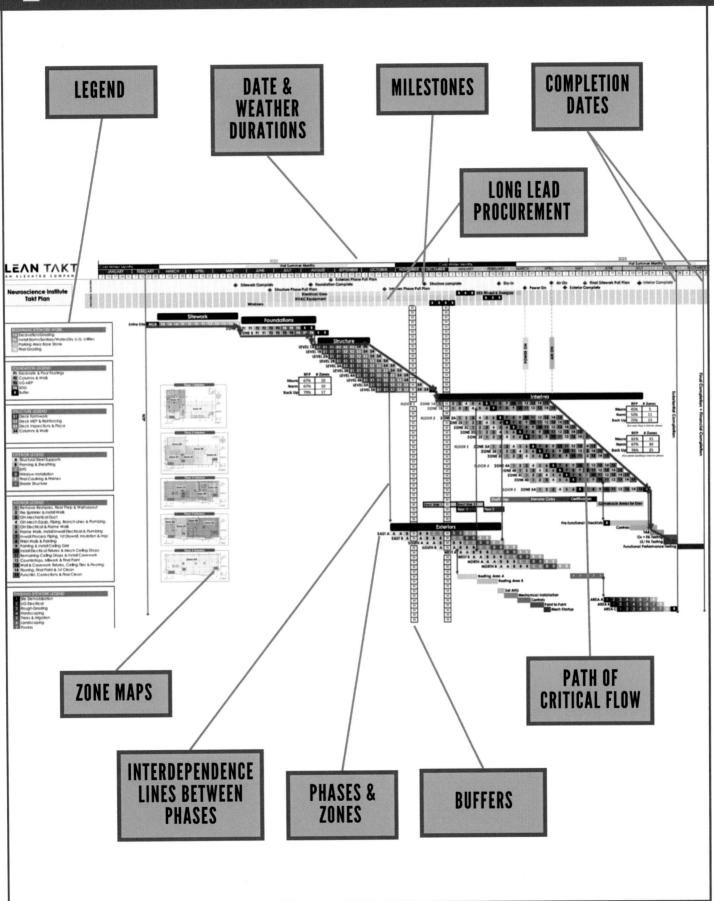

ZONE MAPS

PATH OF CRITICAL FLOW

INTERDEPENDENCE LINES BETWEEN PHASES

PHASES & ZONES

BUFFERS

MINIMUM TAKT PLAN REQUIREMENTS

- [ ] Time on the top
- [ ] Location on the left
- [ ] Trade flow in the middle with colored wagons and a clearly published legend. Wagons are colored. Zones may be, but only if it does not conflict with wagon colors.
- [ ] Weather durations on the top
- [ ] Takt zone maps near phases
- [ ] Name of project with company logos
- [ ] NTP date
- [ ] Substantial completion target
- [ ] Final completion target
- [ ] Financial completion target

- [ ] Buffers to the targets
- [ ] Weather buffers
- [ ] Pre-construction meeting triggers
- [ ] Pull planning triggers
- [ ] Key milestones
- [ ] Long lead and critical procurement
- [ ] The critical three:
  - Permissions
  - Contracting
  - Coordination
- [ ] Interdependence ties
- [ ] Trade flow of each wagon
- [ ] A TPNR if needed
- [ ] You can see the MACRO on one vertical page
- [ ] You can see the NORM on one horizontal page

6 MAKE YOUR ZONE MAPS

Your production plan is in a **time by location** format, so you need to see those locations on your zone maps. Here are some things to keep in mind:

1. Identify your zone quantity from the calculator.
2. Select your zones based on direction, work density, and flow.
3. Remember:
   a. Don't cut rooms in half.
   b. Remember the natural flow of workers.
   c. Keep assemblies together.
4. Identify, mark, and move your flow around constraints.
5. Identify vertical and horizontal zones if needed at this stage.
6. Identify workable backlog.

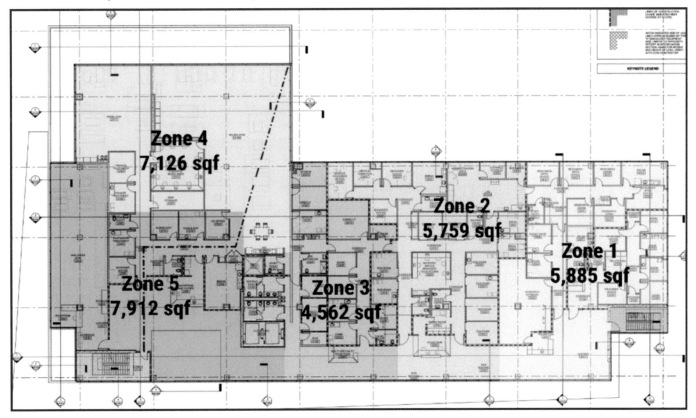

Zone 4
7,126 sqf

Zone 2
5,759 sqf

Zone 1
5,885 sqf

Zone 5
7,912 sqf

Zone 3
4,562 sqf

 Assignment 6 - Sketch out your Macro zones and attach to your macro plan.

7 MAKE YOUR LOGISTICS PLAN

Every production plan needs a great logistics plan to support it. Scheduling an activity is one thing, having the plan, sequence, and overall strategy to execute in alignment with your logistics plan is another. An activity is just an activity shown on paper unless you can actually carry it out with enough access, materials, and connected interfaces.   On your logistics plan I would like to see:

- Installation access
- Installation methods
- Material access
- Interfaces
- General logistical items.

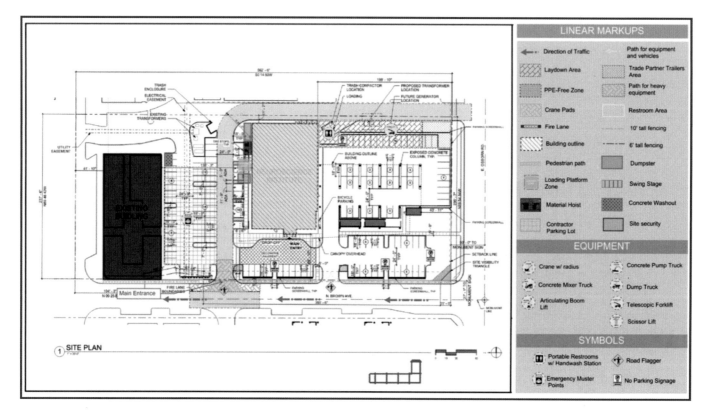

Assignment 7 - Create your Logistics MAP Using the Following gUides

SCAN ME

To help you with this, we've provided a Bluebeam template with an associated toolbox. In addition, here is a blog post and video with full instructions on what to include in your map. The key is to have it reviewed internally and use it to find a problem that you can help the Owner solve. Pay special attention to the public, neighbors, facility staff, pedestrians, and motorists. Your job is to keep your owners and their project off the news.

This link brings you to the video that inlcudes:
The blog post for logistics.
The Bluebeam templates.
The checklists.
Logistics Rules.

1. Download the template.
2. Upload the toolbox.
3. Upload your site plan.
4. Read the guide on the next page.
5. Develop your logistics drawings.
6. Check your plan with the logistics checklist.
7. Check your plan with the logistics rules shown in the following pages.

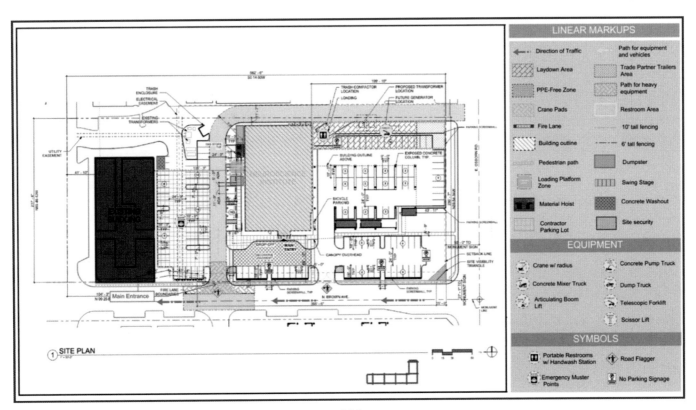

LOGISTICS PLAN - QUICK GLANCE GUIDE

Everyone needs to know where things belong, where things are going, and how to stage materials and equipment. This **comprehensive logistics strategy** includes key tactics for logistical planning of a construction project.

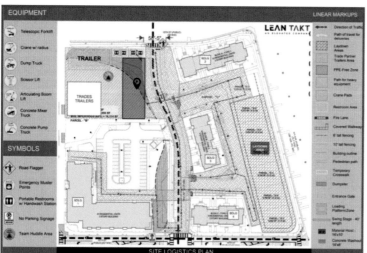

HOW TO CREATE:

There are different ways to create a construction logistics plan using a variety of tools:

- **Excel**
- **Bluebeam**
- **AutoCAD**
- **Revit**

6 USEFUL TIPS

1. Keep your plans **updated**.
2. Use them for your **material staging plan**.
3. **Synchronize** your logistics plan **with** your **deliverable schedule**.
4. Make sure your **operators see the plan** in real time.
5. **Use** these logistics plans **in** your **meetings and huddles**.
6. Make sure **EVERYBODY SEES the plan.**

WHAT TO INCLUDE:

1. Trailer Locations
2. General Site Configurations
3. Flow of deliveries
4. Restrooms
5. Material Laydown
6. Emergency gathering areas
7. Hoist and crane locations
8. Loading platforms
9. Temp water and power

6 KEY TYPES OF LOGISTICS PLANS

SAFETY PLAN
Anything that deals with (or is related to) safety must go here: emergency gathering points, first aid kits, fire extinguishers...

GENERAL SIGNAGE
This must be intentionally designed and has to be clear so everyone knows where they are going. Kind of like an airport, you outline the project.

MOBILIZATION, MAKE-READY, FOUNDATIONS

SUPERSTRUCTURE

EXTERIORS & INTERIORS PHASE

SITE-WORK & CLOSE-OUT

Your logistics plan will change over time based on the phase of the project you're in.

Amateurs study tactics. Armchair-generals study strategy. Generals study LOGISTICS.

- [ ] Review if it is clear and easy to understand.

- [ ] Does it help you to properly control your project?

- [ ] Can you find the following items?

  - [ ] Trailer position and organization
  - [ ] Flow of deliveries
  - [ ] Traffic patterns
  - [ ] Pedestrian patterns
  - [ ] Site security
  - [ ] Equipment mobilization & demobilization
  - [ ] Loading platforms
  - [ ] Pumping
  - [ ] Slick lines & placing booms
  - [ ] The hoist
  - [ ] The crane
  - [ ] Equipment staging
  - [ ] Staging locations
  - [ ] Site signage
  - [ ] Fire lane
  - [ ] Temp water & temp power
  - [ ] Parking lots
  - [ ] Temp fence
  - [ ] Site organization
  - [ ] Site signage
  - [ ] Emergency gathering points
  - [ ] Disaster planning
  - [ ] Emergency personnel access & planning
  - [ ] Lunch area
  - [ ] First Aid
  - [ ] Fire extinguishers
  - [ ] Fire hydrants
  - [ ] Temp Power / Water Locations

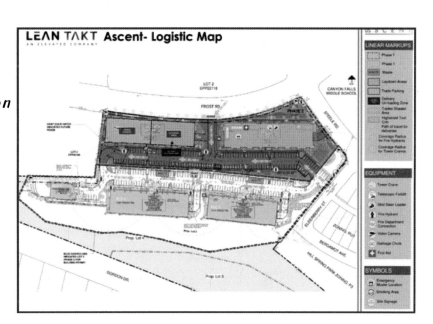

  - [ ] Camera Locations
  - [ ] Rental Show Suites & walking path
  - [ ] Site Address (Address to give 911)
  - [ ] Pump locations
  - [ ] Flow of construction
  - [ ] Entrances to the Job site (2 if possible)
  - [ ] Trade partner offices
  - [ ] Dumpster location
  - [ ] Temp restrooms (Keep them grouped together- do NOT spread them out)
  - [ ] Material laydown
  - [ ] North Arrow
  - [ ] Site Area
  - [ ] Buildings (Directional not letters)
  - [ ] Walking Paths from parking to work sites
  - [ ] Drive Aisles
  - [ ] Smoking Area
  - [ ] Flammable Storage
  - [ ] Fence Plan

Logistics & People

1- Always remember public protection. Treat neighbors like they are your Grandma. If that doesn't land, treat neighbors the way Mr.Rogers would. Won't you be my neighbor?

2- Get workers to their areas of install as your top priority.

3- If you don't let people eat and rest comfortably at lunch, they will get hangry, tired, and hate you. This is basic human care.

4- If you don't provide people with a respectful restroom, they will $&*# on you. If you have access to a clean bathroom at work and your workers don't, that makes you **uncaring** which is the opposite of lean. If that hurts, tough. Do better.

5- If you don't let people smoke, they will sneak around and resent you. Recognize that we all relax in different ways and provide spaces where others are free from second-hand smoke. That isn't your battle to fight.

Logistics & Planning

6- Break the project down into bite-size areas.

7- For logistics, always have A, B, C, & D plans. Never be surprised. You have to plan for everything that has historically gone wrong, so do the research and understand the problems and solutions.

8- All logistics are first created in theory, then realistically. You must have a great plan and it needs to be complete. This will include a:

- Safety Plan
- Mobilization Logistics Plan
- Superstructure Logistics Plan
- Interiors and Exterior Logistics Plan
- Final Site Work Logistics Plan
- Wayfinding Signage Plan

LOGISTICS RULES

Logistics & Access

9- Mind the entryway. The jobsite entrance must be remarkable & set the tone for the job.

10- If you don't tell people where to go, they will go everywhere. Map out access routes-- like an airport.

11- Keep all supply line access ways open & clear.

12- Guard Access Points--These are key interfaces like the hoist, crane, & forklift staging areas. Keep them clean, safe, organized, operational, & flowing with someone appointed to manage them.

Logistics & Materials

13- Bring materials to the site Just-In-Time according to inventory buffers (time & quantity) to lay down yards and staging areas.

14- All deliveries are to be scheduled. No rogue deliveries. Rogue deliveries means rogue staging onsite.

15- Production has more to do with material supply than pace of work. If materials are flowing, work can progress.

Logistics & Production

16- All work must be broken down into phases & zones.

17- Reduce transportation & movement whenever possible. Transportation and motion are waste!

18- Know your interfaces & stacking on a project & confirm they work. Do not perform unsafe or out-of-sequence work.

19- Supplying materials is not the same as doing work. Workers should be installing 30 minutes after the start of the day. Stage materials the night before.

8 CREATE YOUR MODEL VIEWS

The ability to visualize a project in 3D is not only helpful for the builders, it sells well. You and the team need to decide what 3D images you'd like developed for your proposal and interview that will help you to tell the hero's journey story. The images should help you to dig into three problems the Owner has that you and your team can solve.

Here are some things to remember:

1. Select views that will help you to tell your story.
2. You may only need solid massing objects in 3D to tell the story. You usually won't need to get too detailed or fancy.
3. Always consider showing your logistics and how you will protect the neighbors, motorists, pedestrians, and building occupants.
4. You may also consider a 4D schedule to communicate your approach.

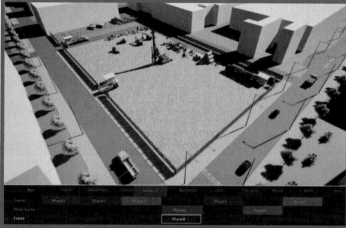

Assignment 8 - Create your Model views with the instruction below and the guide on the next page

1

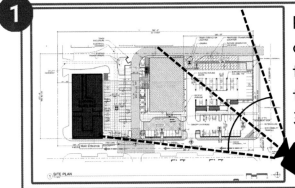

Position the camera view on the logistic map to generate the 3D view.

LOCATE VIEW IN DRAWING

What do you need?

2

- Crane safety ratio
- Pedestrian path
- Laydown Areas
- Path for equipment and vehicles
- PPE-Free Zone
- Fire Extinguishers

THEN SHOW THESE ON YOUR VIEW

Model Views Process Diagram

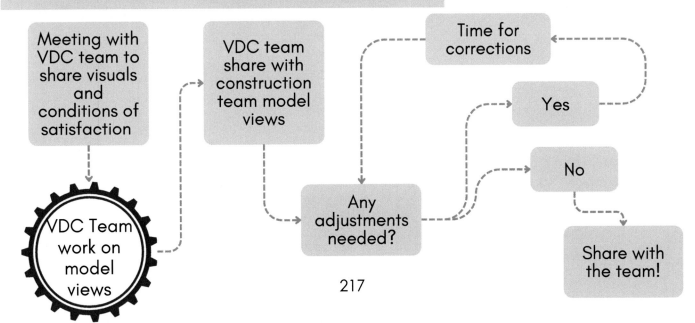

217

VDC - QUICK GLANCE GUIDE

VDC — A process that uses digital tools and technologies to create a virtual representation of the project before it's physically built and throughout construction.

DIFFERENT PROCESSES & APPROACHES USED IN VDC

- Cost Estimation
- Construction Sequencing with 4D Model
- Risk Mitigation
- Coordination and communication
- Facilities management

- Iterative Design Processes
- Sustainability Analysis
- Client Engagement Platforms
- Construction Automation with Robotics

- 3D Modeling
- Digital Collaboration
- Project Visualization
- Clash Detection
- Building Information Modeling (BIM)

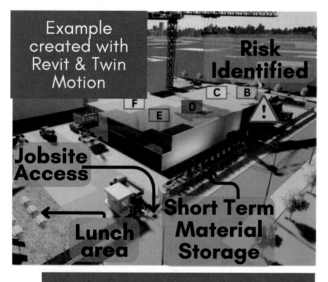

Example created with Revit & Twin Motion

Risk Identified

Jobsite Access

Lunch area

Short Term Material Storage

Model shared with Autodesk Viewer

SOFTWARE EXAMPLES

- Autodesk Revit
- Navisworks Manage
- Tekla Structures
- Trimble Connect
- Solibri Model Checker
- Synchro Pro
- Assembles Systems

HOW CAN I USE VDC ON MY PROJECT?

- 3D Modeling
- 4D Construction Sequencing
- 5D Cost Estimation
- 6D Facility Management
- Integrated Project Delivery
- Augmented and Virtual Reality
- Reality Capture
- Mobile BIM

9 REVIEW THE PLAN

Once you have your macro level Takt plan, zone maps, logistics drawing, and 3D images, the key is to review it with your team to make sure it is accurate. And please remember, this isn't the time to hold back. I want to see red lines, comments, ideas, problems identification, and as much digging as possible.

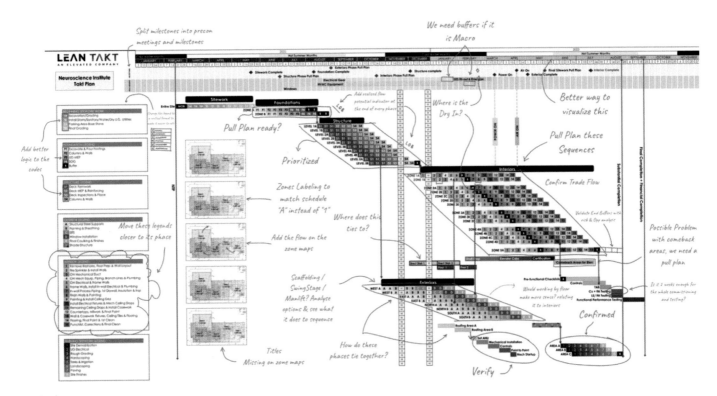

Ask:

Do we have a great plan?

Have we eliminated the client's risks?

Do we see what they care about?

Can they now see how we can help them care?

Are we solving 3 major problems?

Can the builders passionately talk to this plan in the interview?

If our proposal is longer, have we told that story?

Has the team reviewed the plan according to their experience?

Have we identified options to accelerate without hurting trades that we can showcase?

Assignment 9 - Have your Macro plan reviewed

Review your overall plan with the proposal and interview team. You can use the following blog posts to assist you. The purpose of step 9 is to make sure you have a thoroughly vetted plan that stands out in the proposal and interview, solves your client's problems, and solidly begins your planning process.

Use the SCHEDULE REVIEW QUESTIONS blog post to dig into your plan & make sure it's complete. This list has been compiled by main industry experts to help you analyze your plan & approach.

Use the FRESH EYES blog post to help you organize a small fresh eyes meeting with your team & ask them to dig deep into the plan to provide feedback.

10 SHOW YOUR THREE THINGS CLEARLY

The review should provide a comprehensive list of things you can consider changing to better showcase your plan in the interview. This will also refine the three things you want to show the client in the proposal and interview that only your company can prevent or help with. It is time to showcase this on your visuals and send the final product to marketing for binding or the slideshow.

Tips to remember:
1. Showcase these three items clearly with numbers or visuals.
2. Bring them to the client's attention.
3. Be able to speak to them.

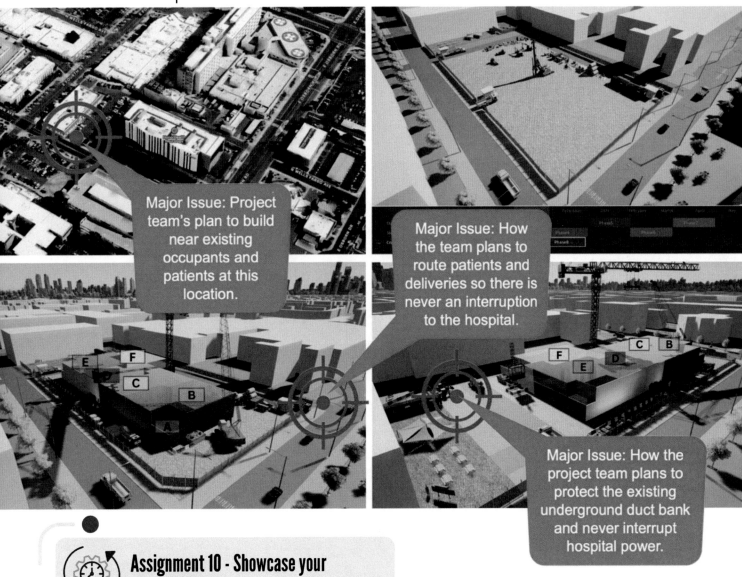

Major Issue: Project team's plan to build near existing occupants and patients at this location.

Major Issue: How the team plans to route patients and deliveries so there is never an interruption to the hospital.

Major Issue: How the project team plans to protect the existing underground duct bank and never interrupt hospital power.

Assignment 10 - Showcase your three things

CONCLUSION

By properly planning and preparing your content for the proposal and interview you have taken your first step in the First Planner System™. You can now be awarded the project and continue your planning efforts.

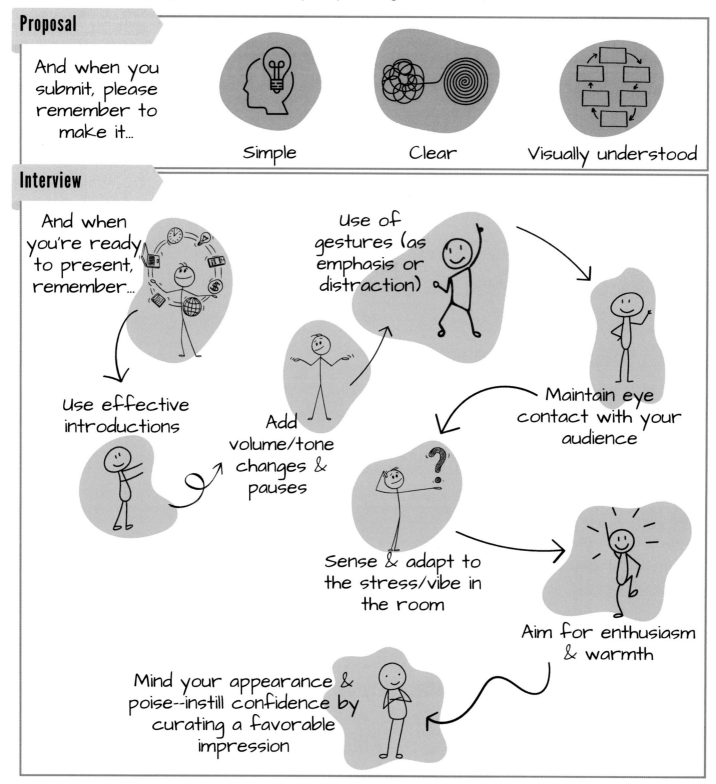

Proposal

And when you submit, please remember to make it...

Simple   Clear   Visually understood

Interview

And when you're ready to present, remember...

Use effective introductions

Add volume/tone changes & pauses

Use of gestures (as emphasis or distraction)

Maintain eye contact with your audience

Sense & adapt to the stress/vibe in the room

Aim for enthusiasm & warmth

Mind your appearance & poise--instill confidence by curating a favorable impression

NOTES ON ACCELERATING THE PRODUCTION PLAN

You can shorten phases by rezoning them with the calculator. For instance, if you take this 7 zone phase shown below and double the zones--which decreases their actual size by half--you gain quite a bit of time in the plan.

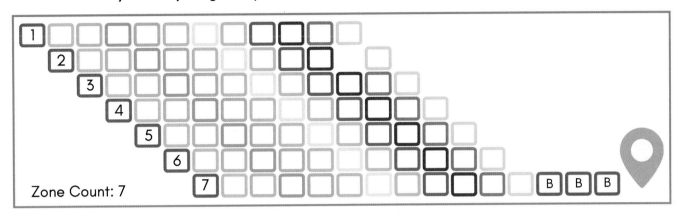

Zone Count: 7

This is helpful when creating project production plans because you can show the owner other options for possible acceleration **without hurting trade partners.**

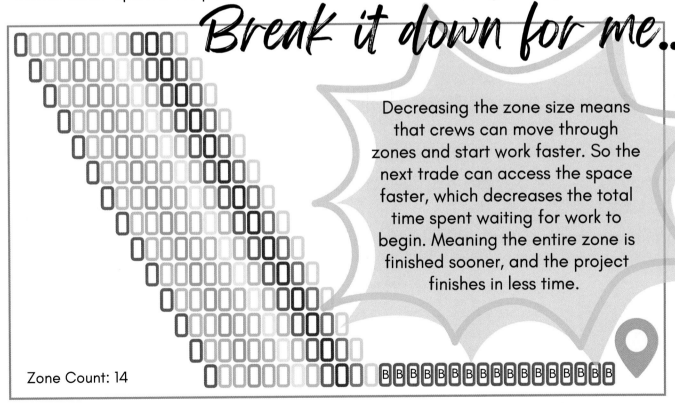

Zone Count: 14

Break it down for me...

Decreasing the zone size means that crews can move through zones and start work faster. So the next trade can access the space faster, which decreases the total time spent waiting for work to begin. Meaning the entire zone is finished sooner, and the project finishes in less time.

Using smaller zones means completing the project or phase faster.

So, if you feel you need to be more competitive for your proposal and interview, you can tell the story of being able to pull the plan back by re-zoning it. As an example, please note the Path of Critical Flow in the Macro plan.

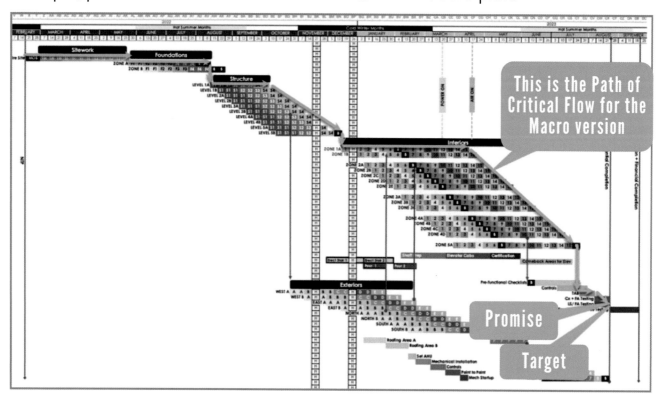

As you can see, the plan can be pulled back quite a bit just by rezoning in the picture below. The only thing to remember is that your team will need buffers at the end of your phases, so you **cannot give away all the time** gained to the Owner. You must leave 2/3rds of the time gained for buffers in the plan.

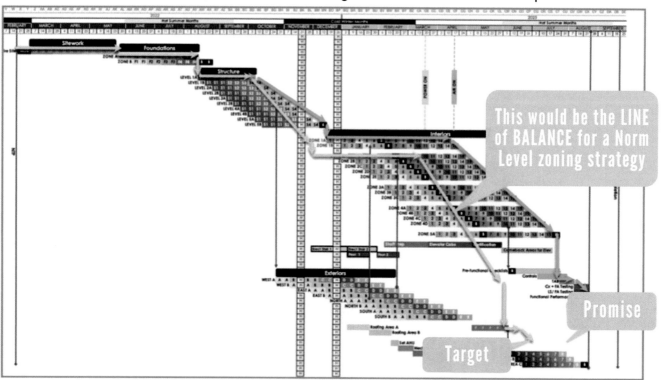

And keep in mind you will always want a backup zoning strategy in case your project ever gets in trouble.

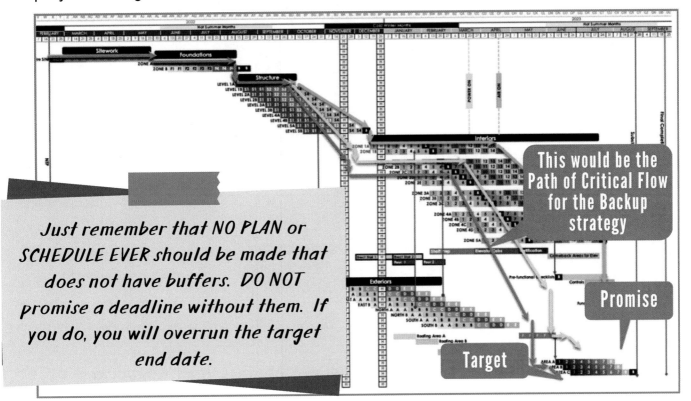

This would be the Path of Critical Flow for the Backup strategy

Just remember that NO PLAN or SCHEDULE EVER should be made that does not have buffers. DO NOT promise a deadline without them. If you do, you will overrun the target end date.

Promise

Target

BUILD THE DESIGN TEAM & SET PARAMETERS

Are we set to work well together?

PROPOSAL PHASE → ADAPT & ENABLE DESIGN → PLAN WITH BUILDERS → PREPARE & START STRONG

Congratulations! You have been awarded the project. You are excited and ready to go. What do you do next? In my opinion you need to build your design and preconstruction team and set parameters early to ensure that team is heading in the right direction. Here is what I mean. You can have the best people, doing the best things, with all the right resources, heading in a completely wrong direction. That is why we need to make sure we are targeting the right production plan, with the right duration, and always keep the team fixed on the right numbers for the project. If we do not do this we will end up with a design outside of our budget and project expectations outside of what is possible.

So the proper outcome of this phase is to:
- Set the right target for the overall total project duration.
- Understand how the general conditions and requirements tie into the overall budget so we do not undercut ourselves.
- Get the team put together and working properly and design to financial targets for the project.

the formula for *success* in DESIGN

226

When you begin your efforts the first thing you should do is build the preconstruction team. At its basic level we will need to get the right people on the team, communicating well, in the right roles, with the right goals, and in the right meetings to progress. Let me take you through some boards that I typically use for this and then we will cap it off with some advice. I will start with board 1.

1. Use this chart to decide on your core or exec team and your clusters.

2. List out the guidelines for communication among the team.

3. Once you draft this out on the top, redline it with the team and do a final on the bottom.

Board 1

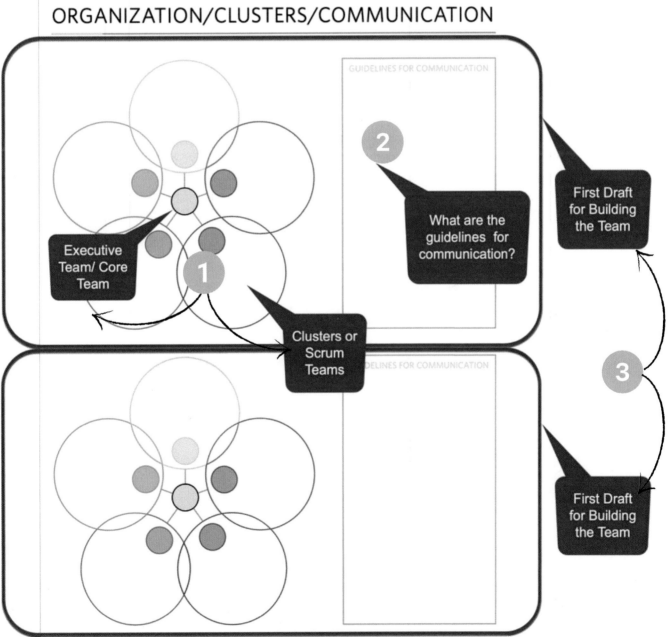

ORGANIZATION/CLUSTERS/COMMUNICATION

GUIDELINES FOR COMMUNICATION

Executive Team/ Core Team

Clusters or Scrum Teams

What are the guidelines for communication?

First Draft for Building the Team

First Draft for Building the Team

The second board is all about setting the right vision for the project with the entire team.

1. Facilitate the team brainstorming the biggest risks for the project.

2. Ask the team what would constitute a remarkable experience for them.

3. Find out what has worked for the team in the past that you can do again.

Board 2

> Gather the team that is now organized and understand what would be a success for this project

CONDITIONS OF SATISFACTION

What is the biggest risk?

1

> Ask the team to brainstorm the biggest risks that they face. This is important for the team to feel you are listening and to transfer any known risks to the build team

What would be a remarkable experience?

2

> This one is my favorite. Ask the team what would be a remarkable experience for them. This is so fundamental and easy. Know what they expect so you can deliver it

What has worked in the past that we can do again?

3

> This really wins over the team. Ask them what they have done in the past that worked very well. That way they feel a part of the process and you can leverage their experience

The third board is all about setting the right meeting cadence for the team.

1. Step 1 – Draft the meeting schedule you think will work for the team and redline it.
2. Step 2 – Propose a more accurate meeting structure and finalize it.
3. Step 3 – Publish your final meeting schedule.

Board 3

1st Draft

WEEKLY MEETING CYCLE

1D SCHEDULE

Use this area to brainstorm how the meeting system will work

2nd Draft

2D SCHEDULE

Propose and redline the system here for final review

Final

FINAL SCHEDULE

Map out your meeting schedule for the project team that they will follow throughout preconstruction

SCAN ME

To access the template, click on this link:

With these things in place, you have a team, roles, organization, communication channels, the right focus, and a meeting structure. If you want to know more about how to organize your team I recommend you reference the book Integrated Project Delivery.

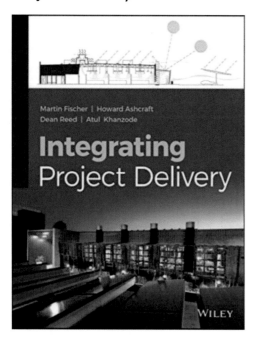

This book discusses how to organize big rooms, build integrated teams, and how to interact as a unified and integrated team.

You will want to consider what clusters or Scrum teams you want and what meetings you want to organize. Here are a few:
- Design charrettes
- Collaborative planning sessions
- Target Value Design meetings
- Weekly progress meetings
- Cluster or Scrum team meetings
- Value engineering workshops
- Report-out Meetings

You may be frustrated that I am not digging deeper into this interesting topic, but if I did the book would triple its current size and likely take years to publish. I would much rather give you this reference and ask you to make sure that your kickoff meeting for pre-construction accomplishes what I have listed above. The bottom line is that a kickoff meeting is like a pre-flight check. On a flight you want to take off properly, ascend, level out, deal with turbulence well, and land the plane comfortably. You need a method to do this for your project and a pre-flight check or kickoff is just the thing for you.

Take-off = Team starting work
Flight – Team working together
Turbulence – Team dealing with conflict
Landing – Finishing the project

Make sure you and your team start well, have a plan to consistently work well together, a method for dealing with conflict, and a way to finish the project well.

Now it is time to discuss setting the right targets and parameters. Your owner likely already knows how much money they have allocated for the project and how long they need it to take based on their pro forma. The trick to understand this and design to it.

Most of the industry should be heading in the direction of Target Value Design (TVD) where the team designs to a target rather than estimating costs after the design is complete. This process involves:

1. Gathering the right collaborative team.
2. Setting a target budget & possibly timeline.
3. Designing to cost.
4. Using lean processes along the way.
5. Iterating often to align with targets.
6. Continuously exploring different value engineering methods.
7. And ending up with a design that is within budget.

This is an amazing process. The key is to make sure that our [the contractor] part of the cost is well understood from the beginning. We do that by creating a Macro level Takt plan, a great initial Logistics plan and estimating our general conditions and general requirements. General Conditions and General Requirements are two categories of costs that are essential to completing a project properly.

General Conditions = Broader operational costs necessary to support the project as a whole.

General Requirements = Specific contractual obligations and logistical tasks required to manage and complete the project.

These may include the following types of costs:

- Project management and supervision
- Temporary facilities
- Site utilities
- Site security
- Safety measures
- Permits and fees
- Insurance and bonding

- Safety measures
- Cleaning and waste removal
- Temporary structures
- And more.

231

It is important to know this early on in this phase because we must know how much of the budget these comprise. What you DON'T want to happen is to underestimate the overall total project duration and realistic project costs and then surprise the team with it too late. That typically looks like:

Concept Design

Schematic Design

Design Development

Construction Documents

- Underestimate the project duration
- Underestimate GC &GR costs
- Report a lower cost to Owner & Design team than what is needed

Owner & Design team design to budget they believe they have

- Contractor realizes the project takes longer and costs more than originally understood.
- A slash and burn value engineering effort takes place to chop design elements from the building
- Owner & Designer are pissed $%#@

What should happen is consistency throughout. The GCs & GRs should remain fairly predictable and up to date throughout. That way there are no suprises.

Concept Design

Schematic Design

Design Development

Construction Documents

- Estimate a correct overall total project duration
- Properly estimate the GC & GR costs
- Report right costs to Owner & Design team

Owner & Design team design to budget

- Overall parameters are still in tact
- No value engineering effort is needed to cover the contractor's mistake
- Owner & Designer are happy to keep the elements they have designed

I will show you how to do this.

Firstly, you will want to refine your Macro level Takt plan and confirm the following:
1. The overall Macro level duration and the path of critical flow.
2. The overall Norm level duration and the path of the critical flow.
3. Major risks and opportunities.
4. How much buffer you will need.
5. Any thought that needs to be given your reference class.

This is what this will look like:

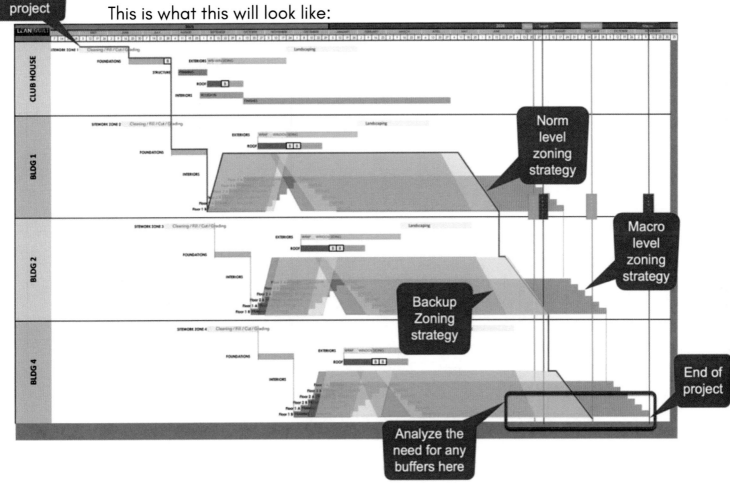

This initial plan will help you to identify how much your salaried positions will cost you throughout the project

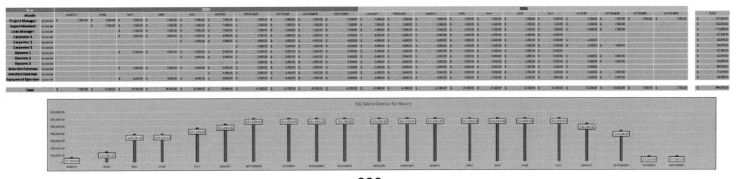

Second, you will need to know how you will run this site. That will require you to refine your logistics plan from your proposal and interview phase. This one may not be as pretty in this stage, but it should be fairly accurate with a few reviews and iterations.

West Fillmore Logistics Map

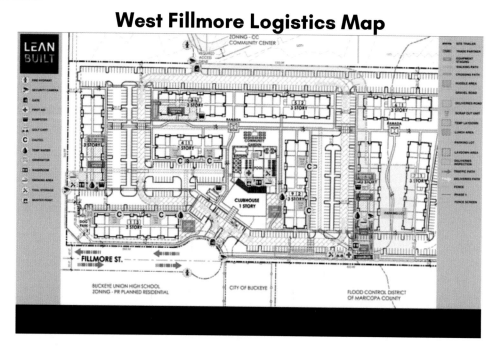

Armed with this information you can identify your GCs and GRs and make sure you are properly estimate the project.

CODE	DESCRIPTION	Unit	Quantity	Unit Price	Estimate	Cost Per SQ FT	Cost Per Unit	Quote	Comments
	LAND				$ -				
00-	LAND				$ -				
00-	SOFT COST				$ -				
	DEVELOPMENT COSTS				$ -				
	CONSTRUCTION COSTS				$ 32,296,223	$ 199	$ 215,308		
01-	GENERAL REQUIREMENTS				$ 3,249,631	$ 20.04	$ 21,664		10.06%
03-	CONCRETE				$ 1,602,000	$ 9.88	$ 10,680		4.96%
04-	MASONRY				$ -	$ -			0.00%
05-	METALS				$ 480,000	$ 2.96	$ 3,200		1.49%
06-	WOODS & PLASTICS				$ 5,013,962	$ 30.92	$ 33,426		15.52%
07-	MOISTURE & DAMPPROOF				$ 3,793,600	$ 23.40	$ 25,291		11.75%
08-	OPENINGS				$ 779,850	$ 4.81	$ 5,199		2.41%
09-	FINISHES				$ 4,091,356	$ 25.23	$ 27,276		12.67%
10-	SPECIALTIES				$ 263,250	$ 1.62	$ 1,755		0.82%
13-	SPECIAL CONSTRUCTION				$ 187,000	$ 1.15	$ 1,247		0.58%
11-	EQUIPMENT				$ 590,000	$ 3.64	$ 3,933		1.83%
21-	FIRE SUPPRESSION				$ 446,000	$ 2.75	$ 2,973		1.38%
23-	MECHANICAL				$ 2,764,529	$ 17.05	$ 18,430		8.56%
22-	PLUMBING				$ 2,343,705	$ 14.45	$ 15,625		7.26%
25-	INTEGRATED AUTOMATION				$ -	$ -			0.00%
26-	ELECTRICAL				$ 2,022,980	$ 12.48	$ 13,487		6.26%
28-	ELECTRONIC SAFETY & SECURITY				$ 84,540	$ 0.52	$ 564		0.26%
31-	EARTHWORK				$ 738,000	$ 4.55	$ 4,920		2.29%
32-	EXTERIOR IMPROVEMENTS				$ 1,161,966	$ 7.17	$ 7,746		3.60%
33-	UTILITIES				$ 818,604	$ 5.05	$ 5,457		2.53%
48-	ELECTRICAL POWER GENERATION				$ 359,000	$ 2.21	$ 2,393		1.11%
18-	FEES / CONTINGENCY				$ 1,506,250	$ 9.29	$ 10,042		4.66%
					$ 32,296,223	$ 199	$ 215,308		

CODE	DESCRIPTION	Unit	Quantity	Unit Price	Estimate	Cost Per SQ FT	Cost Per Unit
01-	GENERAL REQUIREMENTS				$ 3,249,631	$ 20.04	$ 21,664
01-0020	Insurance				$ 602,500	$ 3.72	$ 4,017
01-3530	Site Security				$ 22,509	$ 0.14	$ 150
01-4520	Testing & Inspections				$ 56,000	$ 0.35	$ 373
01-5110	Temp Power				$ 92,000	$ 0.57	$ 613
01-	Temp Cooling				$ 90,000	$ 0.56	$ 600
01-5130	Temp Water				$ 41,400	$ 0.26	$ 276
01-	Dust Control & Soil Stabilization				$ 22,800	$ 0.14	$ 152
01-5150	Job Fuel				$ 81,050	$ 0.50	$ 540
01-5210	Site Facilities				$ 100,750	$ 0.62	$ 672
01-5215	Site & Safety Supplies & Consumables				$ -	$ -	$ -
01-5220	Temp Toilet				$ 49,990	$ 0.31	$ 333
01-5240	Temp Protection				$ 27,000	$ 0.17	$ 180
01-5300	Temp Labour				$ -	$ -	$ -
01-5350	LeanBuilt Staff				$ 1,464,700	$ 9.03	$ 9,765
01-5400	Site Equipment				$ 190,000	$ 1.17	$ 1,267
01-5450	Small Tools				$ 59,400	$ 0.37	$ 396
01-5620	Temp Fencing				$ 69,900	$ 0.43	$ 466
01-5700	Construction Surveying				$ 25,000	$ 0.15	$ 167
01-5800	Rewards & Recognitions				$ 20,400	$ 0.13	$ 136
01-7410	Waste & Recycling				$ 63,240	$ 0.39	$ 422
01-7420	Final Cleaning				$ 115,000	$ 0.71	$ 767
01-	Transport				$ 13,000	$ 0.08	$ 87
01-	SOFTWARE & DEVICES				$ 42,992	$ 0.27	$ 287

You will also want to track your assumptions and clarifications throughout your process of estimating this project.

ASSUMPTIONS & CLARIFICATIONS LOG								
ID	DATE	TYPE	SCOPE	DESCRIPTION	IMPACT	RESP PARTY	STAT	COMMENTS
001	2024-04-25	Assumption	Foundations	All buildings to be construction slab on grade (SOG); conventional reinforced spread footing; 3,000 psi concrete	Cost	Highstreet	Open	-
002	2024-04-25	Assumption	Foundations	ALTERNATE slab option - Post-tension foundation system based on likely results of geotech report	Cost	Highstreet	Open	
003	2024-04-25	Assumption	Foundations	4" on grade	Cost	Highstreet	Open	
004	2024-04-25	Assumption	Foundations	ALTERNATE: Alternate slab integral with post tension system	Cost & Schedule	Highstreet	Open	
005	2024-04-25	Assumption	Foundations	Add crystal in mix to prevent water leaking in from outside	Quality	Highstreet	Open	
006	2024-04-25	Assumption	Structural	All building to be wood framed construction with unit fire separation walls-2x6 frame walls at exterior and corridor/ breezeway.	Cost	Highstreet	Open	
007	2024-04-25	Assumption	Structural	Second and third floors will be 1- 1/2" Gypcrete over plywood- 4x2 open web floor trusses with 3/4" T&G sheathing.	Cost & Schedule	Highstreet	Open	
008	2024-04-25	Assumption	Roof	Roof- Minimum 3/8" per foot slope at flat roofs and 4:12 typical at pitched tile roofs.	Quality	Highstreet	Open	
009	2024-04-25	Assumption	Roof	Roof- Minimum 3/8" per foot slope at flat roofs and 4:12 typical at pitched tile roofs.	Quality	Highstreet	Open	
010	2024-04-25	Assumption	Roof	Roof materials to be pre-painted edge and valley metal	Cost & Quality	Highstreet	Open	

At this point you have set the parameters for your team to follow, aligned with the target, and have built the team.

With ...

THE RIGHT TEAM

USING EFFECTIVE COMMUNICATION SYSTEMS

WORKING TOWARD THE RIGHT GOALS

IN THE RIGHT MEETINGS

WITH THE AMOUNT OF MONEY THEY NEED

You have *what it takes to* 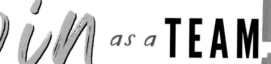 *win as a* **TEAM!**

Before you head into the next stage of design, consider creating a standard way to schedule the efforts of your team. Last Planner® & Scrum are the two methods I will walk you through here.

LPS® & Scrum

1 LAST PLANNER® PLANNING METHOD FOR DESIGN:

In this method, the first thing you will do is perform a **milestone or phase pull**.

1

IDENTIFY END MILESTONE
Identify the ultimate end milestone for the series of phases and milestones.

2

REVERSE PASS
Work backward in identifying activities like work, approvals, procurement, review deadlines, and regulatory durations to obtain major milestones.

3

CONFIRM LOGIC
Add high level summary tags that represent fairly accurate durations. That will help you and team confirm the duration between milestones is correct.

4

REVIEW THE PLAN
Review with the overall team once the pull is complete and redline it with a critical eye.

5

FINALIZE
Work the pull plan backward and forward, then publish. You can now do a detailed pull plan for just one phase that will guide your short-interval work.

The key is to make sure the plan is visual and that the team can make sense of it, review it, and make it right together. I actually don't care how you show this visually--I care that your phases are well defined and not at all vague. I also care that you have thought out the phase requirements so you don't overshoot your milestone date.

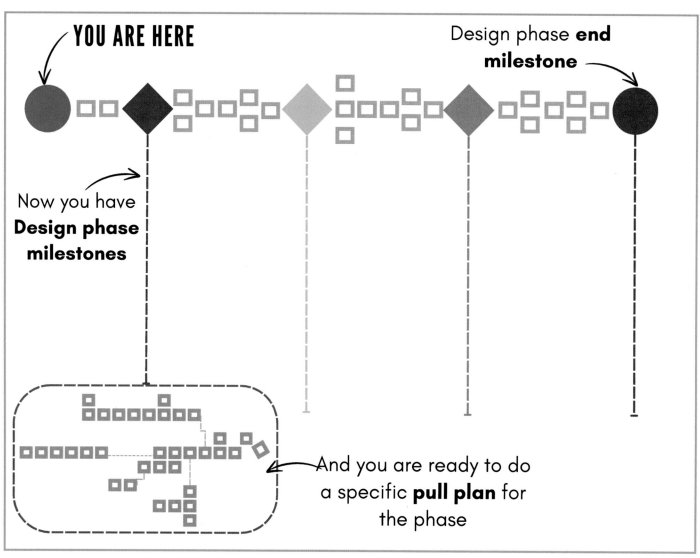

YOU ARE HERE

Design phase **end milestone**

Now you have **Design phase milestones**

And you are ready to do a specific **pull plan** for the phase

Once the phase or milestone pull is complete, you can pull plan the phase itself.

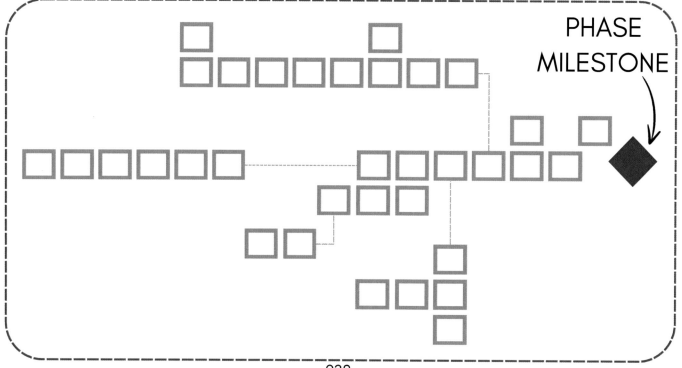

PHASE MILESTONE

Once you have your specific Pull Plan, you can look ahead of weeks and create weekly work plans for the team to follow.

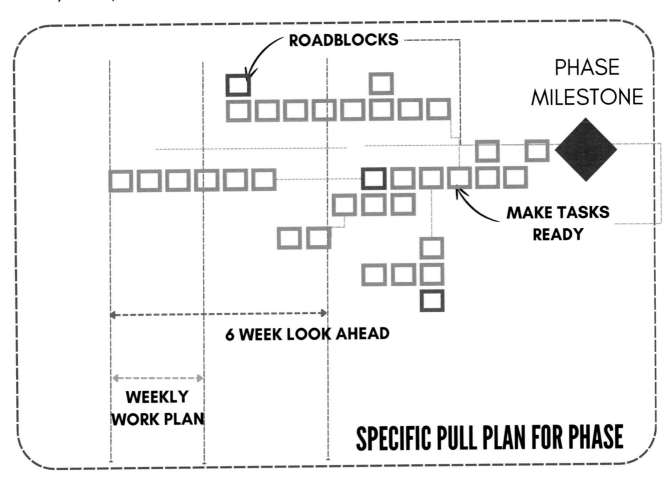

The **6-week Look-ahead** is your time to make tasks ready out ahead, coordinate needs among team members, and find and remove roadblocks.

The **Weekly Work Plan** is your tool to isolate work to be done in that week. This plan is then reviewed by the team and adjusted based on needs and coordination. This is the plan you will implement for that week in pre-construction. Items are tracked daily for status and your Percent Planned Complete score should reflect over 80%

To dig into the details please scan the QR code to the right and check out the video.

With the Last Planner® system, you'll need take time to do the following with the Design team:

- Pull planning,
- Look-ahead planning and roadblock removal,
- Weekly work planning,
- Daily huddles, possibly by discipline or by cluster
- A time to check PPC, identify root causes, and make corrections to the plan.

These can fit into your current system of meetings.

Monday	Tuesday	Wednesday	Thursday	Friday
	CLUSTER WORK		ALL HANDS PLANNING & REVIEW MEETING	BUFFER DAY

Your **daily huddle** and **tracking of PPC** can be done when you work with your cluster

You could do **look-ahead planning** & **weekly work planning** here

The all-hands meeting is where the entire team huddles to coordinate work. The clusters, which may represent different efforts or discipline focuses for design, will then do work as breakouts throughout the week.

The bottom line with this system is to have a pull plan that guides you through the phase, then make work ready 6 weeks out, and make sure everyone knows what their weekly focus is.

PULL PLAN

LOOK AHEAD

WEEKLY WORK PLAN

2 SCRUM PLANNING METHOD FOR DESIGN:

If you are using Scrum, you will begin the same way with a **milestone pull**. You can also do the phase-specific pull plan if you want. The key is to move your activities for the phase and then move them into backlog.

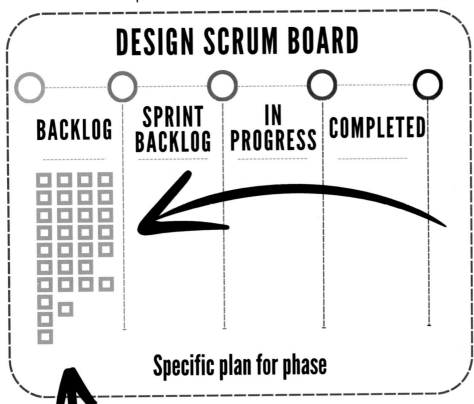

DESIGN SCRUM BOARD

BACKLOG | SPRINT BACKLOG | IN PROGRESS | COMPLETED

Specific plan for phase

Once your activities are in the **backlog**, you can do your **weekly sprint planning** for work to be done that week.

This represents the work to be done in the design phase.

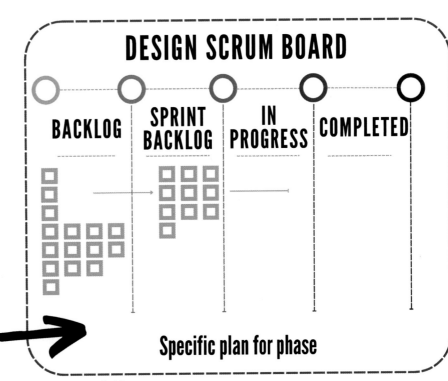

DESIGN SCRUM BOARD

BACKLOG | SPRINT BACKLOG | IN PROGRESS | COMPLETED

Specific plan for phase

Start working tasks to completion.

If your stickies or tags have the right format, you can also use Scrum to make sure you are on track. Here is the format.

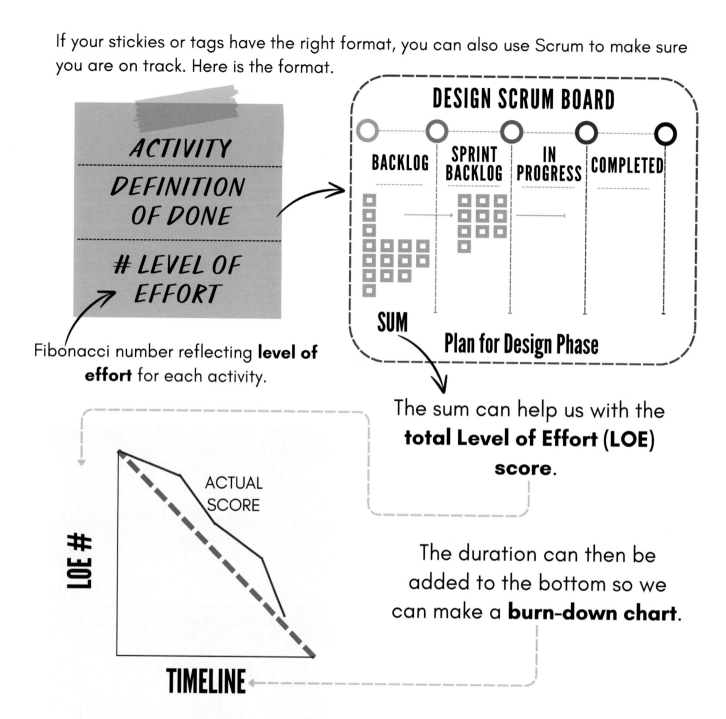

ACTIVITY

DEFINITION OF DONE

LEVEL OF EFFORT

Fibonacci number reflecting **level of effort** for each activity.

DESIGN SCRUM BOARD

BACKLOG | SPRINT BACKLOG | IN PROGRESS | COMPLETED

SUM

Plan for Design Phase

The sum can help us with the **total Level of Effort (LOE) score**.

ACTUAL SCORE

LOE #

TIMELINE

The duration can then be added to the bottom so we can make a **burn-down chart**.

The sum can help us with the total LOE score. The duration can then be added to the bottom so we can make a burn-down chart.

BACKLOG PLANNING

SPRINT PLAN

DAILY HUDDLE

If you have this in place you can follow the Scrum process of planning the work in your Sprint Planning Meeting, checking in daily in Daily Huddles, and closing out the week with a Sprint Review and Retrospective.

Monday	Tuesday	Wednesday	Thursday	Friday
	SCRUM TEAM WORK		*SPRINT PLANNING MEETING*	*BUFFER DAY*

Your **daily huddle** and **tracking of PPC** can be done when you work with your Scrum team work sessions.

Your **Sprint Planning** could be here as well as the Review and Retrospective

For more information about Scrum, please read Felipe Engineer's book Construction Scrum.

As you help you team navigate their work through
these systems be sure to:

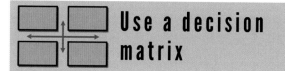

REMEMBER! ↓

Use a decision matrix

Always make sure you are making design decisions in the best possible way and according to a framework. A decision matrix can help you to define alternatives, determine evaluation criteria, assign weights to criteria, score alternatives, compare and decide. I would also add to track decisions well so there is a kept history showing how we arrived at our current state.

Help your design team flow

We must be careful about too much email, too many distractions, batching work, and not utilizing time properly. The problem with meeting design deliverable due dates is not so much about ability, but capacity again. If you are working with a design team, help them to remove waste and improve their environment always.

Always work in one piece flow

Batching work will always hurt the team. Batching design, decisions, design deliverables, and topics in a pre-con and design team will always slow things down. When you plan your work, do one thing at a time, focus, and get it done right then and there.

Create a culture of DDFD

DDFD means Done, Done, Fu*king Done. It means that the habit of doing partial work and saying, "Oh, we're mostly finished with that," is avoided and people are held accountable to actually finish their work.

Control WIP

Control WIP and level work in process. Always level the efforts of the team and control WIP so that cycle times do not extend. The design team must be balanced and healthy for this to work.

Recover delays

If you are delayed according to your pull plan targets, find ways to recover as a team without overburdening people. You cannot afford to be disconnected, siloed, sub optimized, and not able to ask questions about how to recover an effort ahead of a deadline. If if you have a delay, Identity, Discuss, and Solve it.

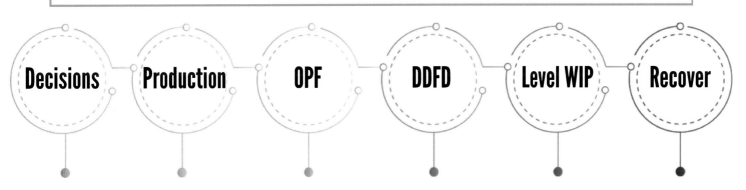

Decisions — Production — OPF — DDFD — Level WIP — Recover

DELIVERABLES AND OUTCOMES

The following are items that should be up and running at this point in the design process.

TRACK EARLY PROCUREMENT

At this point you should have a procurement log attached to your Takt plan and should already be tracking long-lead procurement items. It may seem a bit early, but I assure you it is not. Sketch out how long the procurement takes and work it back from the plan. You can then see when you would have to start any early design assist trade partners.

LOOK FOR EXISTING UTILITIES

Even at this early stage I recommend finding out as much as you can about existing utilities on your project site. Are there any duct banks, comm lines, gas lines, or any other utility on site? If so, it may take months or years to relocate ahead of construction.

REVIEW GEOTECH REPORT

Also review the Geotech report. Find out about the project soils conditions and what preparation must be done. You may find out that as a part of your design effort that you need to design stabilization, shoring, or something else to prepare the project.

ENGAGE VDC

It is always a good idea to engage your Virtual Design and Construction group by this point. They are able to help with design decisions and guide the design model in a way that it can be used for coordination by trade partners.

CONCLUSION

By properly setting up the team and the parameters of your project you can now effectively enable the design team and add a massive amount of value. This is so important because nothing can be successful downstream without the team, the goal, and the approach being clear.

ENABLE THE DESIGN TEAM

What do they need?

PROPOSAL PHASE > BUILD TEAM > > PLAN WITH BUILDERS > PREPARE & START STRONG

In this phase it is your job to support the design team. I know all about the traditional tension between designers and contractors, but there is no room for drama amongst First Planners™. We recognize that design is difficult and that we are perfectly situated to support designers throughout pre-con. Provide these necessities to facilitate their work and leverage the wisdom of builders.

1 REAL-TIME SCHEDULE UPDATES

Real-time means that a response to design changes or progress can happen with minimal delay. Historically our industry has been in a design-react scenario where there are no targets, teaming, or real-time feedback. It would take weeks or months to get pricing, schedule, and constructability feedback to the design team. That does not need to happen any longer. As we use Takt planning for more projects we can simulate changes in a matter of hours on our Takt plans, zone maps, and logistics drawings.

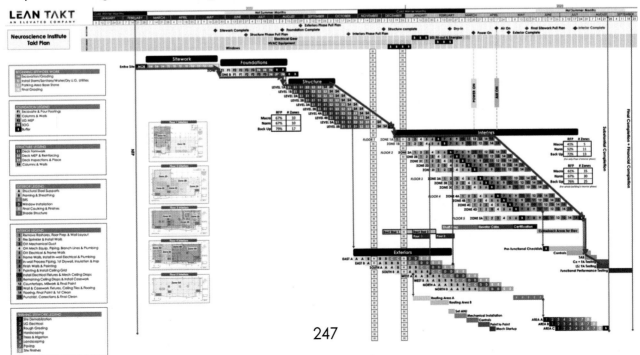

2 REAL-TIME BUDGET UPDATES

We must move faster when providing budget feedback to design teams. In the industry today it takes 3 to 6 weeks to get numbers back from trades for a package of drawings, and by that time it's too late to affect anything. We need to do more partnering with trades, provide quicker estimates, rely more on control estimates, and prioritize budget issues more urgently so that we help steer design and not simply react to it and surprise them with bad news. Here is my process with some ideas to implement positive change.

Effective Cost Estimation

- **Define** project scope based on design and specifications.
- **Gather** essential project information such as design documents and site conditions.
- **Segment** the project into phases for accurate cost estimation and management.

- Use conceptual estimates initially and **validate** with trade partners.
- Stress the need for control estimates to verify and adjust initial figures.
- Bring in Reference Class Forecasting into the strategy so we do not undercut the budget.

Must haves

- **Include** all relevant costs: labor, materials, equipment, and contingencies.
- **Allocate** allowances and contingencies to cover unforeseen expenses adequately--Murphy is real, plan for him.

- PMs / Supers **conduct** thorough budget reviews to ensure accuracy and transparency.
- PMs / Supers **facilitate** clear communication and collaboration among team members.

Actions & Engagement

- Regularly **monitor** and **update** the budget throughout the project lifecycle.
- **Adapt** strategies to mitigate risks and maintain financial health.
- **Share** budget information quickly.

- **Emphasize** the value of feedback and learning from project experiences.
- **Invite** viewers to engage with questions and share insights for mutual benefit.

3 CONSTRUCTABILITY REVIEWS

Constructability reviews have been kind of a joke in our industry for a long time. Rarely is any kind of valuable information given back to design teams for how a contractor intends to build something. This is a such a wasted opportunity! It would be amazing if pre-con teams could provide input on means and methods and how the project will be broken out for construction. Remember, it is up to us to make sure we **design to the work package**, not package work after design.

Effective Constructability Reviews

- **Ensure** that construction designs are practical and feasible to build.
- **Reduce** design flaws and **improve** project outcomes by involving all stakeholders early.
- **Transform** the project with details that reflect the benefits gained by real building experiences.

Must haves

- Start with **clear objectives** and **scope discussions** with the design team.
- Form dedicated review teams including contractors and designers to **catch issues early**.
- **Coordinate** closely with stakeholders to **resolve** issues promptly.
- Use tools like Bluebeam for real-time document reviews and **feedback**.
- **Evaluate** design concepts, feasibility, and potential construction challenges.
- **Consider** material availability, building codes, cost impacts, and sustainability from the start.

Actions & Engagement

- **Document** findings clearly and **share** them across the project team for swift action.
- **Develop** strategies to mitigate identified issues and **update** project documentation accordingly.
- **Monitor** progress to ensure corrections are implemented effectively.
- **Encourage** viewers to adopt proactive review practices for smoother construction processes.

Constructibility reviews aren't just a checkbox; they're crucial for ensuring your construction designs are practical and can be successfully built. Engaging all stakeholders early and using tools like real-time document reviews can significantly reduce design flaws and improve project outcomes. By embracing constructibility reviews, projects experience fewer RFIs, improved coordination, and overall efficiency.

4 EARLY TRADE PARTNER INVOLVEMENT

One of the best ways to support a design team is to call in the experts, the Trade Partners. They have the best knowledge of means and methods, material types, availability, and cost and schedule information. Consider bringing in early design-assist partners for the following trades:

1. Mechanical & Plumbing
2. Electrical
3. Exterior Systems
4. Elevators
5. Specialty Contractors
6. Others as necessary

This will provide the design team the experts they need and you'll have a more realistic production plan and budget.

5 VDC HELP

Our industry currently has a massive problem with wasted effort when it comes to virtual design and construction. We create design models that have to be remade; we redesign areas that could have been coordinated collaboratively the first time. Often we have to coordinate a building twice to respond to the design team and get ready for the structure phase of a project. There is a better way. That way is to integrate our construction VDC efforts with design. I have seen the following work well:

1. Use VDC to make design decisions and to model what-if scenarios.
2. Merge VDC teams so the design model can be used by the trades early on.
3. Use VDC collision detection and model reviews to get a more complete design.

There is obviously so much more to this, but suffice it to say that integration is the key here. Lets do our best to utilize our modeling capabilities together in the most seamless and most useful way throughout design and construction.

6 PERMITTING

Most of the time permitting is handled well by the design team. But the best case scenario is when the design and construction team work together throughout the permitting process. I have found the best practice to be putting together a permitting matrix, map, or strategy from research of the local Authority Having Jurisdiction (AHJ). That permitting strategy can be used in OAC meetings to make sure that design deliverables are on track for and considering permit review durations as a part of the overall production plan. Here are some ideas to consider:

▶ Know that mastering the permit process involves meticulous planning, expert collaboration, and adherence to local regulations for project success.

▶ Start with thorough research on local regulations specific to your project's location and type.

▶ Define project scope early and identify necessary permits during the planning phase to streamline processes.

▶ Conduct a detailed site survey, including topographic analysis and civil design, aligning with local regulations.

▶ Collaborate with knowledgeable architects and civil designers to navigate complex permitting processes effectively.

▶ Schedule a meeting with local authorities to discuss permit requirements and project specifics before application submission.

▶ Prepare and submit permit applications with all required documents and fees to initiate reviews.

▶ Await plan reviews for compliance with local codes; make corrections if necessary before permit issuance.

▶ Conduct inspections using the green tag checklist to ensure adherence to approved plans and specifications.

▶ Obtain final inspections and the certificate of occupancy to legally conclude the project.

▶ Properly close out permits by submitting notices of termination and archiving documents for future reference.

7 VALUE ENGINEERING

Value Engineering is a systematic approach in construction to optimize project value by balancing cost, function, and quality. It involves analyzing functions, identifying value, and implementing cost-effective solutions while maintaining essential features.

Value engineering is often misunderstood as solely cost-cutting, whereas its true aim is to enhance project value over its entire lifecycle, not just reduce costs. We have already discussed this, and if you have followed our advice to properly schedule and budget your project, you should be able to engage in real value engineering efforts.

Information Gathering
This is where the team learns the objectives, constraints, and requirements of the effort and collects data, drawings, and specs.

Function Analysis
This is when the team analyzes the functions of the project or system and determine the costs associated.

Creative Phase
This is where the team evaluates alternative solutions to achieve the same functions with more value and less cost.

Development Phase
This is when the team develops detailed proposals for the alternatives.

Presentation and Implementation
This is when the proposals are presented to stakeholders and changes are implemented.

252

8 USING A3S

Whether it's a simple decision or a value engineering decision at hand, an A3 might be a tool you will want to pull out to support the design team. An A3 is a problem-solving and communication tool in Lean construction, named after the A3 paper size. An A3 consolidates all information to one page to show the complete story and allow teams to see, know, act and make informed decisions together. It is ideal for addressing big problems, strategic goals, or complex issues.

A3 for Success

Problem Statement
Clearly defines the issue.

Current State Analysis
Provides context and current conditions.

Goal Statement
Outlines desired positive outcomes.

Root Cause Analysis
Identifies underlying causes using the 5 Why method.

Proposed Countermeasures:
Offers multiple solution options.

Plan of Action
Details steps to implement the best solution.

Follow-Up & Evaluation
Defines success criteria and KPIs.

Reflection & Learning
Encourages continuous improvement.

COMMON APPLICATIONS:

- **Problem Evaluation:** Addressing issues in processes or systems.
- **Integrated Project Delivery (IPD):** Collaborative decision-making in design and construction phases.
- **Business Decisions:** Structured approach for major business choices.
- **Strategic Planning:** Implementing thematic goals for the quarter or year.
- **Complex Project Issues:** Gathering teams to visualize and solve problems.
- **Scheduling Decisions:** Combining all information into a visual plan.

9 RISK IDENTIFICATION

Risk identification and management is another amazing tool you can provide the design team. You need to be able to see the risks, know where to document them, and what to do about them. The process is simplified here.

IDENTIFY & DISCOVER

- Identify and manage risks to avoid delays, cost overruns, and project failures.
- Use **Fresh Eyes Meetings** and **Risk & Opportunity Registers** to identify and quantify risks in terms of time and cost.
- **Acknowledge** that every project has problems.
- **Bring** them to the surface and **address** them as a team.

DISCUSS & SOLVE

- Risks can significantly affect your career, finances, and project success if not managed properly. **Include** risk identification and discussion in every team meeting.
- **Assign** responsible persons for each risk.
- **Absorb, cover, or remove** risks.
- **Avoid** wishful thinking and always have a contingency plan.

"10TH MAN RULE" FROM WORLD WAR Z

- Have one person in the group **challenge** optimistic assumptions and **prepare** for potential issues.
- Regularly **review** and **address** risks to ensure project success.
- Combine the strengths of **optimists** and **realists** in your team.

DONT FORGET !

Wishful thinking is not allowed in risk management. Identify, discuss, and solve risks regularly to ensure project success. Always have a contingency plan.

DOCUMENTING RISKS

Criteria for Risk Identification:
- *Ensure risks are **documented** where everyone can see them.*
- *Promote **discussion** and **collaborative** problem-solving.*

Daily Habits for Risk Identification:
- **Study** drawings for 30 minutes daily to spot potential risks.
- **Review** the project schedule for 30 minutes daily to identify risks and trigger actions.
- **Conduct project walks** to observe and identify risks firsthand.

Risk Documentation Locations:

Proactively document and share project risks in visible formats like risk registers, schedules, budgets, and planning boards to ensure the team can identify, discuss, and solve issues together, preventing them from impacting project timelines and success.

- **Risk & Opportunity Register**:
  - Log all identified risks.
  - Review and update regularly in team meetings.
  - Assign one person ultimately responsible for each risk.
- **Project Schedule**:
  - Include risks directly in the schedule.
  - Use the schedule as a tool to manage and communicate risks.
- **Project Budget**:
  - Reflect potential risks in the budget and contingency planning.
  - Make financial implications of risks visible to motivate mitigation.
- **Exhibits and Planning Deliverables**:
  - Highlight risks in GMP submissions, bid packages, zone maps, logistics plans, and basis of schedule.
- **Assumptions and Clarifications**:
  - Document assumptions and potential risks in all planning documents.
  - Ensure the team understands which risks need to be mitigated for the plan to succeed.
- **Planning Boards**:
  - Use last planner or Takt Steering and Control boards to display risks.
  - Discuss risks in daily meetings to promote team action and resolution.

CONCLUSION

By properly supporting the design team you can ensure the overall project design is progressing forward in an efficient manner and focused on optimizing the flow through your production system. Remember, how you treat the design team is not only a reflection of you, but also the best way to get the best product. I also want to acknowledge that this section of the book could have been an entire book on its own. I felt it best to cover the high points to keep you heading in the right direction but I recognize that there are other sources you'll need as you dig deeper.

It's all about... SUPPORT

BUILDER COLLABORATION

Does the plan belong to the builders?

| PROPOSAL PHASE | BUILD TEAM | ADAPT & ENABLE DESIGN | | PREPARE & START STRONG |

Hopefully by now your designers feel supported and have what they need to design to a budget. If that is the case then you can keep that pattern all the way to your permitted set of drawings with the confidence knowing that you have been an ideal team player in this pre-construction effort. Now you need to seriously plan this project--and the only way to do that is to plan it with the builders. Meaning the people who will build the project, execute the work, and that actually know how to build. For simplification I will group this section into three categories:

 Gather the Builders - This is where we assemble the planning team and get to work in the right way.

 Make the Plan - This is the process of making the detailed plan. Some of this is covered in our book Takt Planning, but we will provide an overview for you that I believe you will really like.

 Tear the Plan apart - In this part of the process we question our plan, review it, iterate, and try again until it is right.

1 Gather the BUILDERS

So let's get our builders involved. This is important because not doing this will result in your onsite project team doing their own thing and wasting the time in pre-construction. That is unacceptable. The plan must actaully be planned for it to go well. So, the same people building the project have to be the same people planning it. In fact, I will state firmly that it is **immoral and unethical** to hold someone accountable for a project they did not plan. It should never be done. Disagree? Call me. Or better yet, as Gordon Ramsay would say, "Get out!" That kind of dissent cannot be tolerated in this kitchen.

Moving on, in this phase you will execute the following steps:

ENGAGE THE TEAM ASAP

Your builder team may be on other projects while the planning before this project takes place, but we need them nonetheless. In the beginning of this book I shared what Bent and Dan taught us about how projects fail. Without proper planning our project only has a .5% chance of finishing on budget, on time, and as the owner expected. We need to do better--and following the 1/3:2/3 rule is good place to start. If a project duration counts as 2/3 of the overall time, the other 1/3rd should be spend planning.

You will need a PM and a Super at a minimum for this planning. If you cannot get them off the project then the project director, project executive, or operations manager needs to organize the effort and include them at key points throughout the process. This is really a good, better, and best call.

👎 Unacceptable: Make that plan in a silo and dump it on the project team.

✅ Good: Make the plan and have it reviewed by the PM and Super.

👍 Better: Organize the planning with support systems and bring in the PM and Super when possible.

⭐ Best: The industry begins to pay for pre-con and we have a PM and Super planning the project in preconstruction full time.

258

CREATE LEADER STANDARD WORK

There are a few nuanced definitions of leader standard work. What I mean with this item is the standard work each role has during a specific phase of their role. Once you have the right people in your planning effort you need to divide and conquer. Let's assume you have a PM and Super in pre-con. I would break up their roles in this way and detail out the expectations for each:

Project Manager:
- Client Interface
- Organizing design and precon efforts
- Managing budget updates with estimating team
- Run team meetings in precon
- Interface with designers for needed items
- Oversee efforts with Trade Partners

Project Superintendent:
- Project strategy planning
- Planning & scheduling
- Logistics planning
- Constructability reviews
- Project make-ready, permittings, mobilization, and first 90 day planning

Once you know what each person is doing on the team you can outline expectations, standard work items for daily, weekly, and monthly efforts, and be effective as a team and successfully plan the project.

2 Make the PLAN

With these teaming considerations in place, you can now plan your project properly. Get ready, because this is quite a comprehensive process. We will start with the project strategy.

INCORPORATE CONTRACT REQUIREMENTS

Before planning, I highly recommend you reference your prime agreement and Division 1 spec section to fully understand what is required for the project schedule, planning, meetings, progress updates, and the overall strategy of the project. There may be provisions in there that cover weather, buffers, durations for administrative reviews, and the like. Not reviewing these important documents would be analogous to a chef making a meal without looking at the order. Always reference the prime agreement and Div 1 specs to find out what we are contracted to for planning.

PLAN THE PROJECT

We'll use a project from Unitech, a partner from BC, Canada to showcase project planning.

The team started by analyzing the available information and found:
- Construction Drawings & Initial Pass at Procurement Log (shown below)
- Initial CPM Schedule (shown below)
- Trailer Layout (shown below)
- Initial Logistics Plan
- Team Organization Chart

SITE PLANS

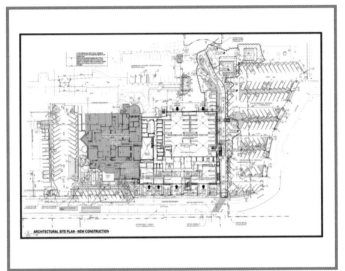

CPM SCHEDULE

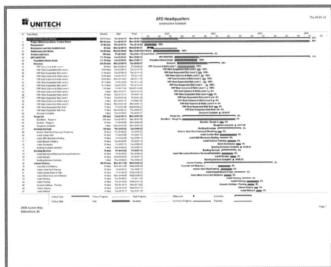

TRAILER LAYOUT

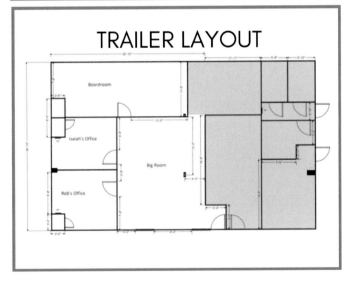

3D MODEL

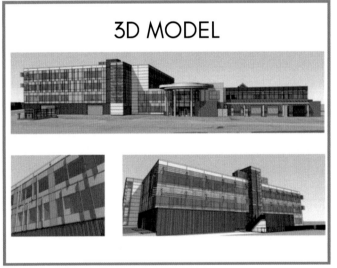

Next we performed a builder review. This means the team put the overall strategy to paper and visually communicated the general approach of the project. I know you cannot see all the details of the image on the next page, but the point is that they pasted the existing information in Miro (can also be on the wall) and sketched out their overall strategy to make sense of it all.

The team:
- Printed the documents available.
- Did a page flip and made marks as they went.
- Listed out all the constraints the project has.
- Looked at how work will flow.
- Got a feel for how it will go together.
- Articulated the early strategic concept.

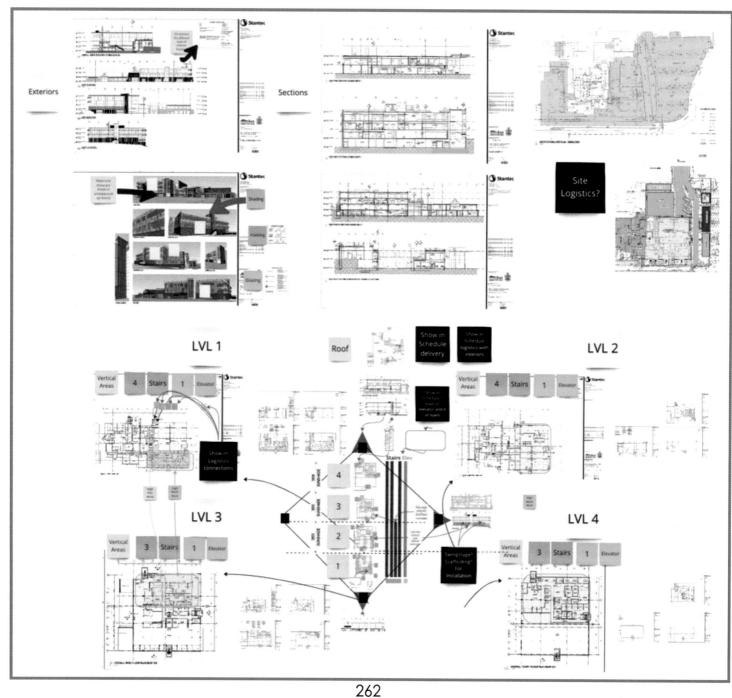

The next step is to complete a general work density analysis. A density analysis is a process where the team creates a scale of work density for all areas of the project. This team isolated the following general scopes of work:

1. Electrical
2. HVAC
3. Plumbing
4. Fire Suppression
5. ICT
6. General Architectural Compontents

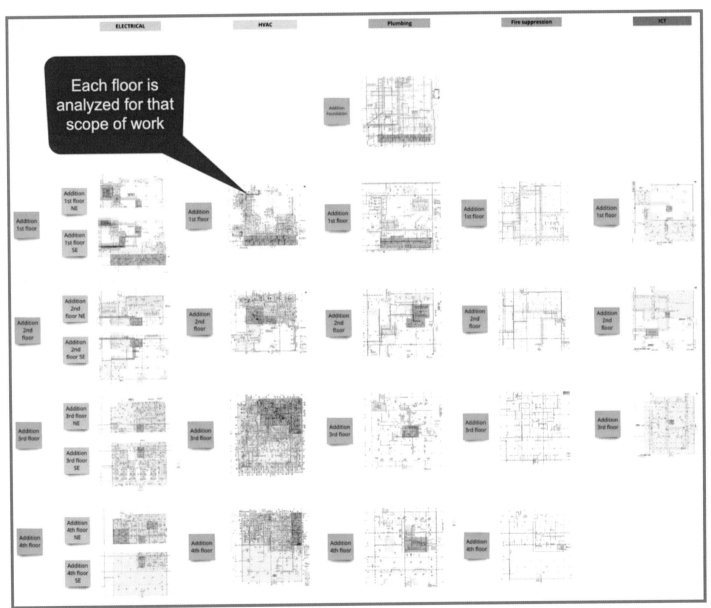

I realize you cannot see the details of these images. That is intentional. For more information about how to do this level of planning please reference our book Takt Planning. It will give you all the details you need. This book is an overview of how the system works.

Once the team overlayed the various work density maps they were able to come up with an aggregate score for all areas of the project.

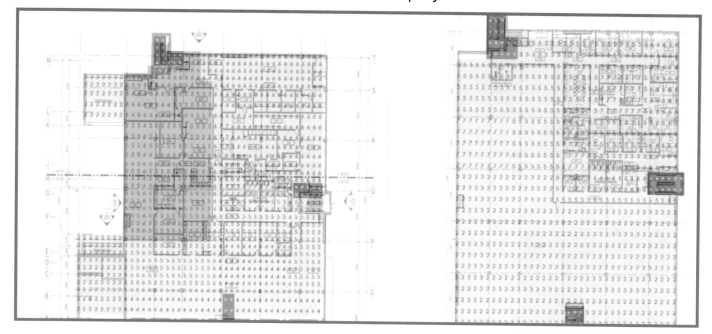

This then enables the team to identify zone sizes and to do a rough draft of your zone maps. Your zones will change as you optimized various strategies, but you will always be able to go back to it and use it as a tool.

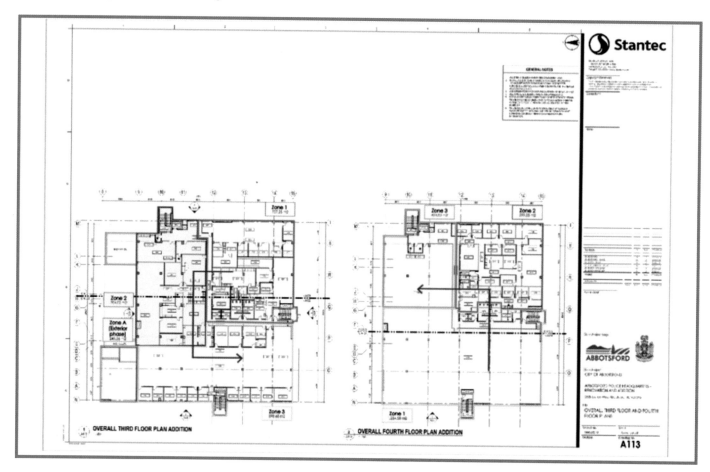

Having your work density analysis and a list of activities in your phase allows you to use the calculator and identify the right zoning strategy for the Macro & Norm level Takt plans.

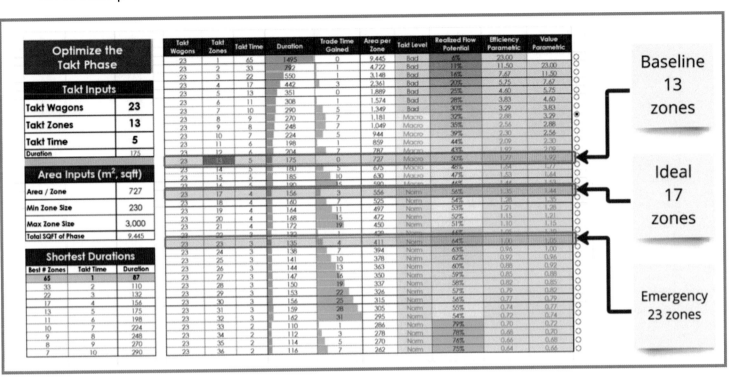

In the picture below, the team is proposing a number of possible phasing and zoning strategies based on the information found from the calculator.

It's always a good idea to sketch out the proposed shape of your Macro level Takt plan before you make it in Excel or inTakt. This helps you to further visualize your plan and save you time as you make it.

This sketching can then help you as you shape it in the application. It should be fairly close to your sketch and be organized in a clear and understandable way. As you can see in the picture below, the team is entering in the sketch into Excel before finalizing sequences and phases.

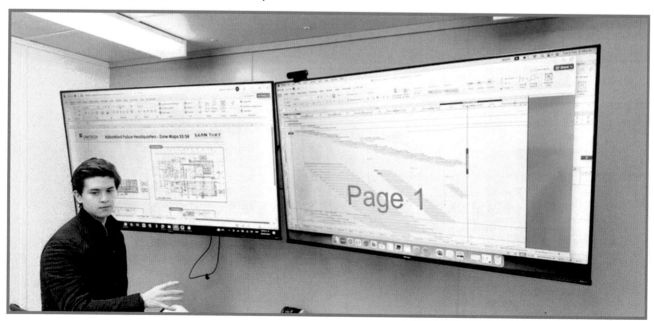

The next key is to discuss the phasing and zoning strategy with the project team and make key decisions that will enable you to create your Macro level Takt plan.

As you can see in the picture below, the team reviewed every part of the initial plan and made review marks for the team to create the base Macro level Takt plan.

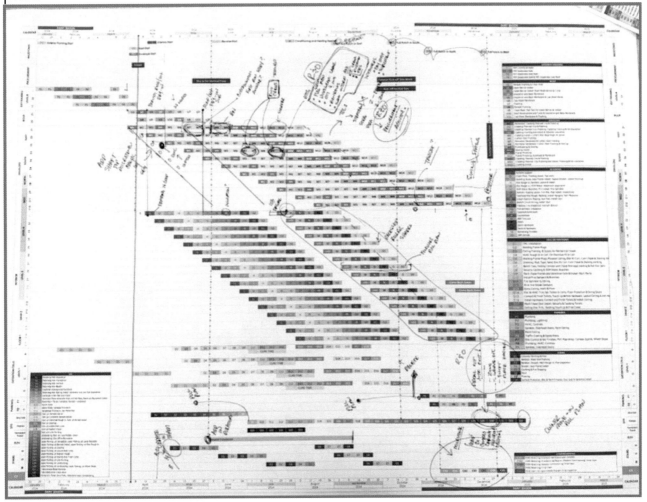

Having this review and input from the project team allows us to finalize the Macro level Takt plan & zone maps and begin working on all other aspects of the initial First Planner™ process.

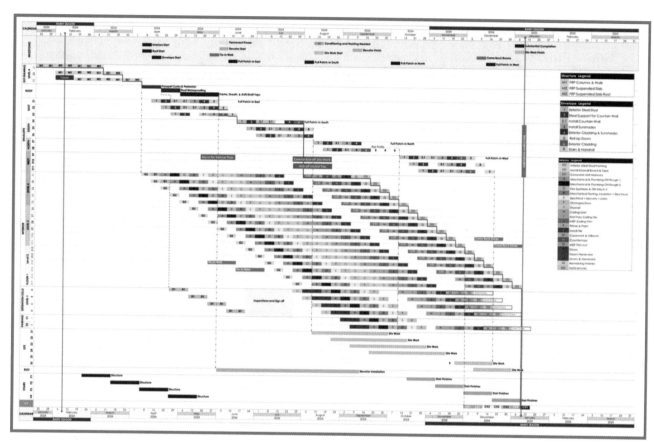

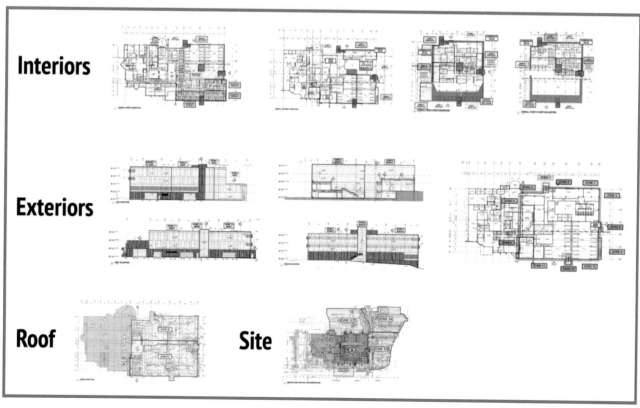

Interiors

Exteriors

Roof

Site

With the Macro level Takt plan you can begin the following activities:
You will begin pull planning each phase with trade partners as they are onboarded and flesh out your Norm level Takt plan.

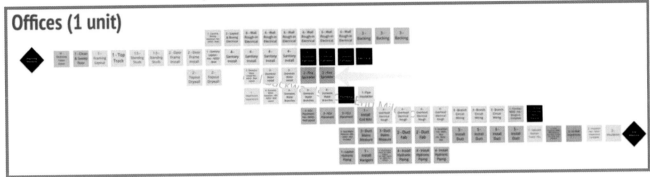

You will create your procurement log and align your supply chain to your production plan.

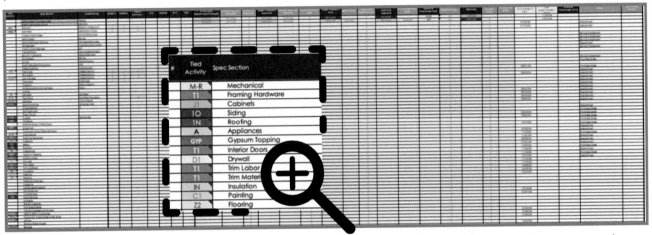

You will align your logistics drawings to match your plan with your phasing and zones.

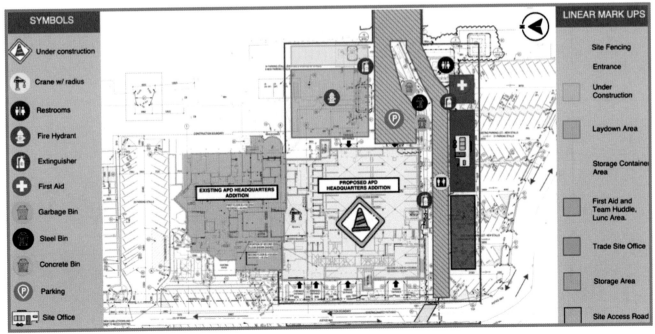

Additionally, you will make sure all of these items are covered in your planning and integrated into your production plan.

Identification & Optimization of Bottlenecks – Make sure you are using your planning documents to find and optimized your bottlenecks or limiting factors. These will normally show up as zones or trade durations.

Detail all Remaining Phases & Sequences – Make sure your overall plan is complete and paints a complete picture of what the project will take.

Add in Weather Indicators – Consider adding in weather days, cold winter months, hot summer months, and other indicators showing dependencies with weather.

Add in Design, Permitting, Buyout, Coordination, and Procurement Durations – No production plan would be complete without adding in the preceding activities showing design, permitting, buyout, coordination efforts, and procurement durations.

Add in Triggers for Pull Planning, TP3 Meetings, and Planning – Add in any key triggers that will remind the team to pull plan, do a pre-con meeting, or plan a phase.

Add Dry-in, Air-on, MEP Completion, and Cx Milestones – Remember that your production plan is not just about structural and architectural features. It is also about MEP systems and commissioning. Detail this out with your team in an clear and understandable manner.

Do another Check on your GCs and GRs – Now that you have involved the builders you have an updated Takt plan and logistics plan. Use these to confirm again that you have properly estimated the general conditions and general requirements for the project.

What would you add

Because you have key members of the permanent project team you can make key decisions. One of those will be what meetings you will have during construction. This is important because it allows you to design your trailer, your other interactions spaces, the flow of information, and the deliverables you'll use to communicate the plan.

These are the meetings I suggest and the ones that will be described in detail in the book Takt Steering & Control:

1. The **Strategic Planning & Procurement** meeting where strategic planning is done with First Planners™.
2. The **Trade Partner Weekly Tactical** where the supers and foremen do look-ahead planning and create the weekly work plan.
3. The **Daily Foreman Huddle** where day planning is done.
4. The **Morning Worker Huddle** where the plan for the day is communicated to workers.
5. The **Crew Preparation Huddle** where crews prepare their portion of work according to the plan.
6. The **Daily Team Huddle** where the project team works together to support flow in the field and remove roadblocks out ahead.

WEEKLY MEETING PLAN SEQUENCE — ELEVATE CONSTRUCTION INSIGHTS SOLUTIONS TRAINING

	MONDAY	TUESDAY	WEDNESDAY	THURSDAY	FRIDAY
5am			NO MEETINGS		NO MEETINGS
	WORKER DAILY HUDDLE CREW PREPARATION	WORKER DAILY HUDDLE CREW PREPARATION	WORKER DAILY HUDDLE CREW PREPARATION	WORKER DAILY HUDDLE CREW PREPARATION	WORKER DAILY HUDDLE CREW PREPARATION
6am					
7am	SAFETY ORIENTATIONS			SAFETY ORIENTATIONS	
8am	TEAM WEEKLY TACTICAL	DAILY HUDDLE	DAILY HUDDLE	DAILY HUDDLE	DAILY HUDDLE
9am				M COORDINA	
10am					
11am		OAC Meeting			
12pm					
1pm	FOREMAN DAILY HUDDLE	FOREMAN DAILY HUDDLE	FOREMAN DAILY HUDDLE	FOREMAN DAILY HUDDLE	FOREMAN DAILY HUDDLE
2pm	STRATEGIC PLANNING & PROCUREMENT	TRADE PARTNER WEEKLY TACTICAL		COORDINATION MEETING PLACEHOLDER	
3pm					
4pm					
5pm					
6pm					

271

I think the design of your onsite trailer is part of your plan for success. You likely need to design and order it early. Customize the trailer based on how you plan to use it. Here are the key steps for this:

1. Understand how your meetings will flow.
2. Map out how you will want to see the visuals to match that flow.

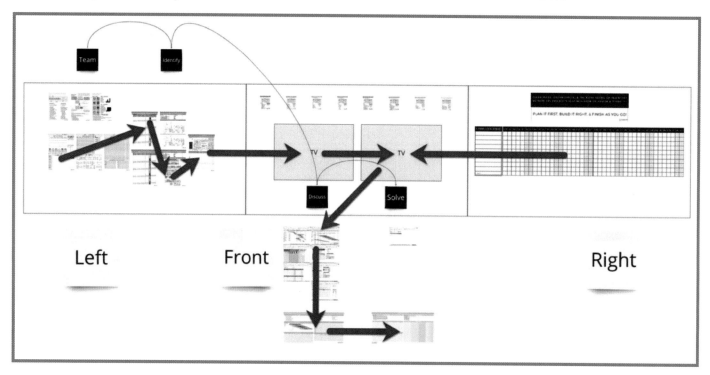

3. Design your trailer accordingly.

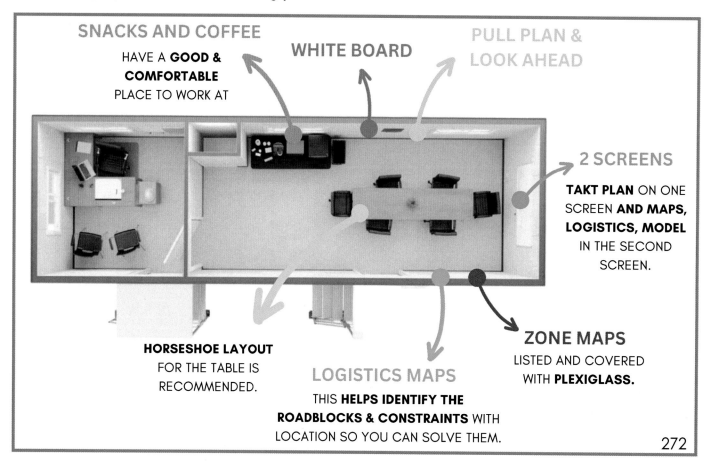

SNACKS AND COFFEE
HAVE A **GOOD & COMFORTABLE** PLACE TO WORK AT

WHITE BOARD

PULL PLAN & LOOK AHEAD

2 SCREENS
TAKT PLAN ON ONE SCREEN **AND MAPS, LOGISTICS, MODEL** IN THE SECOND SCREEN.

ZONE MAPS
LISTED AND COVERED WITH **PLEXIGLASS.**

LOGISTICS MAPS
THIS **HELPS IDENTIFY THE ROADBLOCKS & CONSTRAINTS** WITH LOCATION SO YOU CAN SOLVE THEM.

HORSESHOE LAYOUT
FOR THE TABLE IS RECOMMENDED.

In order to validate the plan for the project you will also need to design your onsite team with intention. I continue to insist that this be done by area and not by scope. That means not assigning someone to a scope like, "All Div 8." It would mean assigning them to building such and such, phase such and such, or floors this that and the other. This is important for what I call geographical control of the project and the effective running of lean systems on site.

This is what that would look like:

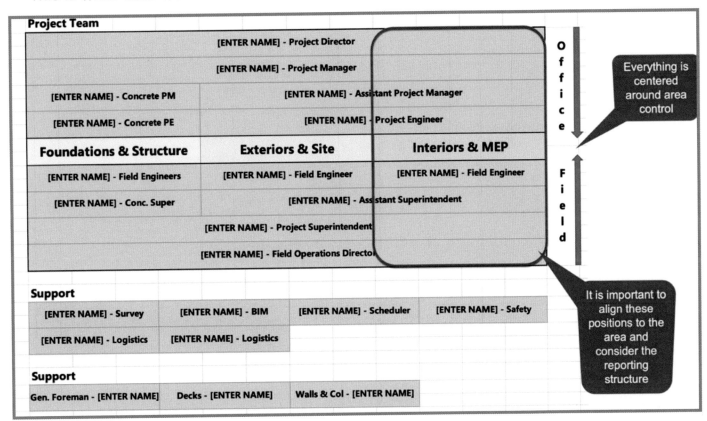

You will notice that this diagram does not focus on hierarchy. It focuses on accountability to the area they are a part of. Everything is centered around the project, phase, area, or grouping of zones, and all positions are aligned to it. It will be important for you and your planning partner(s) to give thought to this and how you want to organize your team.

Organizing your team based on area and not scope will make sure you can maintain operational control throughout the project.

And all of your Last Planner® tools will then be filtered from your Takt plan. Your look-aheads, Weekly Work Plans, and Day plans will then be aligned with your flow.

Look-ahead Plan:

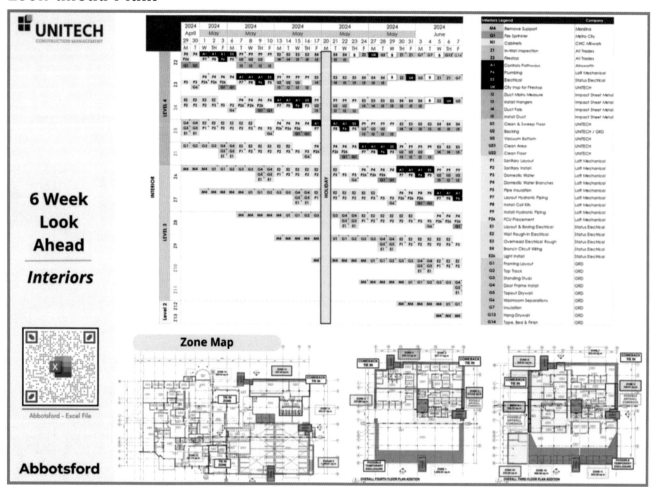

Weekly Work Plan:

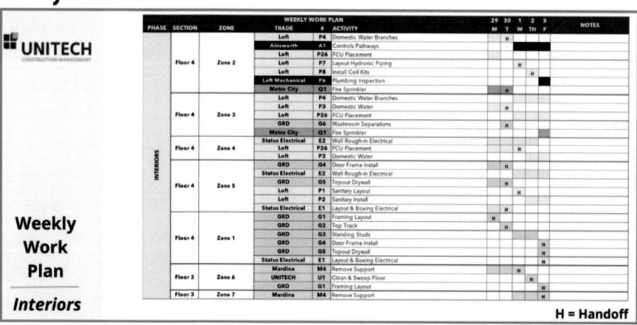

3 _Tear_ it APART

In this part of the phase we need to tear apart the plan and make sure it is correct. This happens when we host our fresh eyes meeting, get trade partner input, log our risks on our risk and opportunity register and establish a baseline for our owner.

1. The Fresh Eyes Meeting or Meetings are designed to gather people that have builder experience--and hopefully experience with that type of building--to review the project and find the problems, risks, and ideas that are needed to make it right.

2. As a part of this process I recommend also getting Trade Partner buy-in ahead of time or during the fresh eyes meeting.

3. Once this review is complete and changes have been made, we will submit it as a baseline to the owner with all other planning deliverables.

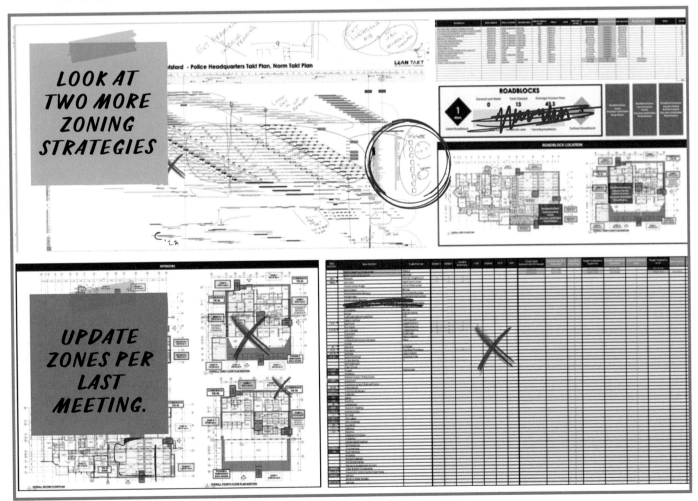

1 ## PREPARE THE RIGHT VISUALS AND FINISH THE PLAN

Prepare the project plan information in PDF's or Excel for presentation on a computer or printout.

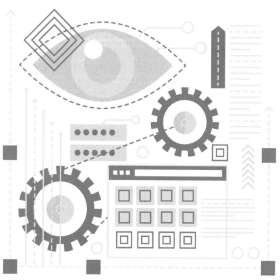

Visuals Needed:
- Takt plan
- Takt zone maps
- Norm Takt plan
- Trailer layout
- Logistic drawings
- Procurement log
- Organization chart
- Risk & opportunity

2 ## EVERYONE IN THE REVIEW MUST PARTICIPATE

- Project team to Foremen need to attend + fresh sets of eyes that have similar experience.
- Everyone adds value.
- Everyone on the project team needs to give real feedback and input.

LEAN TAKT
AN ELEVATED COMPANY

1 PROJECT OVERVIEW

This is when the project team presents their plan with the following deliverables:

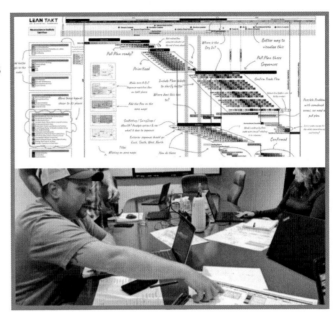

- Takt plan
- Takt zone maps
- Logistic drawings
- Organization chart
- Trailer layout
- Procurement log
- Risk & opportunity register

A project overview that is done and "good enough" is better than one that is "perfect" and late. What we need right now is something we can use to make perfect together.

2 $HIT GLASSES REVIEW

This is where the entire team tries to **break the plan** and find all the risks. This is the most critical part. We must find as many problems as possible right now we can create flow later in the field.

- Focus on problems & risks.
- Positive comments are not allowed.
- Don't make it personal--keep it professional--but pick it apart. Again, pick the plan apart, not the people. Don't be a jerk.
- This is the time to voice all the concerns & doubts about every part of the plan.

277

3 BRAINSTORM

Create a list of solutions and ask what can we do about each risk. All ideas are welcome for each item so it can lead to a real plan. Risks must be absorbed, covered, or prevented-no wishful thinking here.

4 DECIDE

- Create a plan of attack.
- Assign someone to be responsible for each activity.
- Set deadlines for action items.

Do not forget

5 PUBLISH

Everything needs to be shared with the group. All of the information needs to be scaled in a visible format accessible by the team. This should then be reviewed weekly in the team weekly tactical.

Everyone _MUST_ participate in every step!

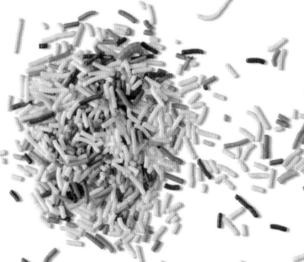

I don't care if the plan is correct the first time. I care if the plan is **visual** and that the team can **make it correct together**. This must be done **before we sign the deal and break ground**.

CONCLUSION

This was the phase to gather your team, make a plan with the people who will actually build the project, and tear apart the plan to make it right. If you do not do this you will suffer on a project where all problems are found in the field and not on paper first. For more information we highly recommend you read the book How Big Things Done.

1 Gather the BUILDERS

2 Make the PLAN

3 Tear it APART

PREPARE TO START STRONG

Are we accelerating when possible?

PROPOSAL PHASE 〉 BUILD TEAM 〉 ADAPT & ENABLE DESIGN 〉 PLAN WITH BUILDERS 〉

The time to go fast is not when you have dozens of trades onsite that are dependent on each other. The time to go fast is when you start. When you have only a few trades and can actually gain time. Follow the list below to prepare your project.

- **Pre-Construction meeting with Owner** – The pre-construction meeting with the owner is key. This meeting will gather the owner and owner's reps with any inspectors to make sure we kick-off the project properly. Schedule it, prepare for it, and follow the guidelines. How you start here will in large measure determine how the rest of the project will go.

- **Schedule Pre-con meetings with all first contractors** – This is huge. You must prepare your first contractors well if they are going to start strong. I usually start this at least 6 weeks before the project starts and I make sure all first contractors are ready.

- **Order all needed supplies** – If you haven't already done so, please order anything you need to support the site early-on:
  - Order signs, job startup materials, and office equipment.
  - Order your safety startup kit from corporate.
  - Order equipment for site support like forklifts, buggies, or other needed logistics items.
  - Order restrooms, hand wash stations, and dumpsters.
  - Order safety stickers.

- **Confirm contracts, insurance, and bonds are in place** – It will be important for you to make sure that contracts, insurance, and bonds are in place for all early trades. Make sure you are tracking this with your buyout so your trades can start well.

- **Schedule key starting activities** - There are key activities on the site that must be scheduled along with your first trades.
  - Call BlueStake.
  - Pot-hole all utility crossings.
  - As-built all underground utilities and provide a Site Utility map for any excavations.
  - Install SWPPP BMPs.
  - Begin building permanent worker bathrooms.
  - Establish a staging yard.
  - Begin daily Forman huddle systems.
  - Begin holding weekly planning meetings.
  - Begin orientations for workers.
  - Set up parking for workers.
  - Schedule trailer installation.
  - Schedule temporary utility hook ups.

- **Post all relevant documentation** - Before you begin you need to make sure any required documents are posted on site.
  - Permits
  - Permit plans
  - Emergency response plan
  - Emergency contacts
  - Critical utility shut-off locations
  - Underground Utility Map for excavations
  - Job specific safety plan
  - Job specific quality plan

- **Send Impact Notice to Owner** - Before you begin work you need to notify the Owner and neighbors. Submit an impact notice ahead of time and make sure everyone is aware that your project is starting.

At this point you have created a system that will produce results--as long as your component score is above 80%.

FPS™ | TPS® | LPS®

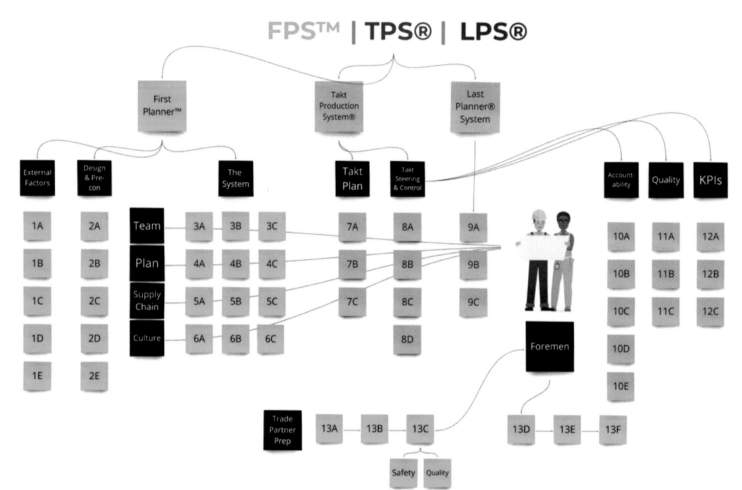

You now have a lean production system.

As previously mentioned, the rest of the overall system will be described in our next book Takt Steering & Control. It will cover in detail Takt Steering & Control, Last Planner® implementation, and these remaining components:

- Holding the Trades accountable in a positive way.
- Ensuring Quality.
- Continuous Improvement.
- Tracking Key Performance Indicators.

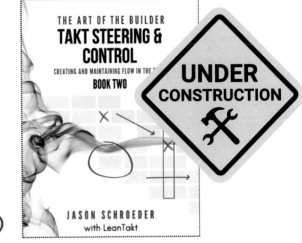

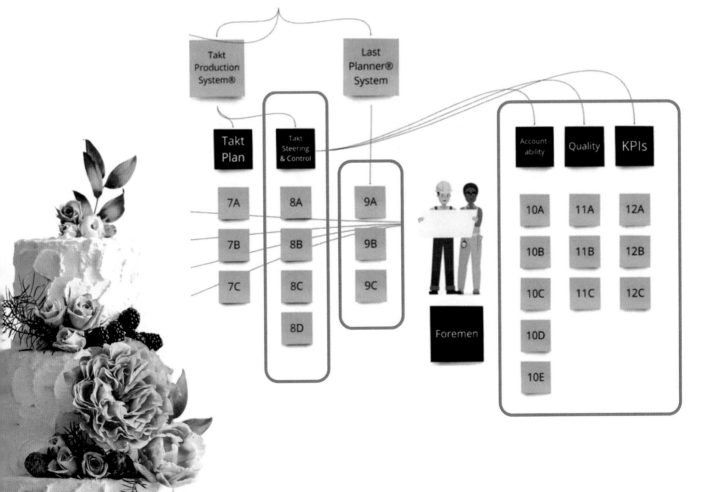

Artifacts:

Most systems can be recognized by their artifacts. When you see the IPCS™ in place on a project you will see certain meetings being held, deliverables being used, and behaviors. Here is a list of what you should find on a project with a lean operating system.

- **Meetings** -
  - Design Meetings
  - Team Weekly Tactical
  - Strategic Planning & Procurement Meeting
  - Team Daily Huddle
  - TP3
    - Buyout Meeting
    - Pre-mobilization Meeting
    - Pre-construction Meeting
    - First-in-place Inspection
    - Follow-up Inspection
    - Final Inspection
- **Deliverables** -
  - Macro Takt Plan
  - Zone Maps
  - Logistics Plan
  - Buyout & Procurement Log
  - Risk & Opportunity Register
  - Team Accountability Chart & Team Balance Tools
  - Basis of Schedule
  - Trailer & Signage Design
  - Well Managed Budget
  - Team Scrum Board
- **Behaviors** -
  - Production planning, not scheduling
  - Review and iterate often, faster, and with transparency
  - Always see risks and anchor to a reference class
  - Enable the work of the Last Planners® at the work package level

CONCLUSION

You may have noticed the absence of topics like RFIs, submittals, pay applications and the like. That is intentional. There are hundreds of books about that. The purpose of this book is to communicate the bare minimum requirements of what it takes to run a remarkable project the lean way. You could theoretically answer RFIs on napkins, review submittals on any platform you like, and make payments in cash if you want to--those things will not change the trajectory of a construction project. Those are administrative tasks. This book is about the art of being a builder.

The construction industry is not for amateur behaviors and amateur training. This is a professional industry with professional people who matter. It is absolutely insane that we do not yet have a standard approach to running remarkable projects. Sure we have concepts that are common like what we find with Taylorism. Sure we have administration. But where is the builder approach? The goal of this book is to provide that. It is time and about time. Please help us to refine the approach by implementing this system on your projects and providing us feedback.

What I said above is important because no one else is coming. There will be no technology, no machine, no other culture, or other species of sentient beings that are coming to save us. It is up to us. No one is coming to save us. If this industry is going to change it will happen with YOU! Yes I am writing to you. No one else is coming. So, this industry changes just as soon as you put your shoulders back, stand up, step up, and decide you will tolerate mediocre performance no longer. It will change when you decide it will. My hope is that this book will help you as you lead us into a future of caring for people, higher productivity, and higher profits.

On we go,
Love,

Jason Schroeder
Founder & COO of Elevate

Made in United States
Orlando, FL
02 October 2024

52297395R00159